Critical Thinking Skills

FOR

DUMMIES®

A Wiley Brand

Critical Thinking Skills

Skills

FOR DUMMIES®

A Wiley Brand

by Martin Cohen

Critical Thinking Skills For Dummies®

Published by:
John Wiley & Sons, Ltd.,
The Atrium,
Southern Gate, Chichester,
www.wiley.com

This edition first published 2015

© 2015 John Wiley & Sons, Ltd, Chichester, West Sussex.

Registered office

John Wiley & Sons Ltd, The Atrium, Southern Gate, Chichester, West Sussex, PO19 8SQ, United Kingdom

For details of our global editorial offices, for customer services and for information about how to apply for permission to reuse the copyright material in this book please see our website at www.wiley.com.

Wiley publishes in a variety of print and electronic formats and by print-on-demand. Some material included with standard print versions of this book may not be included in e-books or in print-on-demand. If this book refers to media such as a CD or DVD that is not included in the version you purchased, you may download this material at http://booksupport.wiley.com. For more information about Wiley products, visit www.wiley.com.

Designations used by companies to distinguish their products are often claimed as trademarks. All brand names and product names used in this book are trade names, service marks, trademarks or registered trademarks of their respective owners. The publisher is not associated with any product or vendor mentioned in this book.

For general information on our other products and services, please contact our Customer Care Department within the U.S. at 877-762-2974, outside the U.S. at (001) 317-572-3993, or fax 317-572-4002. For technical support, please visit www.wiley.com/techsupport.

For technical support, please visit www.wiley.com/techsupport.

Library of Congress Control Number: 2015934517

ISBN 978-1-118-92472-3 (paperback); ISBN 978-1-118-92473-0 (ebk); ISBN 978-1-118-92474-7 (ebk)

Printed in U.S. by Bind-Rite Robbinsville

10 9 8 7 6 5 4 3 2

Contents at a Glance

Table of Contents

Chapter 3: Planting Ideas in Your Head: The Sociology of Thinking 41

Chapter 4: Assessing Your Thinking Skills 65

Chapter 7: Drawing on Graphical (and Other) Tools for Thinking 133

Chapter 8: Constructing Knowledge: Information Hierarchies 159

Part III: Applying Critical Thinking in Practice 175

Chapter 9: Getting to the Heart of the (Reading) Matter 177

Chapter 10: Cultivating Your Critical Writing Skills...............................199

Introduction

Critical Thinking! *Now that* sounds like a good idea. Because it's a kind of souped-up, laser-sharp powerful thinking, just waiting to zap rotten arguments and churn out some pretty brilliant insights instead. And don't worry if people tell you that it is a rather *high-level* kind of thinking, and that only a few can do it, mainly tweedy professors who tell jokes in Latin (*dimidium facti qui coepit habet* — 'he who has begun, has the work half done'), because Critical Thinking certainly isn't like that. Critical Thinking is not just for the tweedy few — but for the curious, the imaginative, the creative many. In fact the only thing that is really deeply mysterious about Critical Thinking is why *everyone's* not doing it. But I've got a theory about that, and it is to do with education and the kind of ways of working that people are corralled into, like so many sheep — supposedly as a preparation for life outside. But life outside is rarely just a business of unreflectively following set procedures and instructions — but rather something where you need constantly to reflect on what you are doing, and why — and act not as a machine, but as a person. So the first skill a Critical Thinker needs to learn is how to think 'the unthinkable', to think outside the box, to 'free their mind' no less.

Sounds idealistic? A bit 60s and hippies wearing flowers? Well, yes, there's a bit of idealism in Critical Thinking, just as there is in all the best things. But there's also a lot of structure, and solid research backing it too. This book will give you what you need of both — plus plenty of opportunities to develop and test your own skills. I've done both my bit of being taught and of teaching over the years, and another rather mysterious thing is why so many people seem to imagine that thinking, let alone Critical Thinking, is something that can be learned by rote: that is, by writing down and memorizing a collection of facts (a body of knowledge) with right and wrong answers. Critical Thinking guides that create obscure distinctions and list technical terms for you to learn are promoting passive, not active, thinking. Rote learning is fine if all you ever intend to do is deal with past problems, but won't get you many new insights or ideas. And, in fact, it is the opposite of what Critical Thinking is all about. Critical Thinking is really a set of transferable skills — learned for one thing, equally useful for another — that cuts across the whole swathe of academic disciplines and is applicable in all spheres of human activity. This is why you will find Critical Thinking useful as part of learning design skills, nursing studies, economics, and even playing good football: it is really a toolbox for making the most of life.

About This Book

In this book you can find both the conventional material on Critical Thinking Skills, which is broadly about avoiding logical fallacies and following the rules of good essay structure, and a lot more besides. Most other books focus on these bits of Critical Thinking because they are easy to talk about, but rather harder to actually get anyone to do. In fact, like philosophy itself (and Critical Thinking is traditionally a branch of philosophy), properly understood the *only* way to learn the method is to use the skills in practice. So what I try to offer here is a kind of map or guide book that will come in handy as you actively start using Critical Thinking in whatever areas you want to. I include enough of the background to the academic debates for you to see the 'why' as well as the 'what', plenty of hands-on tips and advice so that you have the 'how', and I certainly include some opportunities to try things out in practical exercises.

Foolish Assumptions

One of the key skills in Critical Thinking that too often gets overlooked is 'knowing your audience' — and indeed empathising with them. In this case, that means understanding what motivates them. So as I write this book, just as when you write an essay or prepare a report, the crucial thing is to know what the interests and needs of the likely reader are. I assume that you:

✔ Are interested in ideas, and in how to communicate them.

✔ Already know there is a difference between Critical Thinking and just criticising without thinking.

✔ Want to be able to see through a bad argument.

✔ Know how to construct a persuasive argument —
although I don't make any assumptions about *what* you
will be arguing about or the context that you are studying
or working within.

Whether you're young or old, male or female, an engineer or
a philosopher, makes no difference to me — the book is zero
jargon and open access.

You could be a CEO or the prime minister, but you won't get
special sections for that reason. However, I do anticipate
that you might be a student, perhaps starting your studies
or perhaps having progressed to the point where you are
being asked to produce longer dissertations. Because, believe
it or not, Critical Thinking is a skill that even PhD students
often fall short in. This 'thinking gap' is behind a lot of dodgy
research and public policy all over the world. So really, I also
assume that the likely reader has a moral purpose too. You
want to think *better* and more clearly: to get things *right*, not
just know enough to pass the exam.

On the other hand, if you are sort of a reluctant Critical
Thinker, heck, let me have a go at converting you. Because I
know there is an awful lot of boring stuff out there on informal
logic and structuring essays, and I certainly don't intend to
add to it here. So if you are starting off by wanting 'just the
minimum to pass', you've still come to the right place. If
Critical Thinking is sometimes a diet of thoroughly stodgy
skills, here you should find plenty of flavouring has been
added to the stew that makes it all much more tasty.

Icons Used in This Book

I use this icon to point you towards more detailed explanations of important ideas or theories that shed light on Critical
Thinking techniques and skills.

There's a lot of jargon used in some Critical Thinking circles.
I attach this icon near the plain English explanation of a term.

I use this icon to highlight key facts and ideas that — literally —
you may want to remember. If you know it already, sometimes
it will come across more as a *reminder*.

This flags up a simple idea that can be used to achieve both academic Critical Thinking aims (how to dissect an argument, for example) and also broader CT skills such as how to give space to other people to develop their ideas, rather than switch off at the first point of disagreement.

 And last, but definitely not least, this one flags up an opportunity for you to try your skills out!

 I reserve this scary icon to indicate both practical 'pitfalls', and theories that have downsides.

Beyond the Book

In addition to the material in the print or e-book you're reading right now, this product also comes with some access-anywhere goodies on the Web. Check out the free Cheat Sheet at www.dummies.com/cheatsheet/criticalthinking for some helpful tips and hints.

You can also access some fun critical thinking exercises at www.dummies.com/extras/criticalthinking.

Where to Go from Here

You can read this book any way you want — I don't mind if you just try a few bits that seem particularly relevant, or if you plough through the whole thing in one evening (take it to bed with you), or if you skim read it while eating chips and watching TV.

In fact, I'd recommend that you don't treat it as a textbook, with lesson one leading to lesson two, because the smart reader knows — and the Critical Thinker is a smart reader — that information is best digested when it connects to something you have a current, real need to know. Only you can say what it is at the moment you're looking at, or thinking about, or interested in. So use the index, the contents page or that valuable method known as 'flicking through' to find bits that seem relevant to you, and take it from there. (Because I assume many readers will only dip into or out of this book, so I have tried to group material into clearly labeled sections, each with its own 30-second intro, so that you can quickly check out particular aspects as and when you need to.)

However, if you want my advice about where to start, and why not, I wrote the book so I ought to know a bit about it, I'd say some good places to go are:

✔ **Chapter 1:** Because that is where I 'Welcome you to the Arguments Clinic' and say a bit about what Critical Thinking is.

✔ **Chapter 4:** Which is on 'Assessing Your Thinking Skills', because it contains a pretty cool test of the kind that evil employers may give you, and is quite fun too. But don't read if for that reason, because all of the book is fun.

✔ **Chapter 9:** 'Getting to the Heart of the (Reading) Matter': another possible jumping in point.

It sounds a bit serious, but it's also a good place to start as it is through reading that most people get new ideas and develop their views. Don't forget, that's probably why you're looking at this book in the first place. What could be better than just reading this book, than reading it while thinking critically!

Part I

Getting Started with Critical Thinking Skills

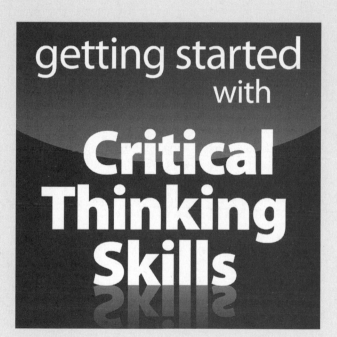

For Dummies can help you get started with lots of subjects. Go to www.dummies.com to learn more and do more with *For Dummies*.

In this part . . .

✔ Find a quick overview of what this newfangled idea called Critical Thinking is really all about, and why everyone's doing it.

✔ Measure your existing thinking skills, and get a big nudge towards broadening your outlook to include emotional intelligence and awareness of everyone's inbuilt biases.

✔ Discover why most people's brains are happier reaching quick answers than they are at reaching the *right* answers — plus tips on how to avoid that tendency for yourself.

✔ Learn how unscrupulous folks, from political extremists to talented advertisers, have always taken advantage of *uncritical* thinkers.

Chapter 1

Entering the Exciting World of Critical Thinking

In This Chapter

▶ Getting the big picture on thinking skills

▶ Picking up cool tips for problem solving

▶ Steering clear of common misconceptions

There goes another beautiful theory about to be murdered by a brutal gang of facts.

—*François VI, Duc de La Rochefoucauld, French writer and moralist (1613–1680)*

*C*ritical Thinking is about pressing points, sniffing a bit more sceptically at issues and generally looking more closely at everything. Not only at factual claims but also, and most importantly, at the ways in which people arrive at their views and ideas.

Harrumph, you may think! Why bother? Good question! I've failed plenty of job interviews in my time by being a Critical Thinker. Equally, the world has no shortage of successful people who scrupulously avoid any appearance of not only thinking critically, but thinking full-stop. My short answer is that being a Critical Thinker is still the best kind of thinker to be, even if it does sometimes mean that you're the odd one out on many issues.

In this chapter I provide an overview of Critical Thinking and what you can find in the rest of this book. I'll also cover the importance of 'reading between the lines' and also set the record straight on what Critical Thinking isn't.

Opening the Doors to the Arguments Clinic

You may well have been brought up not to argue. At school you were probably encouraged to sit quietly and write down facts — I was. When I was five, one teacher even used sticky tape to shut children's mouths up in class! (Yes, I was one of them.) Since then I've had some very enlightened teachers, who encouraged me to use my imagination, to solve some problems or do research. But still not to argue.

So welcome to a very different way of seeing the world — Critical Thinking. This is truly the 'arguments clinic' in which punters can pay for either 5-minute or hour-long arguments (as the famous Monty Python sketch has it). No, it isn't. Yes it is. Still say that it isn't? But, yes it is! (If you like, check out Chapter 17 now to discover ten of the world's most influential arguments — don't worry, I'll still be here when you get back!)

Of course, as the sketch says, this isn't proper argument at all, merely contradiction: nothing like a connected series of statements intended to establish a proposition. If an ability to contradict people is all you come away with after reading this book then you, like the man in the sketch, would be entitled to your money back. Don't worry, here you will find so many new ways of looking at issues that you'll soon be having the full, hour-long arguments on everything under the sun.

My aim by the end of this section is to give you the big picture of Critical Thinking.

Defining Critical Thinking

If you look up Critical Thinking in a dictionary, you see that it's called the philosophical examination of arguments, and I'm a philosopher. But — at the risk of annoying the Ivory Tower experts straight away — I say that this kind of philosophy isn't the sort most of them do or have a clue about. Yes, as Chapter 12 shows, Critical Thinking does have one foot in the realm of logic, in tidily setting out arguments as premises followed by conclusions. But if that were all it was, you might as well give the job to a computer.

No, Critical Thinking is really about a range of skills and understandings, including an ability to play with words, a sensitivity to context, feelings and emotions, and (the hardest skill to develop) the kind of open-mindedness that allows you to make creative leaps and gain insights.

I know that developing these skills sounds rather like a tall order for one book to achieve. But Critical Thinking is also team thinking, and I draw on the ideas of many other thinkers, including a lot of input from my editors at Wiley. As a result, you don't get my opinion of Critical Thinking Skills, but a carefully researched and lively introduction to the subject.

Spotting how the brain likes to think

Professors may sniff, but I prefer to work on exercises that are fun or interesting, which is why I have tried hard to make the ones in this book like that. Here's a rather trivial little exercise, which nonetheless illustrates something important about how the human mind operates.

Should you say 'The yolk of the egg is white' or 'The yolk of the egg are white'?

When I first saw this question, I thought for a minute — and then I gave up and looked for the answers. That's my method with written exercises; it conserves my limited brain power for things like watching TV and eating crisps — at the same time! But I digress (not good in Critical Thinking). This question may form the subject of a 5-minute argument, but it shouldn't stretch to an hour, because neither version is correct: egg yolks are yellow. Boom, boom! Caught you out?

This exercise reveals that people's normal mode of thinking is bound within the parameters of certain rules and systems — due to thousands of years of evolution. In the jargon of psychology, human thinking uses certain *heuristics* (mental shortcuts for solving problems and making judgements quickly).

The trouble is that automatic and well-established ways of thinking can stop you from seeing new possibilities or avoiding unexpected pitfalls. Plus, the great majority of people's thinking goes on without them being aware of it. Although sometimes quick and efficient, in certain circumstances it can rush people to the wrong conclusions.

Critical Thinking is your insurance policy against these dodgy, but more or less universal, thinking habits.

Evaluating what you read, hear and think

The fundamental cause of the trouble is that in the modern world the stupid are cocksure while the intelligent are full of doubt.

—*Bertrand Russell ('The Triumph of Stupidity'*
in Mortals and Others: Bertrand Russell's
American Essays, 1931–1935)

Ingredients that make a Critical Thinker

If you're building a Critical Thinker, à la Dr Frankenstein, here are the abilities and attributes you need:

✔ **Tolerance:** Critical Thinkers delight in hearing divergent views, and enjoy a real debate.

✔ **Analytical skills:** Critical Thinkers don't accept just any kind of talking. They want properly constructed arguments that present reasons and draw sound conclusions.

✔ **Confidence:** Critical Thinkers have to be a little bit confident to be able to examine views that others present — often people in authority.

✔ **Curiosity:** Critical Thinkers need curiosity. It may have killed the cat, but curiosity is the essential ingredient for ideas and insights.

✔ **Truth-seeking:** Critical Thinkers are on mission 'objective truth' — even if it turns out to undermine their own previously held convictions and long-cherished beliefs and is flat against their self-interest.

Critical Thinking is about actively questioning not only the conclusions of what you're reading or hearing, but also the assumptions — be they open or hidden — and the overall frame of reference. (Critical Reading is discussed in detail in Chapter 9.)

Critical Thinkers approach an issue without preconceived assumptions, let alone prejudices, towards certain conclusions. As Professor Stella Cottrell, author of a popular guide to the subject, says, Critical Thinkers are quite prepared to acknowledge a good argument that goes against them, and will refuse to resort to a bad argument even if it looks like the only one available to support them.

Developing Critical Thinking Skills: Reading between the Lines

> *The improver of natural knowledge absolutely refuses to acknowledge authority, as such. For him, scepticism is the highest of duties; blind faith the one unpardonable sin. And it cannot be otherwise, for every great advance in natural knowledge has involved the absolute rejection of authority, the cherishing of the keenest scepticism.*
>
> —Thomas Huxley (On the Advisableness of Improving Natural Knowledge, 1866)

Critical Thinkers know that real debates take place 'between the lines', and, all too often, 'under the mental radar'. The Critical Thinkers' job is to pull the real issues into plain view and, if necessary, shoot them down!

I introduce you here to some of the core skills of Critical Thinking: 'reading between the lines', examining the evidence and quickly deconstructing texts. (The chapters in Part III provide loads more info on how to do just that.)

Challenging people's rationality

Do you know people whose views don't seem to be based on any sort of rational assessment of the world, but rather on

dodgy information easily imbibed — or even on blatant prejudices? Me too. And what's more, at least some of my views —
and some of your views — also fall into this rather illogical
category. The fact is, even though Aristotle called men (not
women, he was emphatically prejudiced) 'rational animals',
people rarely use their rational facility in practice. (I discuss this
subject in more depth in Chapter 13.)

More subtly, people often present good reasons for their positions, but in reality arrive at their views for quite different
ones. The good reasons are irrelevant, as you sometimes find
out if you present some solid arguments that tend to disprove
them. For example, suppose your neighbours buy a 4-wheel
drive, all-terrain car, and insist that it is vital for when the
family goes mountaineering and camping. Yet the fact is that
they rarely go anywhere more remote than the nearest supermarket and hate getting their shiny car dirty. Could the real
reason be that having a tank-sized car bolsters their sense of
self-importance?

Or maybe the government says that it has to charge students
tuition fees — otherwise there won't be enough money for
everyone who wants to go to college in the future. Good
reason! Odd then that the fees system actually costs *more* to
operate than the previous universal grants system. Could the
real reason for the change be something to do with dismantling the political edifice of the welfare state?

Arguments may exist for doing that too, but that's straying
into politics. I'm not saying one way or the other, but I am
recommending the habit of looking a little harder at the
reasons and explanations people give.

Dipping into the Critical Thinking skills toolbox

I think of Critical Thinking as a toolbox. Philosophers have
a long tradition of seeing argument skills as tools (read the
nearby sidebar 'Totting up Aristotle's tools' for more).

Critical Thinking isn't one tool, but lots. Plus, its skills can
do a lot more than most of its experts seem to be aware of —
because most of them come from too narrow a base.

Totting up Aristotle's tools

The most famous writings on 'how to argue' are the 2,000-year-old books of Aristotle. His followers gathered them together and called the collection *Organon* — which is Greek for 'tool'. Interestingly, this title reflects a controversy at the heart of philosophy that has never gone away: is logic the purest form of philosophy or merely a tool that philosophers use? So this obscure bit of Ancient Greek is surprisingly political, taking sides in an educational controversy that continues to rage today.

Logic is a central Critical Thinking tool. You can see the kind of logic that it uses as a *mental screwdriver* with two different purposes: it enables you to take arguments completely apart *and* mend and reassemble them.

Critical Thinking also has creative uses, such as *prototyping* and *brainstorming* (see Chapters 6 and 7, respectively). These 'hammer-and-nails' skills, with plenty of glue added in, are great for creating new solutions and visualising possibilities. Plus, don't forget the social and emotional components of Critical Thinking (which I cover in Chapters 3 and 4, respectively): I like to think of these as the measuring tools in the kit — maybe as the spirit level too.

Philosophical and mathematical logic is a solitary process: one person (or computer) can take on the world. After churning through a formal proof and finding a contradiction, the matter is *closed!* But Critical Thinking involves questioning — challenging arguments, methods, ideas and findings, demanding the context and the background. Therefore, it's a more sociable business, where people explore and create truths collectively.

Ordering your thinking: Reason, analyse and then argue

In that order please! Uncritical Thinkers may start by arguing, and then pause to analyse and finally search for reasons, but making the argument follow the reasoning (not the other way around) is much better.

Which logic for Critical Thinking?

You can encounter plenty of types of logics: Classical logic, Boolean logic, Quantum logic, Sentential logic and how about a bit of Multi-valued logic or Predicate logic too? Sprinkled with Fuzzy logic? No! Breathe again....

Critical Thinking isn't a sneaky way to make students study logic. It's not even a form of logic-lite! A fundamen-tal difference exists between all the usual logics and the one that Critical Thinkers include as one of their tools: *informal logic*. All the other logics are concerned with the form of the arguments, but only informal logic, as the name suggests, is also concerned with the *content* of arguments — with issues and applications.

Philosophers prefer to see Critical Thinking as a course in *informal logic:* the study of arguments expressed in natural language, where an argument being valid isn't enough — the conclusion has to be useful too. The chapters in Part IV are all about that and where I take a good look at the key skills of informal logic (for example, the 'fallacies' that many Critical Thinking experts wax long on). But don't be too excited at the prospect of using logic to conquer the world, because as I explain its powers are strictly limited.

 The difference between a sound argument and a fallacy is often far from black and white. Which isn't to imply that people don't make lots of silly mistakes and lousy arguments. Check out some logical pitfalls in Chapter 16.

On the other hand, don't let any of these concerns put you off using logic skills in your thinking, writing (check out Chapter 10) and speaking (see Chapters 11 and 14), because a little method can go a long way to making your arguments more persuasive and demonstrating the weaknesses in other people's too.

Researchers have often found that when asked, people can't really explain why they hold such and such a view, or what they think would count as suitable evidence for the view. Even more worrying for society, is that these same people are extremely reluctant to have their views challenged. Critical Thinking Skills are your antidote to this very common disease.

Discovering what kind of thinking you do

The one primary and fundamental law of mental action consists in a tendency to generalisation. Feeling tends to spread; connections between feelings awaken feelings; neighboring feelings become assimilated; ideas are apt to reproduce themselves. These are so many formulations of the one law of the growth of mind. When a disturbance of feeling takes place, we have a consciousness of gain, the gain of experience. . . .

—CS Peirce (*The Architecture of Theories, 1891*)

The quote above is about how building on what you already think is vital for future growth. But it brings problems.

A 19th-century American philosopher, Peirce also indentified three kinds of thinkers, which I shall summarise here (a *little* creatively) as follows:

✔ **Sticklers:** People who form their beliefs by tenaciously sticking to whichever view they liked most originally — whatever evidence is presented to them and even however circumstances change. If asked to justify their view, they can be very thorough in finding facts to support it, while also refusing to look into anything that appears likely to run against it. (I write about facts and opinions in Chapter 15.)

✔ **Followers:** People who respect anyone or anything that presents itself as 'authoritative'. They form their view in a group discussion on what they think, say, the professor is saying, or in the absence of an authority figure, on what they imagine is the consensuses view. When they look something up on the Internet, they head for the security of Wikipedia (as they imagine it!) and are reluctant to consult websites run by individuals.

These kinds of thinkers, as Peirce says, are useful members of society, because they aid social harmony and cohesion. (Although they may also be found egging on tyrants and persecuting minorities.) But they aren't useful as far as ideas go.

✔ **System builders:** These are people who try to fit everything into a pre-existing framework. They're a more sophisticated version of the sticklers. Science is obliged — in practice — to operate on a similar principle. System-isers are willing to consider new information, but if it requires dismantling the pre-existing structure for understanding the world, they're likely to reject it. You can read more on how people process information to build knowledge in Chapter 8.

According to Peirce, the smart way to see the world is to accept that everything you know may be wrong and start from scratch if need be. Or indeed end up with all the views on an issue demolished with 'no working hypothesis' left. Only a true Critical Thinker would do such a thing.

Almost all professors of the arts and sciences are egregiously conceited, and derive their happiness from their conceit.

—*Erasmus*

Bertrand Russell ascribes this quote to Erasmus, and I can see why he liked it. Russell was a philosopher prepared to argue unpopular views (such as that war is a bad thing) and was put in prison — twice.

Russell (refreshingly) took on professors and people in authority, but his point of course applies to everyone. Too few people are really open to new ideas, let alone able to take criticism — unless they've taken and really absorbed the lessons of Critical Thinking.

US philosopher William James made a similar point when he complained that many people think that they're thinking when they're *merely rearranging their prejudices.* For Critical Thinkers, discerning thought and prejudice is a vital distinction to make and the first step is becoming more aware of your biases. (I examine this issue in Chapter 2.)

James also recommends that in many areas, people should decide their position on the basis of feelings, even if they have no good or relevant arguments to support it. How logical is that? Well, not at all, but it's not a stupid position either. In Chapter 4 I look at some distinctly non-logical ways of approaching problems.

Professors tend to tell people to 'think', and complain when they don't — but they fail to offer advice on exactly how to do it. For that, students have to rely largely on their own efforts, or maybe turn to specialist experts such as Edward de Bono. He stresses that thinking is a skill that has to be learned. Critical Thinking definitely owes 'pioneers' of thinking skills like him a polite nod, even if the approach here has to be little more, well, scientific.

Speaking of which, here's a scientist to explain about how scientists think:

> *The mere formulation of a problem is far more often essential than its solution, which may be merely a matter of mathematical or experimental skill. To raise new questions, new possibilities, to regard old problems from a new angle requires creative imagination and marks real advances in science.*

> *—Albert Einstein (A. Einstein and L. Infeld, The Evolution of Physics, 1938, p.92)*

Thinking outside the box

This anecdote shows how redefining problems can generate new insights.

A gardening equipment firm challenged a meeting of engineers to use their collective thinking power to come up with a new kind of lawn mower. After some humming and ahhing, the engineers came up with . . . not very much. Some tinkering and slightly novel refinements, but nothing to create a splash in the marketplace.

Then one of the engineers suggested that they return to the original problem; but to 'go back one step' and express it in terms of function. Instead of the engineers thinking about how to *re*design lawn mowers, which meant that their thoughts followed the usual paths, he said they should think about 'machines to help people maintain lawns'.

This small, even niggly, distinction made all the difference. The engineers even created an entirely new product, based on the imaginative insight of one whose son liked playing with yo-yos. They invented the strimmer, which involves a nylon string whizzing around, thus adding a new annoyance to neighbours everywhere. The power of Critical Thinking!

You can read more about *creative brainstorming* in Chapter 7.

Well, he has to come in sooner or later. Einstein's point about creativity is absolutely spot-on. Check out the nearby sidebar 'Thinking outside the box' for an example.

Understanding What Critical Thinking Isn't

The preceding sections discuss what Critical Thinking is, but I now detail what it isn't.

Critical Thinking isn't about putting arguments and debates into formal language or symbols and then spotting logical fallacies in them (despite what many books say). It *is* about how to look at issues and problems in the real world, with all their fuzziness and contradictions, and offer relevant, practical and sharp insights into them. It's a skill that lets you, for example, distinguish right from wrong, choose the best business policy and construct a compelling case for action.

Also, Critical Thinking is far deeper than study skills, those set ways of doing things that lecturers often teach students. Instead, it's about what to do when no obvious answers or set methods are available. Look at it this way: a study skill makes sure that you have pen and paper during lectures; Critical Thinking is about what to jot down.

Quantum physicist Richard Feynman said that science is grounded in the conviction that its own experts are often ignorant of what they profess to be experts about. That statement applies, with knobs on, to Critical Thinking too!

People who claim to be experts in Critical Thinking don't automatically know everything about the vast range of skills and material the subject covers or draws upon. Nonetheless, Critical Thinking is a skill, and so whether you're pretty hot on it or not, you can definitely improve through practice.

Critical Thinking isn't about learning an endless series of 'facts'. Instead, it encourages people to develop their in-built thinking skills by making them active. That's why this book features lots of tricky puzzles (see Chapter 5 for more on puzzles and analogies) rather than platitudes. I want you to start thinking critically and actively from page one. Or from the start of Chapter 2 anyway!

Chapter 2

Peering into the Mind: How People Think

> *We think so because other people all think so . . . or*
> *because we were told so, and think we must think so. . . .*
>
> —*Henry Sidgwick*

*S*ome mysteries are best tackled by digging out and looking at 'the known facts', but not the issue of 'how people think'. This one is best tackled (as philosophers have done for centuries) by asking questions.

For example, when you read something — like this paragraph — whose voice do you hear in your head? Is it your own voice, as the reader, or is it an echo of the voice of the author reappearing through the words — or perhaps both? The neurologist Paul Broks identifies a peculiar thing about writing: it seems to allow other people to access and 'take over the language centres of your brain'. Part of this chapter, the section 'Thinking Logically or Instinctively: Evolution and Consciousness', explains how and why that may happen. Being aware of this is useful when you're trying to understand your reaction both to other people's ideas, and to critically evaluate some of your own theories.

One of the key skills, not only of Critical Thinking but in life generally, is the ability to reflect on your own practices. This chapter is your diagnostic manual for checking what's going on inside your head.

In debates about how people think, a gulf in philosophy has long existed between *conservatives,* who uphold traditional distinctions and assume the brain is a machine (and therefore logical and rational), and *radicals,* who critique that whole approach (and admire the complexity and illogicality of human thinking). This chapter takes a look at these debates — ones that shape all subject areas — so that you can move towards an effective analysis of your own and other people's reasoning. It's important to realise that even scientists aren't immune to making mistakes in this area.

Thinking about how people think: Some thoughts!

We think so because other people all think so; or because — or because — after all we do think so; or because we were told so, and think we must think so; or because we once thought so, and think we still think so; or because, having thought so, we think we will think so.

—Henry Sidgwick

Henry Sidgwick's contribution to understanding how people think (which I started the chapter with) touches upon the key issues, although it's hardly expressed very elegantly. If students wrote like that in exams, they may not fail but they wouldn't get many marks. It's almost rambling — not clear and authoritative at all!

But then English philosopher Sidgwick didn't write those words at all. You can find plenty of people on the Internet saying that he did, but when you look more closely (as Critical Thinkers always should do) you find that the lines are supposed to be insights that occurred to the great philosopher in his sleep, and are in fact as recorded by his relatives, Arthur and Eleanor Mildred Sidgwick. They were probably struck by his idea that thinking is not really an individual matter at all, but rather a complex social phenomenon involving lots of different associations — some of them misremembered and some maybe even imaginary!

I also examine a more specific question: to what extent do logical rules and the methods of rational argument underlie people's beliefs and the judgements and decisions they make? Or, on the contrary, are individuals more influenced by what *other* people think? An understanding of this tendency to groupthink provides you with a key defence against being misled by the opinions of those around you or those in authority, and also a more sophisticated way of interpreting events, debates and decisions.

Read on — but also have a think about what you think about how you think — and then perhaps try not thinking about anything — maybe have a quiet lie down!

Thinking Logically or Instinctively: Evolution and Consciousness

Personally, I don't usually think of myself as having a brain like a lizard or crocodile (unless I've had a particularly bad night's sleep), but in evolutionary terms it seems that I sure do. So if anyone wants to claim that 'the way that we think is what makes us human', they'd better try to work out precisely what humans do differently from animals. As I discuss in this section and throughout this chapter, the debate is as much a philosophical one as a biological one.

In the first part of this section I look at how mysterious the inner world of our thoughts still remains, even as scientists discover more and more about the external world. I first of all look at the different tasks human minds and animal minds are asked to do, and then in 'Jumping to conclusions: The cost of fast thinking' I'll illustrate how sometimes the two kinds of thinking — human and animal — get muddled up and lead people to make rash judgements and silly mistakes.

Buying beans and composing sonnets: Contrasting views of consciousness

Do monkeys think? Do plants? No, or at least not like humans anyway. They just appear to be thinking as they may follow pre-programmed evolutionary strategies; a bit like computers (or *Big Brother* contestants). But, unlike computers, they're 'undoubtedly' conscious of something. For if nowadays scientists agree that the body, indeed the whole universe, is a machine, still no one is quite able to say that a ghost isn't riding along in the centre of it.

One of the most famous philosophers of them all, Descartes, once wrote 'I think, therefore I am', or at least, many people *think* he wrote that. Of course, Critical Readers will check such quotes very carefully and find that actually he said something a little bit different. But as I say, everyone 'thinks' he said that, so in a sense he did. He was suggesting that awareness of the brute fact of existing was the only thing he could be sure of, and he used this nugget not only to get himself up in the morning but also to make sense of and rediscover the world.

Celebrating the human mind

I wrote a book a few years ago that was an investigation of consciousness but went under the rather more appealing title of *Mind Games*. Through such games, I focused on the mysteries that surround the way people think.

The human mind has many inexplicable abilities. It can happily deal with imaginary things that don't really exist, that don't make sense and that can't be explained. Imagine what a disaster it would be if a unicorn ate this book or if it turned out your dad was an alien in disguise! Some people even think the mind can project thoughts instantaneously across distances, cause departed souls to re-materialise and, of course, pass messages directly to a creator God. Yet although mainstream philosophers and hardnosed scientists sneer at such irrationality, that's no reason to throw out the distinction between minds and brains, between consciousness and electrical activity in nerve networks.

The French philosopher was onto something big — and that thing is consciousness, perhaps the central mystery of philosophy. Science can explain many things, but this strange sense of self-awareness it often just dismisses as an illusion.

Humans do many things that animals don't and they do them for complex, socially defined or aesthetical reasons. As the contemporary philosopher-scientist Raymond Tallis challenges his readers, just consider what's going on under the surface with something as commonplace and seemingly simple as buying a can of beans in a supermarket. Why are people buying them? It may be because they've just seen an advert for it, or because it reminds them of some happy times when they were kids. It might be because they think beans are cheap. Surely animals don't have to worry about things like this when they eat grass or gobble up rabbits.

Yet the fact remains that many of the differences between humans and other animals are marginal. The lives of humans and chimpanzees probably looked very similar a few hundred thousand years ago — no tins of beans or supermarkets then, let alone those sonnets and symphonies that philosophers love to cite as proof that humans are something special. Plus humans didn't develop their mysterious minds in an evolutionary blink: The brain evolved over long periods of time, and so Stone Age people must have had pretty much the same kind of consciousness then.

Professor Tallis is near the mark when he says that what's distinctive about humanity is its social environment, bound together by language and tool use. It's utterly different from the world within which animals exist. 'Artefacts, institutions, mores, laws, norms, expectations, narratives, education, training.' And although humans share 98 per cent of their genes with chimpanzees, they share precisely zero per cent of their chromosomes — and chromosomes are what actually do things.

Jumping to conclusions: The cost of fast thinking

In this section I'll look at the theory that actually, people are basically illogical, and because of this they often get muddled up, make faulty judgements and silly mistakes. Understanding how people arrive at their opinions and conclusions gives insights into what people say and think — and can even help you anticipate people's behaviour and responses in advance.

The US professor Daniel Kahneman has written about the psychological basis for judgements, reactions, choices, conclusions and much more. His writings (such as *Thinking, Fast and Slow*) give a significant push to the already pretty widespread view of people as, basically, *irrational* animals. He was even given a Nobel prize for his research!

Kahneman's thesis is that the human animal is systematically illogical. Not only do people mis-assess situations, but they do so following fairly predictable patterns. Moreover, those patterns are grounded in their ancient origins as simple animals. Survival depended on it. Much thinking is instinctive — and hardwired.

He says that people have two ways of thinking:

- ✔ A logical mode (which he thinks is good, of course).

- ✔ An earlier, instinctual mode (which he says is the root of most 'wrong decisions').

The human brain doesn't like information gaps, and so people tend to jump at the first answer/solution that looks good rather than take the time to examine all the data, especially in a world where they receive more information every day than they have time to assimilate. Plus, the human brain loves to see patterns and make connections. Although such traits serve people well in many ways, sometimes they mislead people too.

For example, thinking is a complex biological process and requires a lot of energy: the human brain uses up 20 percent of an adult's total energy, and for children it gobbles up almost half their body's energy! (Try multiplying two two-digit numbers in your head while running: 23 × 47 anyone? You're sure to slow down both in your running and your caculating. So, because thinking gobbles up precious mental resources, the body is programmed to avoid it. Instead, human beings have developed, over many thousands of years, a range of built-in, 'off the peg' methods for reaching decisions.

You might want to say that the example of the multiplication sum 'slowing down your running' is a bit dodgy — maybe that it is the distraction rather than the mental energy that causes any slowing down. Certanly, don't accept anything just because an expert says so! However, the notion of being distracted itself indicates a sort of limit in human thinking powers. That's partly why we admire people who can, say, balance on a monocycle on a rope while juggling!

The problem with fast thinking however is that often it means people don't solve the right problem — they solve the easy problem. A celebrated example is the 'bat and ball' quiz.

Test yourself! A bat and a ball together cost £1.10. The bat costs £1 more than the ball. How much does the ball cost? (Answers at the end of the chapter.)

Encountering human illogicality: The Linda Problem

The Linda Problem, one of the most celebrated quizzes in psychological research, is an experiment in unintended bias. It's used to illustrate how illogical everyday judgements are ridden by fallacies anchored in evolutionary history. The original experiment, by two psychology professors, Amos Tversky and Daniel Kahneman was elegantly simple. At the outset, participants were given this information:

> Linda is thirty-one years old, single, outspoken and very bright. She majored in philosophy. As a student she was deeply concerned with issues of discrimination and social justice, and also participated in anti-nuclear demonstrations.

On the basis of this character sketch, the researchers asked student volunteers to rank the likelihood (probability) of Linda having one of a list of possible jobs, ranging from 'teacher in an elementary school' to 'insurance salesperson' by way of 'works in a bookstore and takes yoga classes'. They had provided a stereotype, and waited to see if the research participants would be influenced by it.

The context seemed to be that of matching a psychological type (as per the short description) to a career choice. By implication, the research was asking the students

questions like: Would you be surprised to find a bright philosophy student working in a bookshop and doing yoga?
Certainly, for me, the answer to that is 'no', and the students
were no different. This process, in which people use stereotypes to arrive at conclusions, has a fancy name in psychology called the 'representativeness heuristic'. That's an
off-putting term but it basically just means 'basing judgements
on typical things'. People make a lot of decisions more-or-less
subconsciously by applying preconceived stereotypes.

Being a psychology experiment, however, the researchers
tucked away a sneaky trick. One of the jobs in the list, 'bank
teller' (the American term for bank cashier) was entered
twice: the first time high up the list just as 'Linda is a bank
teller' and the second time at the bottom of the list as 'Linda
is a bank teller and active in the feminist movement'.

In essence, therefore, the question being asked of the participants, and that you can ask yourself now, is: drawing on the
earlier description of Linda's character, which of these two
statements do you think is more likely?

  ✔ Linda is a bank teller.

  ✔ Linda is a bank teller and is active in the feminist
    movement.

Tversky and Kahneman wrote their description of Linda to
make it seem highly *likely* that Linda was active in the feminist
movement, but *unlikely* that she'd have taken a job in a bank.
Thus, nearly all the students considered the first option, of
Linda becoming a bank teller, to be improbable. But by linking
the unlikely element of the description of Linda to the likely
one, the researchers found that a full 89 per cent of students
were persuaded that the description 'Linda is a bank teller
and is active in the feminist movement' was plausible, and
certainly *much more so* than the simpler claim.

Yet here's the catch — how can Linda being a bank clerk of
one particular kind be more likely than her being a bank clerk
of all possible kinds? Oops! That's illogical.

In fact, as the logicians say: *the probability of a conjunction
is never greater than the probability of its conjuncts.* In other
words, the likelihood of two particular things happening must
be less than just one of them happening. Your being hit on the

head by a flying pig tomorrow is very unlikely, your being hit on the head by a flying pig tomorrow *and* getting rained on is a bit less likely again, no matter how rainy a bit of the world you live in. It's kind of an iron rule, like 2 + 2 = 4. Don't argue with it! (A *conjuction* is two or more things joined together in some sense, and a *conjunct* is just one or other of the things.)

To cut a long story short, simple logic seems to dictate that Linda being a bank teller *tout simple* is more likely than her being a bank teller *and* a feminist. But Tversky and Kahneman drew much more general conclusions than just that people don't understand formal logic. They declared that the result was solid evidence of the illogicality of human thinking. The research has been cited many times since to wag a cautionary finger at those who see human beings as rational creatures who use the lessons of experience to learn and improve their navigation of life, and to make most people look dumb instead.

However, you don't have to rush to agree. On the contrary, many possible arguments can be made as to why the second description is more likely than the first one, and why that 89 per cent were quite entitled to say so. It all depends on the way words work, which is rather more complex than Tversky and Kahneman, let alone subsequent logicians, seem to have allowed. (For more on this famous and revealing experiment, read the nearby sidebar 'Another possible way to argue for intuition against logicians'.)

A CLOSER LOOK

Another possible way to argue for intuition against logicians

Critical Thinkers always need to ask why the mathematical model of the probabilities is so at odds with human intuition. Another way of modelling the Linda problem is to argue that when one of the categories includes two pieces of information, by *implication* all the categories do too. In this case, by adding 'and is a feminist' to the description of Linda

as a bank teller, the researchers also added a rider to each of the other descriptions. It might be the implication that she is not a feminist. At the very least, it would be something like 'and there is no information about whether or not she is a feminist'. In that sense, as far as these jobs go, her status as feminist or not isn't known — it's undetermined.

(continued)

(continued)

When no information is available for an undetermined value like this, the conventional way is to make it being true or false equally likely — that is to compute it with the value 0.5. (That's how mathematicians calculate the odds of something that in everyday language is said to be 'evens', or 50:50.)

With real life being full of uncertainties and many possible career paths being available, Linda's job is very hard to predict, and so all the options must have a very low probability, even her being an elementary school teacher. In those numerical values so beloved of logicians, you can for the sake of argument put the likelihood of her being a bank teller at 0.01 (1 in 100) and the chance of her being the teacher at 0.1 (1 in 10). On the other hand, her being a feminist is almost certain — the description makes it so: call it 0.9 (9 in 10).

Thus the prediction that 'Linda is a bank teller' can be represented as $0.01 \times 0.5 = 0.005$ (5 in 1000) and 'Linda is a bank teller and a feminist as $0.01 \times 0.9 = 0.009$ (9 in 1000), in which case, unambiguously, the extra information *increases the likelihood* of the latter option. If the maths is treated this way, then, just as almost all the students insisted, Linda being a feminist bank teller really is more likely than her being a bank teller who may or may not be a feminist.

This way of recalculating the options brings the logic into line with intuition, which is how such things should be done, rather than vice versa. I'm not saying it *is* the right way to look at things, mind — what do you think?

Considering the power of group thinking

Consider for a moment, if you'd be so kind, why you're reading this book: perhaps it's a project of your own devising to become more logical. Or, on the contrary, perhaps this book is part of a kind of extreme groupthink — brainwashing even — an effort by society to make you think a certain way! Outlandish idea perhaps, but that's one possible implication Professor Deanna Kuhn draws from her research into psychology and education. She is concerned that as a society people spend much of their time and effort determining what they believe but seem to care little about how they come to believe what they do.

Questioning your beliefs

The question as to the extent people are in control of their decisions, and the extent to which they simply follow other people, is important to Deanna Kuhn.

She believes that Critical Thinkers should see thinking *as a form of argument,* because individuals' beliefs are chosen from among alternatives on the basis of the evidence for them. However, her research caused her increasingly to question the extent to which individuals actually do hold their beliefs on the basis of evidence, instead of as a result of social pressures.

 Deanna Kuhn's rather alarming conclusion is that many people don't or can't give adequate evidence for the beliefs they hold. Worse! People are unwilling or unable to consider revising their beliefs when presented with evidence against them. Kuhn holds that reasoned argument requires, at the very least, this ability to distinguish between the theoretical framework and the physical evidence.

Cascading information

 Cascade theory is the idea that information cascades down the side of an informational pyramid — like a waterfall. If people don't have the ability or the interest to discover something for themselves, they find that adopting the views of others is easier. This act is without doubt a useful social instinct and an individual relying on information passed on by others is often quite rational. (After all, thinking is difficult and energy-sapping, as I explain in the earlier section 'Jumping to con-clusions: The cost of fast thinking'.)

 Unfortunately, following wrong information is less rational, and that's what often happens. People cascade uselessly in everyday ways, like so many wildebeest fleeing a non-existent lion. A lot of economic activity and business behaviour, including management fads, the adoption of new technologies and innovations, not to mention the vexed issues of health-and-safety regulation, reflect exactly this tendency of the herd to follow poor information.

There are two possible, but conflicting, strategies, for coping with the tendency of people to unthinkingly absorb and follow duff information:

✔ Some people suggest that society needs to encourage a range of views to be heard, even when they're annoying to the 'majority'. For instance, allowing people to deny global warming or to let teachers decide what they're going to teach.

✔ Other people say that society needs stricter control of information to stop the spread of 'wrong views'. This view is the one currently cascading down the pyramid.

For a great example of cascade theory, check out the nearby sidebar 'Don't snack on chips while reading this!'

Don't snack on chips while reading this!

One of the best examples of information cascade is the entirely false consensus around the danger of so-called fatty foods, despite it having no medical or scientific basis.

The theory originates to a single researcher called Ancel Keys, who published a paper saying that Americans were suffering from 'an epidemic' of heart disease, because their diet was more fatty than their bodies were accustomed to after thousands of years of natural evolution. In the following years, results from four other countries appeared to confirm that a high-fat diet coincided with high rates of heart disease.

Unfortunately for this theory, prehistoric 'traditional diets' turn out not to be especially 'low fat' after all, and in the most relevant period of a hundred years before the supposed 'epidemic' of heart disease, Americans had actually been consuming large amounts of fatty meat, and so the epidemic followed a reduction in the amount of fat consumed — not an increase.

The problem is that the human brain is quite good at seeing things the way it wants to see them, rather than the way there really are. It can even see patterns in raw data — that don't exist. For example, Keys simply excluded the many countries that didn't fit his theory (like France and Italy with their oily but healthy cuisine), and the obvious factor for higher rates of heart disease that people were now living long enough to develop heart disease (rather than being killed off by things like diseases). But the cascade had started. Soon (despite the protests of specialist researchers about the lack of good evidence) hardly any doctors were prepared to speak out against such an overwhelming 'consensus'.

In fact, in recent years, large-scale studies in which comparable groups have been put on controlled diets (low-fat and high-fat) appear to show that the low-fat diet seems to be unhealthy! But no one is quite sure why.

So the next time someone says that 'all the experts agree' — even if they're philosophers, Nobel Prize winners or even TV personalities — don't be so sure that that proves anything at all.

Watching How the Brain Thinks

Wouldn't you love to be able to see a great brain — such as Einstein's, Copernicus's or Robbie Williams's — thinking? To watch as the neurons spark into action and they solve another mystery of the universe like: 'How are space and time related?', 'Maybe the Earth goes round the Sun!' or 'Why don't I have hit records anymore?'

It's important for Critical Thinkers to know whether they really can think freely — or are only churning through data, more or less efficiently, in the manner of a very complicated computer. In this section I look at some of the arguments for thinking that the human mind is actually more complicated than that — and by implication capable of achieving more things.

'My nerves are playing up': The brain at work

Francis Crick, the 20-century British biochemist who played a key role in the discovering of DNA, imagined he'd solved the mystery of how human beings think. He put it all down to nerve cells and molecules. Many academics take what seems a small step from this conclusion to assuming, as Stephen Pinker puts it, that the 'mind is a system of organs of computation designed by natural selection to solve the problems faced by our evolutionary ancestors'.

Raymond Tallis, however, is appalled by this 'Darwinization of our understanding of humanity' as well as by *neuromania* more generally, which he defines as the almost ubiquitous use of what's offered as the latest brain science to (supposedly) reveal how the human mind works. The stakes are high too, he warns, muttering about the awful lessons of history, when societies adopted policies based on pseudo-science and applied them with great cruelty against millions of individuals. (I say more about this in Chapter 3.)

Can scientists really read thoughts in the brain?

Neuroscience — the science of the brain — is all about new technology. Raymond Tallis is a medical man, and he points out rather revealingly that fMRI 'brain scanners' aren't infallible and can be rather imprecise; they certainly can't pinpoint particular thoughts placed in minds by the social scientists.

Forget all those colour pictures in magazines of people's brains working as they are shown pictures of 'loved ones' — or maybe fast food. Because Tallis accuses the experiments with brain scanners as being laughably crude and 'mind-numbingly simplistic'. For example, even the best scanners operate by measuring blood flow, which varies over timescales of seconds — but the real activity of the brain, the electrical changes in the busy neurons, is measured in milliseconds. Experiments in which subjects may be shown photographs of friends on the one hand, and lovers on the other, and researchers take the 'differences' in the brain scans to indicate the 'unconditional-love spot' sound amazing. Yet when more mundane experiments are done with subjects being asked to, for example, tap their fingers, researchers can deduce nothing from the brain scans about finger-tapping. So what are the chances of discovering anything about grand emotional reactions?

Neuroscience *is* very good at showing things like light getting into the brain through the eyes and triggering nerve impulses. However the gaze looking out remains another matter entirely. After all, as Tallis says, 'it is a person that looks out, not a brain'. Even neurophysiologists allow that the seen object that people construct isn't really there, but is created by the brain. But this is paradoxical — the brain is shaping the world that's it shaped by? Philosophers in particular should remember that the world is an undifferentiated mass until the mind splits it up into discrete parts.

Neuromaniacs see the mind as being nothing more (or less) than the human brain, and the brain itself as a machine. They even assume the presence of a central controller, a little person inside the big person — something akin to the program that runs in a digital computer.

But perhaps the brain and the mind aren't the same thing. Raymond Tallis refreshingly puts the contrary argument that in fact human thinking is incredibly, unbelievably complicated. At a biological level, the brain reacts in unpredictable, even chaotic, ways, and is being constantly altered by individual experiences.

The consequence of this alternative view for Critical Thinking is that issues are seen as being open and multi-dimensional, rather than settled and black-and-white. Truth is seen as coming in shades of grey, from various sources rather than being delivered 'once and for all' by an expert.

'I don't wish to know that': Preferring stereotypes to statistics

A point that Daniel Kahneman, the contemporary American psychologist, makes is that all people have a tendency to let stereotypes trump statistics. For example, if two people in your street got burgled last year, whatever the official claims about such things your assessment of the level of crime is probably too high.

Newspaper headlines provide a similar kind of distorting perspective on the world: if your paper runs a series on 'Women attacked at night walking home', while my paper runs a series on 'Why walking is good for the health', we end up with two quite different views on the same matter, based on a partial and misleading kind of 'evidence' (what we've read in the paper).

The power of the mass media to distort, if not quite *all* human thinking certainly people's assessments of risk, is shown in public anxiety over things such as children being attacked by strangers on the way to buy sweeties, or train stations being blown up in terrorist attacks.

But that's partly to do with the statistical nature of risk assessment. Humans just don't get stats! Try this problem out. Here's the data:

- ✔ A census classifies 85 per cent of men in a city as 'European' and 15 per cent as 'indigenous'.

- ✔ A witness to a street robbery identifies the assailant as 'indigenous'.

- ✔ The court tests the reliability of the witness, and he's able to identify correctly people as being either 'European' or 'indigenous' 80 per cent of the time, but he mistakes people's origins up to 20 per cent of the time.

Without being prejudiced one way or the other (of course), but having limited resources, in which community should the police prioritise its search for the street robber?

Perhaps this tendency of humans to prioritise prejudice over facts has something to do with many of the world's problems today; just a thought!

Getting Inside Scientists' Heads

I realise that this heading may produce for some people a scary image, of miniaturised Raquel Welch and Donald Pleasance being injected into a scientist's ear. So you'll be glad to know that this section actually is about getting a handle on the kind of material that you need to analyse and evaluate in many areas of life. Because Critical Thinking requires you to not only handle information effectively, but to put it into a wider context, and even, when necessary, to treat it sceptically.

The conventional view of science is of a steady progression from crude guesses to sophisticated knowledge, propelled by ever-more ingenious techniques and machinery. Science, like a majestic river, heads in only one direction, and if foolish humans attempt to erect barriers to its progress, at some point in time their obstructions are swept aside and the great wave of discovery flows on.

I take a look at this traditional approach, which involves conjecture and refutation, and also at a view that challenges it: paradigm shifts. Uncritical thinkers just want to take whatever is said or written by a scientist as the plain facts of the matter — but more sophisticated thinkers recognize that across the whole sweep of human knowledge, facts keep changing! A textbook that was a pretty good guide thirty years ago, is likely to be substantially flawed by today's standards. This section explains why.

Engaging with scientific convention

Much of the history of Western philosophy assumes a steady, comforting process: knowledge exists and just needs to be identified rationally. When firm foundations have been established, the rest of the edifice can be constructed without needing to worry about one or other bit of it later being shown to be wrong.

But this picture ignores the complexities and inconsistencies of 'real life'. Whatever people may like to think, in science, experiments don't lead to new theories, because all historically significant theories (and quite a few insignificant ones too) agree with the facts. As every politician and spin doctor knows, lots of facts exist and if you want to you can choose them to bolster your theory. Scientists are no different. *But they think they are.*

Trusting conjecture and refutation

Conventionally speaking, people suppose that when experiments are conducted to test theories in reality, and the results don't accord with those anticipated, the theory is disproven.

But some philosophers (called *critical rationalists*) reject this view — that thinking coolly and logically about the world is the route to true knowledge). Thinkers such as Karl Popper argued that no 'theory-free', infallible observations exist, but instead that all observation is theory-laden and involves seeing the world through the distorting glass (and filter) of a pre-existing conceptual scheme.

Popper writes:

> *If we are uncritical we shall always find what we want: we shall look for, and find, confirmations, and we shall look away from, and not see, whatever might be dangerous to our pet theories. In this way it is only too easy to obtain what appears to be overwhelming evidence in favor of a theory which, if approached critically, would have been refuted.*

Yet, in a way, the 18th-century philosopher David Hume was even more radical than Popper. He concluded that science and philosophy alike rested less upon the rock of logic and human reason, but rather upon the shifting sands of scientific fashion and aesthetic preferences.

Hume's approach is exactly that of the Critical Thinker — taking nothing as given but insisting on the full application of reason in all areas — ignoring and standing free from conventional opinion. Certainly, this made him unpopular in many circles, but it also gave him some great insights into many issues.

Thinking in fits and starts: Paradigm shifts

None of us can function without a set of assumptions. You can't make sense of this book unless you assume I use words the same way that you do, or that the book is read from front to back, rather than, say, from the bottom of the last page backwards — and it would seem pretty silly to start any other way (unless you live in China!). Scientists start off by making a whole load of assumptions when they try to do anything too — they have to do this. But many of these background assumptions are just guesses — and many of them get abandoned later. Worst of all, starting assumptions tend to block off other alternatives and can stymie progress.

Although a somewhat wooly terms these days, a *paradigm* is a kind of picture or way of picturing something. In its simplest form the theory of *paradigm shifts* claims that scientific knowledge proceeds in fits and starts, with theories fighting to the death, as it were, against each other, instead of as a smooth process of the accumulation and refinement that people like to imagine.

Instead of being logical or rational, scientists find that the old theory has become too complicated and cumbersome to modify, and so they collectively abandon it. Or else a split emerges between followers of one theory and another, which is eventually decided in favour of the new theory for any number of reasons, none of them particularly scientific. This abandonment of a longstanding way of seeing an issue towards a new way is the paradigm shift.

When Copernicus first cautiously suggested that perhaps a better way to understand the workings of the universe was to suppose that the Earth and the rest of the planets went around the Sun, rather than the Earth staying put and everything (including the start) rotating round it, the maths went against him. The fact was, the Moon, the Sun and the planets' movements could be better calculated and predicted using the old system, even if it was quite complicated. The Church authorities insisted that the facts (the mathematics) should decide the issue — but a few scientific radicals, like the famous astronomer and physicist Galileo, preferred the simplicity and elegance of Copernicus's new theory and campaigned in public for its acceptance.

Which side would you support — the traditional view of the universe, well supported by the 'facts and figures' — or a trendy new one which clearly needed a lot more work before it could be considered even a competitor?

Answers to Chapter 2's Exercises

Here are the answers to this chapter's exercises.

Pricing bats and balls

Fast, instinctive thinking jumps out with an answer: 10 pence! Alas, the answer is wrong. Check the maths — the bat cost £1 *more* than the ball, which means that the ball must be a real bargain at just 5 pence (bat = £1.05, ball = 5 pence to total £1.10). Slow thinking is required to come up with the right answer — as well as distrusting your intuition.

Looking for the robber

Given the numbers in the scenario, most people assume that the smart place to start looking for the attacker in the incident is among the indigenous community, because of the witness testimony, even though a 'possibility' clearly exists that the witness may have made a misidentification.

But suppose that 10,000 white people live in the city and just 1 'indigenous' one. The best strategy is then a slam-dunk for the police, isn't it? But then remember that the witness sees 'indigenous people' 20 per cent of the time. The evidence isn't so persuasive now, is it, because the witness will often say someone is indigenous when they aren't. The 'mathematically' correct answer to the original scenario is that a substantially higher probability exists that the villain involved in the street robbery was European rather than indigenous — so the police should be looking for a European robber. Mathematicians use a technique called Bayesian analysis to get an exact figure, but the important thing is to be aware of the general issue. The reliability of the identification of the robber as indigenous is, in this case, 41 per cent, only about half the 80 per cent reliability people comfortably opted for 'without thinking'.

Astronomical wrangles

You can be forgiven if you think this is a bit of a no-brainer — of course the Earth goes around the Sun, and so you support the new-fangled theory. But when you do that, you have to accept that you are throwing out any pretence that you think scientific matters should be settled on the basis of the facts and figures and evidence.

This is what the radical philosopher, Paul Feyerabend, meant when he argued in his books that in science, *the only rule is that there are no rules*, and what's more, that only by breaking rules that scientists have been able to make the progress for which they are — later on — praised.

Chapter 3

Planting Ideas in Your Head: The Sociology of Thinking

> *Faced with the choice between changing one's mind and proving that there is no need to do so, almost everybody gets busy on the proof.*
>
> —JK Galbraith (Economics, Peace and Laughter, 1971)

*M*ost people offering their views on something think that they're presenting 'just the facts, Sir', helping others to avoid errors and 'see the light', so to speak. But plenty of others — such as experts in public relations (PR), marketing and political campaigning — see their jobs as — planting new ideas in the public mind.

Now, of course, some ideas are good and socially beneficial (for example, that we need to keep rivers unpolluted and help sick children get the necessary treatment) and many others are harmless, but certain ideas are dangerous and harmful. Unfortunately, history indicates fairly convincingly that the nastiest ideas seem to be the easiest to plant! They spread like brambles while the more delicate blooms of human culture wilt and fade, if they're not actually strangled. As a Critical Thinker you need to know how to spot these pernicious ideas so that you can investigate and challenge them.

In this chapter on the social dimensions and consequences of how people think and argue, I invite you to jump into my time machine, return to the first half of the 20th century and consider the sociological insights of one Mr Hitler — and how the Nazis used propaganda to win mass support.

You may not be surprised to see that I include that master manipulator here, but I wonder about your reaction on discovering that even in the freedom-lovin' West, censorship and control of the news 'in the public interest' is never far away? Therefore, as well as discussing how politicians and advertisers influence you, I also look at how the BBC tries, and sometimes fails, to be 'balanced', and why Critical Thinking skills are vital to the wellbeing of society.

Asking Whether You're Thinking What You Think You're Thinking

Many people say that even if they don't know much about many things, at least they know what they like. But no, sorry sucker, hard luck! What they like, indeed what anyone likes, is often not their decision or choice at all. On the contrary, what people like is one of the things most susceptible to outside influence.

This section is about how social forces shape people's views, for example in the economic and marketing spheres.

Knowing how outside forces work on people

Outside forces can mould not only, say, people's musical or cinematic tastes or their political opinions, but also all those practical consumer choices that define people — something that marketing experts know very well. When you answer questions like these — you aren't really dealing with practical matters at all. Rather, you are responding to other people and trying to project a particular image of yourself:

> ✔ What kind of car do you think you need? Does it really need room satnav, seats for six children and kangaroo bars on the front?

> ✔ What kind of restaurants would you eat at? They all do food, but some you would probably rather starve first than go in.

> ✔ And clothes. Most people (yes, even me) wear the same sort of things all the time — almost a uniform. When Auntie buys me a jumper with a loud checkerboard design, I can't imagine wearing it! I'm a fashion victim — but so are you, and our ideas about the kind of shoes, socks and shirts we think are 'smart' or 'cool' to wear are not quite as free as we usually imagine.

Yet isn't it odd that a forgotten photo of me a few years back shows me wearing exactly one of those ghastly checkerboard jumpers! How could my tastes have been so bad then! For more on advertising, see the later section 'Understanding how advertising works'.

Influencing people's opinions

If you think I'm exaggerating about the power of social forces in this context, reflect for a moment on how your own views and tastes keep changing! Maybe you used to have a favourite pair of yellow, crimplene 'slacks', enjoy watching Terminator films and eat lots of popcorn. Now you think such and such is really unfashionable, and you say popcorn has long ago lost any appeal, just like the films it used to go with.

Far from tastes and opinions being things that people carefully arrive at after due consideration, they seem to be more like fashionable (or not) clothes that people change regularly. Sometimes people change entire preference sets almost overnight, particularly if their circumstances change — for example, when they go from being a radical student studying international economics to landing a lucrative job as a trader in a bank.

One journalist I know went from being the features editor on a right-wing tabloid to being deputy editor on a 'hard-left' magazine. Within a few weeks, this person's trademark trouser suit and coiffured hair-do became jean jackets and a crew cut. Circumstances alter values, even for the most independently minded person.

Consumer demand

According to JK Galbraith, the great 20th century economist, *consumer demand* (the sum of all the decisions everyone takes about the things they feel that they can't get by without, such as lunch, cars or smart phones) has very little to do with a person's individual needs and everything to do with everyone else's behaviour and opinions. Or, to be more precise, with a small group of powerful influencers' opinions.

So what sort of people are these influencers? Well, consider the business networking site LinkedIn. It's grown to be one of the web's biggest and regularly sends out emails presenting the views of a what it calls 'top influencers', usually sorted into categories such as 'Green Business' or 'Fortune Women' (the latter means women who run big companies, by the way, not women offering to read people's fortunes in their palms — pity!).

Anyway, these influencers have thousands of followers on the social networks and blogs. (I have, by comparison, three, and one of them is me under a pseudonym.) Thousands, you say? Sometimes hundreds of thousands — millions occasionally! Therefore, the 'logical' conclusion must be that their views are important.

I'm not saying that, for example, when Richard Branson states that 'polo neck jumpers are cool', millions of people immediately pop out to the shops to buy one. Influence is more subtle. As Galbraith explains, what really influences people is much more difficult to be aware of, but involves two key social forces: emulation and advertising. These forces shape all our views, even when we write essays, so a Critical Thinker needs to always be aware of them.

Emulation

Emulation is the desire to keep ahead of the neighbours, or to be more precise, to keep up with the *peer group*. This desire is so universal that it seems only 'normal' to be like that and, frankly, antisocial not to be! Teenagers are obvious examples — they *have to have* those floppy trainers, the electronic devices and the Che Guevera posters. Okay, maybe not the posters . . . though Grandpa may still want one.

But adults are no better! They have to have the family cars with satnav and the 5-minute Italian ravioli meals in the low-energy freezer compartment ready for when they get home. Even Critical Thinkers have their hidden weaknesses: for things like watching documentaries and for old bicycles and dried fruit. But maybe I'm wrong about the typical Critical Thinker — after all, I'm not a marketing expert. Nonetheless, if you buy a book on Critical Thinking skills on the Internet these days, a computer algorithm *will* soon link you to other 'products you may be interested in' — and put ads for them under your nose to tempt you. What kinds of things have been popping up recently on web pages to tempt you?

Galbraith explains consumer choices by saying that demand for a product and the desire of a company that produces goods (or services) for a market are locked in a feedback cycle — as production increases, so too does need for the product, or something like it. Hence the developed world's problem with people over-eating, why electronic devices demand ever larger chunks of people's time and even why cupboards never have enough room for everyone's shoes or coats.

Advertising

The second key force Galbraith identifies is *advertising*. This is at its most effective when it talks about things that you already have some sense you may want — when it persuades you to buy this brand rather than any other.

But in terms of economics, its significance is its role in creating *new* wants, *new* desires. (I talk much more on how advertising works in the later section 'Manipulating Minds'.)

Thinking and Indoctrination: Propaganda

This section is all about the Three Ps — Prejudice, Propaganda, and Public Relations. The gold standard for Critical Thinking is usually said to be balance, depth of understanding, and accuracy — and certainly the 3Ps sit uncomfortably with that. Even so, of course, the issues are not black and white — publicity for a good cause we salute, and when is a strong conviction a prejudice and when is it a courageously held view?

Originally, the word *propaganda* meant 'planting ideas' and was quite a positive notion. Teachers plant ideas in children's minds, for example. The hate propaganda of the Nazis changed all that though, and in the 21st century, nearly all governments eschew propaganda and instead pay lip-service to the values of a free and independent voice for teachers, the press and TV. Even so, they make sure that education and the media, especially the news media, are firmly under government 'supervision', which can quickly become control.

'Here's what you think, comrade': Russia and China

In Russia, the brief flowering of different viewpoints that President Gorbachev encouraged in the 1980s (called *glasnost* or 'opening up') was soon replaced by ruthless suppression of independent voices, in favour of a centralised system.

Snooping on snapshots and selfies

In 2014, the London *Guardian* revealed that the British and American governments were routinely reading people's emails and even checking photos that teenagers swapped on mobile phones. As a result, the British secret services visited the paper and insisted on destroying the hard disks of the computers from which the story was drawn — all 'in the public interest', of course! This was accompanied by some scary advice about how

Bad People could listen to conversations by focusing lasers on the journalists' coffee cups. (What do cups of coffee say to one another I wonder!)

The scariest thing about the whole incident, however, is that before the paper ran its story, it had already asked the government to check it over. When a paper seeks government approval for its stories, there's no longer a free press.

These days, this revolves around the official Russian state news agency, led (at the time of writing) by Dmitry Kiselev (a former talk show host notorious for his charming suggestion such as that gays' hearts should be incinerated in ovens). Under such centralised government guidance, the Russian media majors in one subject — praise of the Russian president.

No wonder the current president, Vladimir Putin, has achieved ever higher popularity ratings at home, busy waging mini wars to 'protect' ethnic Russians and creating laws such as one against 'homosexual propaganda', which opponents say has caused an upturn in homophobic violence and threats. Not a new idea, of course: Hitler also increased his popularity when he targeted gays, making them wear a special pink triangle. (Later on, many homosexuals died in the concentration camps.)

Countries such as China stress a different kind of news management. Printed stories are carefully checked to be 'safe and suitable' for public consumption and thousands of people are paid to monitor Internet chat sites and discussion boards for signs of 'undesirable' political comment. The government pays teams of watchers to note the names and IP addresses (electronic details that identify the geographical location of computer users) of anyone posting 'dangerous' views or 'misinformation' and many an anonymous (that's what they thought!) surfer later receives a sinister 'knock at the door'.

Mr Hitler appealing to the Man in the Street

If you want to know about how governments can manipulate their citizens' minds, you have to know about Hitler. Hitler and his henchman, Goebbles, made propaganda into a science — and since they were very proud of what they were doing, they leave Critical Thinkers lots of insider information on just how it all works. Both knowledge and analysis of Hitler's techniques is invaluable for Critical Thinkers for spotting similar things that go on today.

Adolf Hitler was originally a not-very good watercolour artist and a very disgruntled demobbed soldier. However, his speciality was propaganda and mass-suggestion. In his autobiography, *Mein Kampf* (1923, which translates as 'My Struggle') he writes:

> *The art of propaganda lies in understanding the emotional ideas of the great masses and finding, through a psychologically correct form, the way to the attention and thence to the heart of the broad masses. . . . The receptivity of the great masses is very limited, their intelligence is small, but their power of forgetting is enormous. In consequence of these facts, all effective propaganda must be limited to a very few points and must harp on these in slogans until the last member of the public understands what you want him to understand by your slogan.*

For more on how Hitler manipulates with emotion and what he thought of the public, check out the later sections 'Appealing to Feelings: The Psychology of Argument' and 'Manipulating Minds and Persuading People', respectively.

Mein Kampf is surprisingly readable. It opens with an engaging, even amusing, account of his arrival in Vienna from the provinces, aged 15. This technique is used to create the image of the personable, charming Mr Hitler who so impressed some Western statesmen. It also connects to the style of personal narrative that modern-day politicians often substitute for discussion of political programs — like Hitler, to win over voters by appealing to their emotions rather than their intellects (see Figure 3-1).

You often read about the almost hypnotic effect Hitler had on his audiences and of his extraordinary skills as a speaker, but I think the truth is rather more prosaic than that. (Look at one of the old clips showing him speak if you don't believe me!) Using the age-old technique of saying one thing in public and doing quite another in private, Hitler based his political messages on a shrewd and realistic assessment of popular opinion and the views of 'the man in the street'.

Hardly anyone today can be found who says that they like his message, but that only makes it more worrying that in a few years under Hitler's marketing, the Nazis went from being a handful of disaffected ex-soldiers meeting in a pub every week, to a mass movement of millions, capable, in due course, of seizing control of one of the world's most intellectually sophisticated nations.

Figure 3-1: Sticking to your beliefs isn't always easy. This famous image shows a crowd of people giving the Nazi salute, with just August Landmesser refusing to do so.

Even though the death camps came only at the end of Hitler's period in government, the Nazi doctrine (which always and unambiguously anticipated them) was initially embraced by many in the Western democracies as a fine thing. (See the nearby sidebar 'What the papers said about Nazism'.)

What the papers said about Nazism

Hitler says he learnt the black arts of propaganda from the English. He credits the British War Office for showing him to limit messages to a few points, devised specifically for mass consumption, and repeated with indefatigable persistence.

The London newspapers admired him. When Adolf Hitler became Chancellor on 30 January 1933, the British newspaper magnate, Lord Rothermere, produced a series of articles acclaiming the new regime. The *Daily Mail* criticised 'the old women of both sexes' who filled British newspapers with rabid reports of Nazi 'excesses'. Instead, the newspaper claimed, Hitler had saved Germany from 'Israelites of international attachments' and the 'minor misdeeds of individual Nazis will be submerged by the immense benefits that the new regime is already bestowing upon Germany'.

(continued)

(continued)

Before war eventually changed its minds, the British government wasn't unduly concerned that in *Mein Kampf* Hitler suggested killing ethnic minorities, 'Reds' and disabled people. In fact, the *Daily Express* enthusiastically covered the visit of the former British Prime Minister Lloyd George to see the newly declared German *Führer* and uncritically reported his comments:

I have now seen the famous German leader and also something of the great change he has effected.

Whatever one may think of his methods — and they are certainly not those of a parliamentary country, there can be no doubt that he has achieved a marvelous transformation in the spirit of the people, in their attitude towards each other, and in their social and economic outlook.

(Extract from the report published in the *Daily Express*, London, September 17, 1936)

The moral is, don't believe everything you read in the papers!

Appreciating the Difficulties of Staying Impartial

The earlier section 'Asking Whether You're Thinking What You Think You're Thinking' shows that many apparently 'free' choices have been subjected to outside influences. A natural conclusion to draw from this social power is how difficult people can find being neutral, that is, to avoid 'taking sides', on any issue.

In this section I tell the story of how the British Broadcasting Corporation (BBC) threw out its charter, which stipulates balance and impartiality, and turned reporting about climate issues into propaganda for a particular cause. It campaigned against human burning of fossil fuels, such as oil and coal.

 As you read this section, think about the way public opinion is influenced by the media (within which the BBC is just one important player) — who in turn are influenced by their perception of public opinion!

Being neutral . . . up to a point: The BBC

All BBC staff carry an identity card proclaiming the BBC's first mission, to be independent, impartial and honest. Yet, as a 2007 BBC report, gnomically entitled 'From Seesaw to Wagon Wheel' (subtitled more helpfully: 'Safeguarding Impartiality in the 21st Century'), acknowledges, impartiality is easier to talk about than achieve.

As the BBC report says, recent history is littered with instances of mainstream opinion moving away from the prevailing consensus. Examples include the change of monetarism from being advocated by a few right-wing economists to a central feature of every European government's economic policy. Or the increasingly widespread Euro-sceptic views towards the European Union or the apparent drop in support for multiculturalism among the UK's politicians. What's a neutral BBC reporter to do when covering such subjects?

Things are hotting up: The BBC and climate change

The BBC report notes that climate change is a particular subject where dissenters can be unpopular:

> There may be now a broad scientific consensus that climate change is definitely happening, and that it is at least predominantly man-made. But the second part of that consensus still has some intelligent and articulate opponents, even if a small minority.

In fact, using the term *climate change* is a prejudicial way to frame the debate, because everyone agrees that climate changes — all the time. In fact, the subject is *manmade global warming!* Specifically, the government's view that it's happening and is caused by over-consumption of fossil fuels — such as coal.

The debate about how to approach many issues concerning the human impact on the environment has often been vexed and highly politicised. This issue has a huge impact on everyone — not so much because of the higher temperatures but because of all the new taxes on energy, the changes in the way energy is being generated and in the way food is grown (this last directly affecting some of the world's poorest countries most).

The BBC's report says that its policy on the issue should be that dissenters' voices can still be heard, because the BBC's role isn't to close down this debate: impartiality 'always requires a breadth of view' and 'bias by elimination is as dangerous today as it ever was'. It even adds that the BBC has many public purposes — 'but joining campaigns to save the planet isn't one of them'. Instead, programme-makers should reflect the full range of debate that such topics offer, scientifically, politically and ethically.

Struggling to find a consensus

All Critical Thinkers need to take note of the BBC's message for its programme-makers: areas of consensus need to be treated with 'proper scepticism and rigour', to avoid rushing around trying to keep up with ever-changing public opinion.

However, the alternative to reflecting a range of views is to try to find the 'consensus' view and that's the direction the organisation went. Alas, finding the consensus view is by no means as easy as many people imagine. Just think, how would you obtain a 'balanced view' on complicated not to say highly political, matters?

The BBC started off, by holding, it said, a high-level seminar in Exeter, 'with some of the best scientific experts'. After this, it came 'to the view that the weight of evidence no longer justifies equal space being given to the opponents of the consensus'. Thus, whereas previously news reports and documentaries may have said that *many scientists believe* that burning coal and oil is causing the ice caps to disappear (cue, pictures of drowning polar bears in the *Daily Mail*) and even the towering Himalayas to melt, now the BBC simply stated such things as fact.

Researching the experts' views sounds a good way to approach many matters. But a Critical Thinker has to look sceptically at this sort of 'appeal to authority'. In this case, when you do look closer, you find a little bit of 'spin' seems to have been added to the message. For a start, the BBC report doesn't mention that the seminar was partly funded by the UK government and organised in conjunction with a lobby group called the International Broadcasting Trust, both of which had a particular policy aim of increasing coverage about human environmental damage.

Likewise Exeter is a nice town, but it's an awfully long way from Broadcasting House in London. However it is the base of the UK government's research unit whose job is to produce evidence of the effects of human-made global warming.

That's some of the background set-up, the funding and the organising in question. But more importantly, who *were* the invited experts? When people asked how they were selected, the BBC went to court to prevent this information ever becoming public, to keep their 'sources' secret. This action perhaps reveals that the BBC knew it was on very weak ground. But the court granted the request.

Unfortunately for the BBC, an Italian climate sceptic found all the names of the people at the expert conference on a long-forgotten web-page. The list showed that far from a representative sample of scientific opinion, the meeting consisted of: scientists whose jobs revolved around proving the theory of human-made climate change; plenty of campaigners whose commitment to the cause of fighting global warming was in inverse proportion to their expert knowledge; and groups with financial interests such as British Petroleum. Oil companies, despite what you may have read many times, are one of the big winners of the 'coal is bad for you' policy, because for example they own most of the world's gas reserves — and very few coal mines!

These experts' evidence, however well intentioned, was almost certain to come to only one conclusion. Consensus was obtained at the expense of genuine debate. Critical thinkers don't do that sort of stuff.

Appealing to Feelings: The Psychology of Argument

Do you think what you think you think? Not likely! And nor do any of us. It turns out instead that we mostly think what we feel. You bet that 20th-century master of all the dark arts of propaganda, Adolf Hitler, knew this very clearly and so in this section I look first at how propagandists use emotional responses to bypass the reasoning part of the brain — for good or evil or just to sell washing powder. Foregrounding this technique is a crucial first step for Critical Thinkers in getting back to rational argumentation, which is where the marks, if not the votes are.

In the second section, *Grabbing the attention of the gullible*, I explain how one reason for Hitler's popularity was that he understood his audience, or to be more precise, that he recognized the different elements of it. Unfortunately, his comments on the public mind then are as true today as ever, and thus are essential for anyone seeking to persuade others of a certain point of view to bear in mind.

Using emotions to powerful effect

One of Hitler's all-too-influential ideas is that slogans are a much better way to influence mass opinion than arguments, and debate is always best avoided. (That's right, what you are studying in this book, which is all about the importance of real debates and well-founded arguments has almost nothing to do with influencing popular opinion.)

Instead of facts, much of *Mein Kampf* comprises pages upon irrelevant pages of Hitler's early years, views on clothing, descriptions of the appearance of Jews and so on. This is because *Mein Kampf* is a new kind of political philosophy — it's not a work of rational argument but of irrational or emotive appeals.

It was the first of a new kind of political manifesto that used the kinds of methods and pulled the kinds of levers that marketing experts use, rather than plodding through formal arguments backed by boring old evidence!

The reality that voters are persuaded less by arguments than by feelings is illustrated quite unambiguously by Jutta Rüdiger, in this account of her feelings after she heard Adolf Hitler speak in Düsseldorf in 1932.

> *I must say it was an electrifying atmosphere. . . . Even before 1933 everybody was waiting for him as if he was a saviour.*

Then he went to the podium. I remember it all went quiet, and he started to speak in his serious voice. Calm, slow, and then he got more and more enthusiastic. I must admit, I can't remember exactly what he actually said. But my impression afterwards was: this is a man who does not want anything for himself, but only thinks about how he can help the German people.

Grabbing the attention of the gullible

Hitler writes that the politician (and equally campaigners, journalists and advertisers) aiming to influence opinion should aim to attract attention, and should definitely not be in the business of trying to educate people. The initial approach, the attempt to get people's attention, should be 'aimed at the emotions and only to a very limited degree at the so-called intellect'. After all, as he says with great cynicism:

> *All propaganda must be popular and its intellectual level must be adjusted to the most limited intelligence among those it is addressed to . . . . Consequently, the greater the mass it is intended to reach, the lower its purely intellectual level will have to be.*

Hitler, now truly into his role of a pioneer 'spin doctor', analyses in some detail the audience for propaganda, which divides into three groups:

- ✔ **Those who believe everything they read:** Naturally, this group of the gullible is the largest, which has social and you may say practical advantages. It's also obviously at the heart of most of the tragedies of human history. As a reader of this book, you don't fit in this category.

- ✔ **Those who have ceased to believe anything:** This group is smaller, composed of people who previously belonged to the gullible, but who've been upset by events and have shifted to the opposite extreme where they no longer believe anything and instead suspect everything. Hitler writes that

> *They hate every newspaper; either they don't read it at all, or without exception fly into a rage over the contents, since in their opinion they consist only of lies and falsehoods.*

These people are very hard to handle, since they are suspicious even in the face of the truth. Consequently, they are lost for all positive, political work.

Are you a total denier? Or do you belong instead in this last group?

✔ **Those who examine critically what they read and judge accordingly:** In other words, a subtle critical thinker.

Here's what Hitler has to say about these people:

Most of them in the course of their lives have learned to regard every journalist as a rascal on principle, who tells the truth only once in a blue moon. Unfortunately, however, the importance of these splendid people lies only in their intelligence and not in their number — a misfortune at a time when wisdom is nothing and the majority is everything! Today, when the ballot of the masses decides, the chief weight lies with the most numerous group, and this is the first: the mob of the simple or credulous.

The Critical Thinkers group is always bound to be the smallest in Hitler's assessment. It consists of

the minds with real mental subtlety, whom natural gifts and education have taught to think independently, who try to form their own judgment on all things, and who subject everything they read to a thorough examination and further development of their own. They will not look at a newspaper without always collaborating in their minds, and the writer has no easy time of it.

The masses are gullible and easily led, and so Hitler says that through education and control of the press, the State has to 'prevent these people from falling into the hands of bad, ignorant, or even vicious educators'. Well, he'd know!

Spotting prejudice dressed as science

I've said quite a lot about how propaganda avoids formal arguments and tries to go behind the scenes, as it were, to appeal to the emotions, but many campaigns do use at least the appearance of factual, maybe even scientific, claims to compel people to accept their conclusions. In this section you can find out about one of the most influential 'bad arguments' in history, and one of the nastiest — and have a go at trying to counter it.

Nazism is a philosophy with only one plank — prejudice. It was successful because prejudice, against other races or religions, or against old people (or young people!) or sick people, whatever it is, however outrageous, however irrational, is never deeply buried in the human psyche.

Hitler launched his early tirades, as he would his later wars, against all sorts of imagined categories of 'inferior humans', such as the Slavs, the 'negroes' and even his later allies the Japanese and Italians. Hitler explains the significance of his theories on pure blood to the German public with a crude pastiche of Darwin's evolutionary theory:

> *Any crossing of two beings not at exactly the same level produces a medium between the level of the two parents. This means: the offspring will probably stand higher than the racially lower parent, but not as high as the higher one. Consequently, it will later succumb in the struggle against the higher level. Such mating is contrary to the will of Nature for a higher breeding of all life. The precondition for this does not lie in associating superior and inferior, but in the total victory of the former. The stronger must dominate and not blend with the weaker, thus sacrificing his own greatness.*

How would you push back again this argument? It's not a new view, that much-respected historical figure Plato used a very similar line in one of his books, and nor is it a view that disappeared with Hitler after the war, but instead has been used (in a different form), for example, in the US against Native Americans and in European countries against disabled people.

The tragic fact is that the Nazi political platform did attract mass support. Particularly, you may be surprised to know, among women. Although the Nazis official programme insisted that women should have no say in matters outside the organisation of household life and the bringing up of children, Hitler himself noted that women's votes got him into power (though plenty of men helped too!).

Nazi policy in everyday practice

As well as different races and religions, the Nazis also wanted to 'eliminate' deviant artists, trade unionists, gypsies, homosexuals and the disabled — all in order to make German society 'healthy'. Therefore, Hitler planned to take up the ancient notion of *breeding* better people. His nasty, 'ideal state' not only outlawed contraception but also forbade procreation for anyone on his list of undesirables. In fact, he ruled out children for most of the citizens under one or other prejudice!

Some arguments in Critical Thinking books, like The Times Cryptic Crossword or a *Suduko* puzzle, can seem too artificial to be worth sorting out, but there are plenty of real arguments that do matter. Here's just one example of what this particular policy meant.

Liselotte Katscher was a nurse and she writes about doctors in a hospital — I expect not very different and no better or worse than anyone else — who propelled by the force of Hitler's argument, participated in the forced sterilisation of a 16-year-old girl called Henny:

> Henny was examined by a doctor who diagnosed a slight feeble-mindedness — in my opinion it was only a slight feeble-mindedness, and they decided that she should be sterilized. I thought about it a great deal at the time, and I felt sorry for the girl, **but it was the law, and the doctors had decided.** I personally took her to the maternity ward in the hospital where it took place. But I never got rid of the doubt in my mind that the decision was too harsh. . . . The tragedy was that she was released very soon after this, then got a job and met a nice young man, and was now not allowed to marry him because of her sterilisation.

Note the point in bold — how many people have the courage to oppose 'the law' and expert opinion? Indeed, most of the time, they'd be wrong to do so!

Manipulating Minds and Persuading People

In this section I look at another 'nasty but true' lesson from Hitler, and then in 'Understanding how persuasion in society works' I plunge into current thinking in marketing and consumer advertising, and show how the 'persuaders' can be split into three main varieties, each with their own particular technique. The section *Recognising the language of persuasion* takes this a bit further and explains how psychological factors such as the technique known as *emotional transfer* can be used to make sure you don't actually think what you think you think.

The final section *Spotting the techniques being used on you!* contains some really useful techniques that you may like to try to spot.

Ever wondered why politicians are so dogmatic, and just repeat one point all the time? Hitler was sure he knew the answer: 'As soon as you sacrifice this slogan and try to be many-sided, the effect will piddle away, for the crowd can neither digest nor retain the material offered. In this way the result is weakened and in the end entirely cancelled out.'

Hitler saw the general public as being so slow to pick up on ideas that speakers had to repeat and repeat them. He also realised that the best propaganda appears not to be political at all. He advocates the 'cleansing of culture' in all fields, from theatre to the press, so that everything served to perpetuate only 'healthy' ideas — and he of course decided what was healthy.

Here, in the area of manipulating public opinion, *Mein Kampf* makes its most distinctive, if poisonous, contribution to political theory.

Understanding how persuasion in society works

The goal of most media messages is to persuade the audience to believe or do something. Hollywood movies use expensive special effects to make viewers believe that what they're seeing is real. TV and newspapers use images — which may not be quite what they appear — as well as several techniques — such as carefully selected short quotations from identified sources — to make readers believe that the story is accurate. Every time one word is used instead of another, and every small twist of grammar, subtly affects the way you interpret and receive information and messages.

Language defines and shapes the world, and language is far from neutral. The experts in the 'language of persuasion' are the people who work in advertising, public relations and campaigning:

- ✔ **Advertisers:** The most straightforward group — they seek to persuade people to buy a product or service. They usually present their message in plain sight — as an advert! — making it much easier to keep a certain critical distance from the message.

- ✔ **Public relations:** These experts 'sell' positive images – maybe of a political organisation, or of a commercial brand on behalf of a corporation, government or other organisation, and they like to do this selling covertly. A certain brand of computer may be used by the hero in a film, an ambitious politician appears in a TV documentary talking about their love of nature.

- ✔ **Campaigning (or 'advocacy') groups:** Also want people to 'buy' into particular beliefs or policies, and although they use up-front and straightforward advertisements for their views, they also try to skew debates in their favour, so that by the time representatives are actually interviewed on the show, or in the press, their views have already been presented to the reader or viewer as 'facts'.

The one constant between all these groups is that they all use the 'language of persuasion'.

Recognising the language of persuasion

The trick with the language of persuasion in advertising or campaigning more generally is to link a product or idea with something else that the audience is known to already like or desire, something full of positive associations. A breakfast cereal is linked to a beautiful young woman walking through a field of flowers, for example.

On the other hand, political and advocacy campaigns often link to things the audience is known to dislike or fear. Think about how many times you've seen the following images used:

- ✔ **To sell 'protectionist' policies on trade:** Unappealing images of foreigners, or scary images of shuttered factories and sad-looking citizens queuing for food handouts.

✔ **To sell the idea that taxes on energy should rise:** Official reports warning that the Amazon is drying out, that many coastal cities will disappear under the waves and tropical diseases invade your home town.

✔ **To sell organic alternatives:** Health-food companies have used tales of children dying from pesticides.

These horror scenarios are irrelevant to most people's lives today. But the persuaders know that messages are more powerful when they're stated indirectly — when the association is implied. Psychologists refer to the process as *emotional transfer*. I include several of the most common persuasion techniques in the next section.

Spotting the techniques being used on you!

Here are some sneaky techniques that you may well be exposed to every day. Keep an eye open and see who's trying to persuade you of their views, using these kinds of methods. Think of this list as beautiful people being warm and fuzzy!:

✔ **Everyone else is doing it:** The so-called bandwagon effect. People do like to follow the crowd! Which book is best — see the one that's selling most. Which restaurant has the best food — this one has the most clients in it! So when an advertisement shows a lot of fun-looking, happy people doing something, everyone wants to 'be part of it' too. Politicians use the same technique when they claim to speak for 'everyday people', and of course 'hard-working families'.

✔ **Be like your hero:** The views of beautiful people, famous people, successful people and role models of various kinds are much more interesting than just anyone's views, and campaigners of all stripes know this. The exception, of course, is when the message is about 'everyone thinks such and such', when a celebrity is a less suitable advocate and dull Mr and Mrs Brown seem very convincing. Naturally, in an advert Mr and Mrs Brown are actually actors – not plain at all!

✔ **Trust me:** Often people want an expert view. How many boxes of detergent have been sold because the actor recommending it put on a white coat and black-rimmed specs? Just as in a hospital, uniforms reassure, and the appearance of being part of an expert group is all that matters.

Many areas of current public controversy, such as 'are fossil fuels causing the planet to overheat' or 'can alternative health techniques ever work' are regularly supposed to be settled merely by producing evidence of a large majority of experts on one side of the issue. (Don't forget: sometimes, 'plain folks' can also be experts, as when a housewife endorses a brand of washing powder.)

✔ **Weasel words:** Remarkably little can be said if you know how to slip in the odd weasel word! Lawyers, politicians and scientists have all great skill in using these. Unproven, exaggerated and outrageous claims can be made, as long as they're accompanied by words such as may, can, could, some or many. Watch for those giveaway words that render the claim in the passage more or less meaningless.

✔ **Flattery:** That nice method of polishing egos. People selling you something are the nicest people in town. They admire your taste and judgement: 'You know a good thing when you see one!', 'You demand quality', 'You deserve the top of the range!'

✔ **Warm and fuzzy:** Ah! Looking at images of families on holiday, kids playing with pet animals can be relied on to produce those 'warm and fuzzy' feelings in the viewer, especially if aided by great music, pleasant voices and maybe some visual special effects too — cue 'pink sunset' over ocean!

Answers to Chapter 3's Exercise

Check out some of my thoughts on this chapter's Try This exercise.

Hitler on eugenics or breeding people

In style, this argument is a 'scientific' one, though not a very good one. Suppose that Hitler is right — that when two people, ah, breed, and the result is offspring not as good as the best parent but better than the worst. Hitler's idea was to take all the best specimens in Germany and get them to breed, while forcibly stopping all the rest. Go for a moment with that. But then what would happen? Clearly the best specimens would still be breeding with the not-quite-as-good, and so the quality would still drop.

So the logic of the argument is to allow only a handful of people to breed, and to build up a new 'super gene pool' from this handful. This would require 'in-breeding' — relatives marrying near relatives. This practice is pretty universally discouraged, because the gene pool degrades and children are born with illnesses.

This way of looking at Hitler's argument is taking it as it stands and extending it. The extension isn't ridiculous, but merely logical. It leads to what looks like a contradiction 'on his own terms'.

Another possible objection is to ask how come any 'high quality' specimens are even left at the time Hitler was writing? If random mixing of genes drives out excellence in favour of mediocrity, this process must have ruined the Aryan stock long before Hitler arrived to save the nation!

But the best way to look at arguments like this is to challenge the underlying assumptions. Here, Hitler is really advancing his view that 'The right of personal freedom recedes before the duty to preserve the race'. This is a general principle that continues to be actively debated in modern societies and whose implications continue to be controversial. You can refuse to accept this kind of starting assumption.

Chapter 4

Assessing Your Thinking Skills

> *I do not know what I may appear to the world, but to myself I seem to have been only like a boy playing on the sea-shore, and diverting myself in now and then finding a smoother pebble or a prettier shell than ordinary, whilst the great ocean of truth lay all undiscovered before me*
>
> — *Isaac Newton (as recorded in Memoirs of the Life, Writings, and Discoveries of Sir Isaac Newton, 1855, by David Brewster)*

*N*ewton was a pretty clever chap, but a key part of his cleverness was being open-minded and curious, and thinking in unconventional ways. These are the hallmarks and the key skills of the Critical Thinker. And the good news? Everyone can develop them. So, if you can read only one chapter in the book — make it this one! It offers an overview of all the aspects of thinking that people often overlook. For too long courses supposed to help you think have plodded through various kinds of 'rules' and exercises that use only a tiny, narrow kind of 'thinking'.

In this chapter, I explain why these days informal logic is moving away from its focus on dissecting arguments that seem valid but aren't, towards a view of truth and the appropriate use of arguments that puts a much greater emphasis on the context. The skills needed turn out to be much more social than mathematical.

After all, if arguments are restricted to those involving clear propositions, most of the issues people encounter in real life, or most of the mass messages they're bombarded with every day, aren't 'arguments' at all! Traditional Critical Thinking too often focuses on what's in an argument — and neglects to look at what's been left outside, whether inadvertently or deliberately. This chapter helps you to avoid that pitfall!

Discovering Your Personal Thinking Habits

This section concerns the theory that because humans are animals that live in groups, their minds have a tendency to think *sociocentrically,* that is, to think like everyone around them.

First of all, this section tips you off about what's too often wrong with education, and why it fails to give people any real training in Critical Thinking. Then, you get a chance to find out how *you* measure up to the ideal, with my own specially crafted thinking test. Don't worry; it's quite fun and definitely an eye opener.

Identifying the essence of Critical Thinking

It's true that no one seems to have heard of him nowadays, but this section gives you a taste of the views of the man who, in many ways, started the whole Critical Thinking ball rolling about a century ago, and whose ideas continue to influence the way the subjects is taught now.

Over a century ago William Graham Sumner published a ground-breaking study of 'how people think', which blended elements of sociology and anthropology, called *Folkways* (1906). Sumner is not particularly well known, but he was a remarkable man, a true *polymath* (expert at everything), with a keen interest in public affairs.

Despite the title, the message of his study is anything but whimsical: he says that people's thinking skills are systematically drained out of them in schools, colleges and the workplace! Sound plausible? The trouble is, modern education is rooted in assumptions about the need to turn individuals into citizens ready to play a role in society. As he puts it:

> *Schools make persons all on one pattern, orthodoxy. School education, unless it is regulated by the best knowledge and good sense, will produce men and women who are all of one pattern, as if turned in a lathe. An orthodoxy is produced in regard to all the great doctrines of life. It consists of the most worn and commonplace opinions which are common in the masses. The popular opinions always contain broad fallacies, half-truths, and glib generalizations.*

> —*William Graham Sumner (Folkways, 1906)*

Everyone is like this — fortunately, you're now aware of it! The solution, or antidote, according to Sumner is a hefty dose of Critical Thinking skills in life and in education:

> *Criticism is the examination and test of propositions of any kind which are offered for acceptance, in order to find out whether they correspond to reality or not. The critical faculty is a product of education and training. It is a mental habit and power. It is a prime condition of human welfare that men and women should be trained in it. It is our only guarantee against delusion, deception, superstition, and misapprehension of ourselves and our earthly circumstances.*

> —*William Graham Sumner (Folkways, 1906)*

For Sumner, education should be about an insistence on what he calls 'accuracy and a rational control of all processes and methods', coupled with a habit of demanding logical arguments to back up all claims along with an indefatigable willingness to rethink, and if necessary to go back and start again.

The true Critical Thinker waits for solid evidence, weighs claims coolly and resists appeals to prejudices. Such people, Sumner says, make the best citizens.

Testing your own Critical Thinking skills!

To discover how *you* measure up to Sumner's ideal, try out the test in this section. After all, tests and Critical Thinking skills seem to go hand in hand, like fish and chips, or maybe Dracula and garlic.

I looked at lots of these tests in order to prepare this one, but I should straight away confide to you that I think most of the standard tests are nonsense. No kidding, really I do.

The questions conventionally used to measure Critical Thinking skills range widely across a lot of areas — verbal skills, visual skills and of course number skills — but I doubt whether they measure anything that deserves to be called Critical Thinking. More important than that, plenty of recent research indicates that such tests are poor indicators of how anyone may do in any real-world job or situation. The tests only seem to show how good you are at doing, well, tests!

Nonetheless, lots of people do think such skills are terribly relevant and important, and they certainly tell you *something*, even if its only how well you'd do in a Critical Thinking skills paper. Naturally, a true Critical Thinker will always try new things and be quite happy to tackle tests like this both in the spirit of fun and to discover something about their own thinking patterns and preferences. So here's one to try. The time allowed for the ten questions is 30 minutes. You can find the answers at the end of this chapter — but don't cheat!

Question 1: Brain teaser

A famous architect builds a hexagonal holiday house in such a way that windows on each side point south to catch the sun. The first day that the new owners are in the house, they're amazed to see through the windows a large, furry animal slowly walk right round the house!

Two skill-stretching queries are: What colour is the beast? And how do you know?

(a) It's brown, because most large furry animals are brown.

(b) It's black . . . because bears are black.

(c) It's white . . . because of the specifications for the windows of the house.

(d) There's no possible way to answer this and if this is Critical Thinking, it's stupid.

Question 2: Word pictures

Each picture is made up of words, but also represents a common saying. Can you see what the everyday adage is?

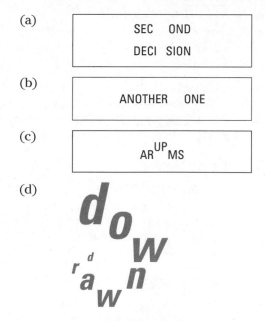

(a)
> SEC   OND
> DECI SION

(b)
> ANOTHER   ONE

(c)
> AR ^{UP} MS

(d)

Question 3: Spot the fallacy!

In the following example, try to pin down the precise problem with the argument. (For more on types of argument errors, check out Chapter 16.)

Many vegetarians believe that killing animals is wrong. If they could have their way, anyone who eats meat should go to prison.

    (a) Slippery slope

    (b) Begging the question or circular argument

    (c) Straw man

    (d) *Non sequitur*

    (e) *Ad hominem*

(Tip: Don't worry if you haven't a clue what these are about — it's just jargon. But that's one thing a lot of these tests measure. Skip to the answers now, if you want a quick decoding of the language in this question.)

Question 4: Spot another fallacy!

In the following example, try to pin down the precise problem with the argument. (You can check up on the definitions for the argument types in the answers as well as find out in more detail about some more in Chapter 16.)

Tea and coffee both contain caffeine, which is a drug. Excess caffeine intake has dangerous side effects, potentially including heart attacks. Therefore, drinking tea or coffee is dangerous.

    (a) Slippery slope

    (b) Begging the question orcircular argument

    (c) Straw man

    (d) *Non sequitur*

    (e) *Ad hominem*

Question 5: Type-casting

Which one of the following scenarios best describes a situation in which emotion rather than logic or rational thought has been allowed to decide the outcome?

    (a) Mary hates looking at herself in the mirror. She thinks she has got too fat! So she decides to take up jogging.

(b) Someone has just telephoned the college to say that they've planted a bomb in one of the buildings. Even though nothing like it has ever happened before, the school principal orders all the students and staff out of the buildings and tells everyone to go home.

(c) Mark has a job interview at a Silicon Valley computer firm and wants to look the part at his interview. He buys some computer magazines and looks at the pictures in them of the kind of people who seem to work in high-tech businesses, and tries to make himself fit that style.

(d) Jenny wants to buy a new car, but the model she likes best and can afford has high carbon emissions. She worries this may be the kind of buying decision that if lots of people took would contribute to climate change and be bad for the planet. She wants to 'be the change' she believes in, so she gets a different car that's less suitable for her needs but has a better environmental 'footprint'.

(e) The publisher is amazed at the new sales figures for Critical Thinking books, which are much higher than anyone had predicted. It decides in future to take very little notice of anything the marketing folk in the firm say.

A CLOSER LOOK

What do intelligence tests really measure?

The intelligence test taken by most students in the US, known as the Standardised Assessment Test (SAT), is an extraordinarily accurate indicator of . . . how wealthy students' families are!

If you start at families all living on between $0 and $20,000 (about £12,000), which in the US is considered very poor, the average SAT score of college-bound students is 1,326 (out of a possible 2,400). Jump to the $20,000–40,000 bracket, and the scores go up to a whisker over 1,400. In the next bracket, the scores edge up, and the same again all the way in jumps of $20,000 to the families with more than $200,000 income a year. The students coming from these 'rich families' typically score just over 1,700 points.

(continued)

(continued)

You can interpret these figures in several ways, of course. One (that suits the rich people) is to suppose that rich kids *are* smarter than poor kids. Perhaps people suggest that the parents are richer because they're smarter, and their skills have simply been 'passed on'.

A second explanation may be to say that the richer you are the better the education you get — better schools, extra tutors and so on — and so your scores go up for that reason. The SAT is recognised, despite originally being designed to treat everyone taking it equally, as being very much influenced by the amount of training students have had in taking the test. As with conventional exams, the success of students depends to some extent on their teachers' skills.

The third way of looking at this issue is to say that the test isn't measuring 'intelligence' or 'problem solving' so much as social class. Social class would tend to follow incomes. But wouldn't it be a disgrace to filter access to the best colleges by measuring which social class students come from! Such a thing would be really rather scandalous, yet that's unmistakably the lesson of this research. (A very similar kind of thing can be said for using conventional exams (such as the UK's 'A levels') as a way of deciding who should go to colleges too.)

Question 6: More type-casting

Jenny designs wallpaper for a big home decoration business. She's good at her job, but is caught out when a new and enthusiastic man joins the company and asks her for ideas for a new marketing campaign for the wallpapers? Marketing and advertising aren't her area of expertise at all.

Should she:

(a) Find out what other wallpaper manufacturers are doing to market their designs, and arrange to chat with people in the marketing department to get their views and share a few ideas. (Brainstorm it too, maybe.)

(b) Email the new man in marketing (copy to the CEO, colleagues) that she's the wrong person for this task, because she knows nothing about marketing. Suggest that if he can't think of anything himself, he should look around for someone with the right skills.

(c) Politely acknowledge the request for info, and promise to deal with it as 'a priority'. Then make sure she's not available until long after the decisions have all been taken anyway by someone else. After all, they'll probably be better qualified to handle it anyway.

Question 7: Business skills

You're stressed out about the mountain of work piling up and realise that you can't possibly finish it all. What's the smart way to meet the challenge?

(a) Do the best you can, if necessary working evenings and weekends, and skipping meals, to get it all done in some form or another.

(b) Send a note to everyone involved stating clearly that your workload is excessive and you can only do a proper job if some of the deadlines are extended and less new work is set.

(c) Recognise that it is your feelings that are the key factor — you feel tired and stressed! Reduce your working hours, take more time off, have proper meals and maybe go somewhere nice at the weekend too.

Question 8: Time management

In your job you always seem to have several tasks to complete by the end of the week. What's the most efficient way of organising your time?

(a) Be linear: Take the jobs one thing at a time, not starting a new task until you finish with the one at hand.

(b) Multitask: Tackle everything at once, because this stops you getting bored and some areas overlap, thus immediately saving time.

(c) Recognise that the problem isn't your way of working but the amount of time you have. Take a strict look at your daily timetable and clear out all the unnecessary jobs and commit yourself to putting in extra hours until the backlog is cleared.

Question 9: Justice for TV watchers

Have a look at this argument:

In Britain, every household pays the same amount for their televisions, regardless of how rich the household is, or how many TVs they have — or how much they watch them! Surely this is unfair. Instead, TV should be made a subscription service so that those who watch the most pay the most. This wouldn't only be fairer, but could also bring in more revenue.

Which of the following arguments uses the same principle as the one above?

(Hint: The question isn't about whether the argument is a good one or not, but rather about its structure.)

    (a) Things should only be available free to people if they can't afford them otherwise.

    (b) Discounts on bus and train fares should be available to people who travel most.

    (c) Rich people should pay a surcharge on their houses to help poor people who don't have a home at all.

    (d) Television channels should be funded by general taxation so that the richer you are the more you pay.

    (e) Internet sites that make a lot of money from advertising shouldn't be able to charge for access.

Question 10: Car rentals

Take a deep breath: here's the maths question!

Bodge-It Rental Cars rent out cars at a cost of £19.99 per day plus free mileage for the first 100 miles. An extra charge of £1.00 applies for every mile travelled over 100 miles.

Luxury Limos charge £100.00 per day for just taking the car out of their showrooms, and 20 pence for every single mile travelled.

How many miles would you need to travel before it paid for you to hire a Luxury Limo?

    (a) 101

    (b) 131

(c) 151

(d) 171

(e) It's *always* cheaper to hire Bodge-It

Bonus question: The riddle of the old-fashioned brew

Hint. This is another maths question and is based on a question for one of the big Critical Thinking testing organisations.

The Munchkins family makes tea following the traditional rule: 'warm the pot, and add one spoonful of tea per person plus one for the pot'.

The family used to buy a packet of Green Lion tea every week but because Grandma came to live with them, their tea buying has gone up. Now, every fifth week they buy an extra packet of tea.

Your question is: how many people were at home before Grandma arrived?

Busting Myths about Thinking

You know how your mind sort of glazes over when asked to list all the major exports of Bulgaria? Or to calculate how long a swimming pool will take to fill if a tap drips at the rate of 2.5 cm cubed every minute? But there are people who can do such things and you've probably got used to the idea that they're the smarties in the packet. In this section I describe some misconceptions that people have about thinking, rationality and logicality, and put in a word for some very different ways of seeing intelligence.

Accepting that sloppy thinking can work

In this section I look a scientific look at unscientific thinking, splitting it into two main types, and pick out when it has to be avoided, and when, maybe, it should be allowed a little more space.

Psychologists distinguish between two kinds of errors that people make when reasoning:

✔ **Motivational or 'hot' illusions:** These stem from the influence of emotions and assessments of personal interests upon the reasoning. For example, most people assume that their views now will stay the same for the foreseeable future, and fiercely defend them, even though, in reality, most people's views change and evolve all the time.

✔ **Cognitive or 'cold' illusions:** Stem from errors in your reasoning: things like mixing up correlation and causation (two things may keep happening together but that doesn't actually mean one *caused* the other) or having an unconscious bias in favour of information which fits with your existing views.

Many researchers consider that because both kinds of errors are so common, indeed almost universal, they must have some kind of evolutionary purpose, indeed advantage, for the human species.

What most people would call sloppy reasoning allows for quick responses and so may increase the chance of survival in situations where a lack of time or of background information can be fatal.

Plenty of research also suggests that people who distort assessments in favour of their own self-interest, perhaps inflating their achievements and capabilities in job interviews or in reports, do better in life. Perhaps, paradoxically, self-deception can enhance people's motivation, mood and even productivity.

That being said, cognitive illusions can also lead to unwise decisions and errors due to unrealistic assessment of risks or plain wishful thinking, or from self-deception (check out the nearby sidebar 'Everyone's a bit better than average'). The errors may lead to conflict due to resentments created by prejudice, scapegoating and so on. Other unconscious biases may lead to the phenomenon known as *attitude polarisation,* which is when two sides with perhaps only minor differences end up much further apart, because each side interprets information in distorted ways that reinforces their prejudices.

Cognitive illusions are kinds of Trojan horses that unscrupulous salespeople or politicians can use to manipulate you. For example, politicians trying to worry people about an issue, say unemployment or immigration, may use scary music and images in a commercial, because the sensation of fear generates biases that favour their position.

Trumping logic with belief

One of the most pervasive illusions from which everyone suffers is *belief bias*. This is the tendency to accept the logic of an argument not so much by a dispassionate Critical-Thinker-style analysis of its structure, but simply by an instinctive, knee-jerk assessment of the plausibility or otherwise of the conclusions.

In one study (by Jonathan Evans, Julie Barston and Paul Pollard) people were asked to evaluate arguments expressed in formal style — as *syllogisms*. (A syllogism is an argument which consists of two premises, or starting assumptions, followed by a conclusion which is supposed to follow logically on from it.)

The researchers were really investigating the extent to which people simply accept arguments they encounter that support existing beliefs, without any real examination. This idea (also explored in Chapter 2) connects to the one about the human brain being 'hard-wired' after aeons of hunting wildebeest

---

Everyone's a bit better than average

According to Thomas Gilovich, a professor of psychology at Cornell University in the US, a survey of one million high-school seniors found that 70 per cent thought they were above average in leadership ability, and only 2 per cent thought they were below average. Nor did people grow out of their unrealistic self-assessments — a similar exercise involving university professors found that 94 per cent thought they were better at their jobs than their run-of-the-mill colleagues!

Other studies reveal that most people consider themselves to be happier, more fair-minded, more skilful behind the wheel and so on than 'the average person'. Plus, of course, most people think that they're much less likely to fall into such silly errors than other people.

with sticks, to take short cuts rather than hang about to be gobbled by lions.

Here are some example syllogisms of my own to try: ask yourself which of these arguments is logical and valid?

> ✔ All dogs have fur.
>
> ✔ Boa is a python.
>
> ✔ Therefore, Boa doesn't have fur.

Valid or invalid?

> ✔ Some cats like milk.
>
> ✔ Toby is a cat.
>
> ✔ Therefore, Toby likes milk.

Valid or invalid?

> ✔ Red berries are dangerous to humans to eat.
>
> ✔ Raspberries are a kind of red berry.
>
> ✔ Therefore, raspberries are dangerous.

Valid or invalid?

I don't make you wait for the answers: neither of the first two arguments is valid. Although pythons don't have fur, the first argument hasn't proved that — it doesn't even look like it will! So, I hope you weren't taken in. In the second argument, you may have been tempted to 'give the argument some rope', because Toby probably *does* like milk if he's a cat. Nonetheless, if all you know is that 'some' cats like milk, again the conclusion isn't proved.

The third argument is sort-of-valid. I say sort-of because the wording contains a bit of fudge. The first premise 'Red berries are dangerous to humans to eat' is true in one sense and not true in another. Far too many arguments depend on such ambiguities!

Anyway, with this one, if you take the claim as being that *all* red berries are dangerous, the argument is valid, even though the conclusion isn't true. Confused? That's because in logic, a valid argument means that if the starting assumptions are true, then the conclusion must be too; so yes, *if* all red berries were really dangerous the argument is fine. In real life though, the first premise isn't true. In real life only *some* red berries are dangerous (and raspberries aren't one of them).

The common-sense intuition to take the starting statement as saying only that 'lots of red berries are dangerous to humans to eat' makes the argument invalid, because you can't draw any conclusions in this case about any particular kind of red berry.

Confirming the truth of confirmation bias

Confirmation bias is the tendency of people to focus on evidence that confirms their existing views and to ignore or discount information that may challenge those views.

Scientists, for all their reputation as dispassionate sifters of data, often fall easy prey to this bias — repeatedly rejecting experiments that come to the 'wrong' conclusions. The history of science is full of cases in which scientists carry out an experiment to prove their theory, but if the results come back disagreeing, instead of rethinking the whole theory, they suspect the experimental set-up.

Some great scientific discoveries arose through such behaviour, but also many erroneous ideas and theories were perpetuated long after they should've been abandoned.

If the problem of confirmation bias sounds rather abstract, consider this example. Mind-boggling sums are directed at developing drugs today that are supposed to help cure illnesses — and the scientists are often given the task of proving that the drugs really work. However, if the studies find that they don't work, neither the scientists nor the manufacturers benefit — therefore they tend to repeat the studies until they get a more positive result. This one is then carried forward. As a result, zillions of zlotys are spent on remedies that don't really work — and may actually be harmful!

So-called *egocentric biases* — distortions due to people having an inflated opinion of their own work or importance, for example — naturally lead to other sorts of biases:

✔ **Argument from authority:** Where someone assumes that he must be right because he's confident that he knows more than his opponents on certain topics.

✔ **Ad hominem (or directed 'at the person') arguments:** Where the views of others are dismissed out of hand, perhaps in a condescending or even insulting manner. This bias may lead people to errors in their recall or selection of facts. Who does the washing-up? 'It's always me!'

Argumentative self-control and Critical Thinking

Problems like these ones mean that Critical Thinkers also need to take a course in what's sometimes called *argumentative self-control*. This involves developing a psychological understanding of what makes people tick, alongside a logical understanding of the structure of arguments.

A good place to start is with some great tips prepared by two Dutch professors, Frans van Eemeren and Rob Grootendorst, as what they call 'a code of conduct for reasonable discussions'. These appear in a book, alarmingly called *Advances in Pragma-Dialectics* (2002), where they set out their 'ten commandments' to guide anyone in a debate. Here's my take on their 'best' four ideas (the others become rather technical and even repeat the same broad points). Therefore, to explain your approach to argumentative self-control, you can, if you like, say that you're following Martin Cohen's Four Commandments, though it doesn't have a great ring, I admit.

✔ **Rule 1: Don't stop your opponent from advancing a new position or challenging your position.** The authors call this the 'freedom' commandment, and it underpins many of the others.

✔ **Rule 2: Both sides must defend and justify their positions when asked to.**

✔ **Rule 3: Don't attack positions that no one has put forward.** No matter how much fun it is and how clever it makes you look!

✔ **Rule 4: Don't use anything except arguments to advance your position.** For example, don't appeal to people's sentiments, let alone their prejudices or fears.

Rules for arguments are all very well, of course, and few people disagree with the general principles. But arguments in the real world aren't so easily sorted out. After all, they often happen because people make genuine mistakes, or have been misled by some erroneous information — such as something they heard on the radio or read in the newspaper or in Wikipedia! Add in distortions caused by strong emotional attachments and you have a rule book that isn't really sufficient for sorting out many arguments.

Above all, conscious efforts to observe the rules of argumentation are rarely sufficient to prevent 'honest mistakes'.

'It's only logically consistent, Captain': Practical wisdom is virtuous

The ability to 'recognise salient facts', 'open-mindedness in collecting and appraising evidence', 'fairness in evaluating the arguments of others' and so on all look pretty useful and should help avoid mistakes in life. Funnily enough, the list of good instincts looks very like Aristotle's ancient 'intellectual virtues', written over 2,000 years ago (for background, see the nearby sidebar 'Getting practical with Aristotle').

Crucial to this section is Aristotle's *practical wisdom,* which he says is 'a virtue and not a technical skill'. Practical wisdom deals with change and variety. Thus it's the part of the soul that forms needed opinions. Aristotle's Big Idea is that the character (*ethos* in Ancient Greek) of the arguer is crucial. Similarly, the French philosopher, Montaigne, also says that argumentational virtues are so sensible, that once learned, they become a sort of 'second nature'.

Getting practical with Aristotle

Aristotle's tips appear in a section of his *Nicomachean Ethics,* where he identifies two parts of 'the soul': one irrational and the other rational, that grasps a rule or principle.

He subdivides the rational category again: now one part studies the eternal truths of science and mathematics and the other, which Aristotle calls the 'calculative part', deals with the practical matters of human life.

Another virtuous habit useful for anyone involved in an argument is the ability to contemplate potential objections and alternative views. Doing so offsets the two-fold tendency of humans: to overlook what contradicts their existing beliefs and views; and to rest comfortably on sources confirming their biases.

The English philosopher, John Stuart Mill, expressed this attribute plainly in *On Liberty* (1859). He states that playing devil's advocate is the duty of all thinkers: that is, to throw themselves into the 'mental position of those who think differently'. If they don't, even if they're well-educated, expert arguers and their conclusion is right, they don't know why they're right, because they haven't considered the arguments fully, deeply, equally and impartially.

In their book *Logical Self-Defense* (2006), Ralph Henry Johnson and J Anthony Blair see this problem as arising because 'the act of reasoning is rarely carried out in a situation that lacks an emotional dimension', that is, personal interests and involvements often distort the way people treat information and the way they argue, and emotional commitments make it harder to look at an issue from someone else's point of view.

Exploring Different Types of Intelligence: Emotions and Creativity

This section looks at two important but much neglected kinds of intelligence: the emotional and the creative kinds. Did you hear about IBM's powerful computer — the one that outfoxed the world's top chess masters? Well now it's struggling to develop these intelligences too. So keep ahead here.

Thinking about what other people are thinking: Emotional intelligence

According to Daniel Goleman, who popularised the term in his 1995 book *Emotional Intelligence: Why It Can Matter More Than IQ, emotional intelligence* is a mix of self-awareness coupled

Thinking emotionally for success

In his research, Daniel Goleman found that although the qualities conventionally associated with leadership — intelligence, determination, vision — are part of the recipe for success, on their own they aren't enough. The most successful people, he says, have a different kind of intelligence to the one schools normally harp on about: emotional intelligence.

Plus, Goleman believes that these skills can be developed; they aren't fixed at birth. Five million, yes, five *million* people have bought his book and so it's obviously a rentable business. (Critical Readers should note that Goleman isn't an academic as such — his background is as science correspondent for the influential newspaper, the *New York Times*.)

with the ability to manage yourself, motivation and empathy. Good leaders have social skills, in short. He contrasts it to conventional intelligence, for example the ability to understand a complicated comment — what psychologists call *threshold skills:* you have to have them, but it's what comes afterwards that makes you successful, or not.

Emotional intelligence skills

Goleman suggests that emotions play a much greater role in thought, decision-making and individual success than is commonly acknowledged.

He argues that the skills of emotional intelligence, which he sums up as self-awareness, altruism, personal motivation, empathy and the ability to love and be loved, is the key to success in life. Whereas other psychologists (for example, see the views of Daniel Kahneman in Chapter 2) want people to ignore their instincts and be more rational, Goleman wants them to tune in to their intuitions and trust their gut feelings. Check out the nearby sidebar 'Thinking emotionally for success' for more on Goleman.

Within the family, with friends and in the workplace, emotional intelligence (some people call it EQ, for emotional quotient, to contrast it with intelligence quotient, or IQ) means being able to listen to, predict and understand other people, and to know the right words to say.

Here are four tips for raising your EQ:

- ✔ **Spot emotions:** Be aware of other people's emotions. Try to notice and read nonverbal signals such as body language and facial expressions in those around you.

- ✔ **Reason with your emotions:** Use your emotions to guide your thinking, for example to help you prioritise. A common error is to give too high a priority to trivial things that are urgent, and neglect important things that don't have an obvious deadline. Using your EQ can counteract this tendency.

- ✔ **Understand emotions:** Emotions can conceal a wide range of causes. For example, if someone is getting angry, it may be because of what you've just done or are currently doing (which may trigger a defensive response from you). But it may also be because they just had some bad news (say, a speeding ticket on the way to work) or maybe they're just overtired. (In Dostoyevsky's famous book, *Crime and Punishment,* the detective Porfiry Petrovich displays great emotional intelligence and empathy in his investigation of Rodion Raskolnikov.)

- ✔ **Handle your emotions:** The ability to do this is the final key aspect of emotional intelligence. For example, an athlete may be tempted to perform a celebratory trick in the last lap — and maybe lose their focus — and the race. This actually happened at the 2006 Winter Olympics when snowboarder Lindsey Jacobellis made the mistake of celebrating her gold medal before actually having actually won it and ended up with her face in the snow.

EQ not IQ

Unlike IQ, which is gauged by highly standardised tests (such as the Stanford-Binet ones), EQ doesn't lend itself to any single numerical measure. After all, by definition it's a complex, multifaceted quality representing such intangibles as self-awareness, empathy, persistence and social skills. Some aspects can, however, be quantified. Optimism, for example. According to some psychologists, how people respond to setbacks — optimistically or pessimistically — is an indicator of how well they succeed in life.

A brief history of emotional intelligence

1930s – Edward Thorndike describes the concept of *social intelligence* as the ability to get along with other people.

1940s – David Wechsler suggests that affective components of intelli-gence, that is, the ability to deal with moods and feelings, may be essen-tial to success in life.

1975 – Howard Gardner publishes *The Shattered Mind*, which high-lights the concept of multiple intelli-gences, which are the different ways people interpret and interact with their surroundings. Conventionally, intelligence is thought of as interac-tions via things such as language and logical-mathematical analysis, but there are many other ways too, such as spatial representation, musi-cal thinking, kinaesthetic intelligence to do with the sense of shape and touch, and varieties of emotional intelligence.

1995 – The concept of emotional intelligence is popularised after pub-lication of Daniel Goleman's book *Emotional Intelligence: Why It Can Matter More Than IQ.*

The good news is that emotional intelligence involves skills you can learn, such as ambition to achieve and emotional self-control, both of which build on underlying EQ skills such as self-management. This ability to manage yourself — to have self-awareness and self-regulation — is the key to managing others. For employees, how a leader or manager makes them feel plays a large role in their level of motivation. For custom-ers and clients, how they feel about their interactions with the people in an organisation often decides their feelings about the place as a whole.

One way to boost your self-awareness is to undergo an evaluation by people you know well and trust as regards your emotional characteristics and competencies. There are some nice (and quick) tests on the internet, for example, which ask things like 'do you regularly help people by pointing out their errors and faults?' Try popping over to: www.proprofs.com/ quiz-school/story.php?title=how-selfaware-are-you for one I did really badly on!

Finding out about fuzzy thinking and creativity

Being logical is good for some kinds of problems and being emotionally in tune is useful for many more. But plenty of situations require something rather harder to pin down: creative insight.

In these kinds of situations, lots of possible answers can apply: in a sense, anything goes and the more the merrier too. It's not just at advertising confabs looking for new marketing strategies, or design consultancy brainstorms coming up with new ideas for the local supermarket car park that benefit from creative insight, but so too do hard-nosed economists trying to work out how to reboot the economy, and even doctors wondering why so many people seem to be getting colds!

Yet in many situations people still want to end up with something that commands wide acceptance, rather than just their own idiosyncratic opinion or view. In such cases, creative thinkers have to be prepared to risk losing arguments and admit that they've gone up blind alleyways.

Creativity is unstructured and unpredictable, which can be difficult if you're more used to analytical and logical approaches. With creative thinking it is important to be able to cope with risk, confusion, disorder and feeling that you're not progressing quickly. For example, many important breakthroughs in science and innovation have resulted from dreams or daydreams when the innovator wasn't trying so hard to find the answer. The rewards of creativity are golden — and not just in the arts!

Nurture your creative side: start by jotting down any inspirations — good or bad (you can weed them down later). Remember, ideas can also slip away very easily (see also Chapter 7).

Answers to Chapter 4's Exercises

Here are my answers to this chapter's test.

Feedback on the Critical Thinking skills test

1: Brain teasers

The point of this little teaser is that the important information is present in the dull-looking line about the windows all facing south. The house must be at the North Pole, and the furry animal is thus white — a polar bear. It's easy — but unwise — to overlook the dull.

2: Word pictures

Each picture is made up of words, but also represents a common saying. What are they?

(a) split second decision

(b) one after another

(c) up in arms

(d) downward spiral

3: Spot the fallacy!

Slippery slope arguments are ones where someone plays on the fact that often the line between two things is hard to draw, but nonetheless, there is a generally accepted difference to be respected.

Begging the question or circular arguments assume at the outset what is supposed to be demonstrated later on.

Straw man arguments pose ridiculous examples only to easily knock them down later.

Non sequiturs, from the Latin, are claims that do not actually follow in any logical sense.

Ad hominem, again from the Latin, are arguments which attack the person making the claim, rather than deal with what they are saying.

You can legitimately say that this argument contains many fallacies, but I claim that the 'Straw Man' is the most relevant one to note. No vegetarians argue this and so the claim that they do is, well, made of straw.

4: Spot another fallacy!

This fallacy is 'begging the question' meaning that it is a circular argument. The idea is that the explanation used to back up your point relies on the assumption of what it's supposed to be proving.

5: Type-casting

I'd plump for (d) — Jenny and her new car — but honestly, you can make a case for most of them being rooted in 'irrationality'. These questions are popular in Critical Thinking tests, but they're really rather subjective.

6: More type-casting

Well, I think you can guess that (a) is the 'politically correct' answer, especially in business circles. After all, she may not know about marketing but she does presumably know what's good about her designs. But in the real world, I have sympathy for the 'directness' of response (b), and in the very real world, the person who uses the third tactic I suspect will be the one who goes furthest!

7: Business skills

The correct answer is (c)! Amazed? But that's the view of most business-skills authorities who offer such questions. In the real world, I suspect answer (a) will get you further.

8: Time management

I think the correct answer is to prioritse — which I didn't put in here! Call it a trick question.

9: Justice for TV watchers

This is a very confusing question. It seems to be about 'ability to pay', but in fact, it isn't. Literally, the argument is those who use a service most should pay most. (If poor people watch lots of TV — they should pay most!) The only argument here putting that line is argument

(c) which seems to be saying the opposite: 'Rich people should pay a surcharge on their houses so as to help poor people who maybe don't have a home at all.'

It would be easy to misread the question and plump for argument (d) 'Television channels should be paid for by general taxation so that the richer you are the more you pay.' I'd call this almost a trick question.

10: Car rentals

It's 151. It took me absolutely ages to work it out. Turn it into an equation, though, and it's easy to solve:

$$50 + (\text{mileage} - 80) - 1 = 60 + (\text{mileage}) - 0.5$$

(Note that multiplying by one is just for demonstration purposes.)

Bonus question: The riddle of the old-fashioned brew

The key thing here is that the amount of tea being drunk is up 25 per cent. You also know that Grandma is one person. One person thus requires one extra packet of tea every fifth week, which is a complicated way of saying that one packet of tea lasts one person five weeks, or that one person would be drinking one fifth of a packet in a week.

So previously, when one packet lasted a week, five spoons must have been in the pot, which corresponds not to five people but four people plus that extra spoon 'for the pot'. The answer is therefore four people, and previously four spoons of tea must have been in the pot.

I've seen people discussing questions like this one on the Internet: they sometimes get the right answer — but for the wrong reasons, which may be okay in a test but not in real life. One person advising all the others even stated confidently that the 'spoon for the pot' was 'completely irrelevant'. But of course, it isn't!

Part II
Developing Your Critical Thinking Skills

Data   Information   Knowledge

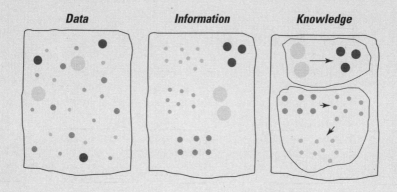

In this part . . .

✔ Get plenty of 'no holds barred' exercises in thinking. By the time you've finished reading what I've got on analogies and puzzles, the Times Cryptic Crossword will look like stuff for kids.

✔ Road-test your skills on 'thinking in circles', so you'll be ready to tie the next genius you meet up in knots.

✔ Get the inside track on mind mapping, along with a whole bunch of practical tools for thinking more effectively.

✔ Wonder no more what all the fuss is about in terms of different levels and kinds of thinking. Synthesising is something to do with music, right? Nope! Synthesising is a skill that you will need to climb to the top of the knowledge pyramid.

Chapter 5

Critical Thinking Is Like ... Solving Puzzles: Reasoning by Analogy

● ●

In This Chapter

▶ Creating compelling comparisons

▶ Spotting dodgy analogies

▶ Carrying out thought experiments

● ●

> *By three methods, we may learn wisdom: First, by reflection, which is noblest; Second by imitation, which is easiest; and third by experience which is the bitterest.*
>
> —Confucius

*W*ith this chapter's title I don't mean to imply that Critical Thinking is literally another term for solving puzzles, but instead that the two actions share areas of similarity. The connection is that solving puzzles, like Critical Thinking, involves the use of insight, of creative imagination — the tool that produces that famous 'Eureka' moment (see the nearby sidebar 'Eureka!'). If Critical Thinking is using the same kinds of hidden abilities as puzzle-solving then it's clearly doing something right.

Brilliant insights are the stuff of legend, whether they're in science, business or the arts. No one really knows the secret to obtaining them — despite the huge number of books offering tips. But certain strategies do seem to be related, and I take a look at some of them in this chapter. I guide you through the world of analogies (like the one in this chapter's title), discuss how to make effective comparisons (and how to recognise false ones) and describe some thought experiments that employ analogies and bring people towards thinking critically.

Investigating Inventiveness and Imagination

Creative insight is linked to the imagination, and to people's in-built ability to make connections between two quite different things.

Take the skills of the imagination. People aren't taught them very often; they're always the poor cousin to learning the 3Rs — reading, (w)riting and (a)rithmetic. When I went to school we *did* do a little bit of art, and reading and writing at least included making up stories. But nowadays, because governments are focusing on making education more business-friendly, art is often reduced to being part of computer studies and writing is all about spelling and grammar.

Eureka!

'Eureka' isn't an expression indicating that someone is a bit smelly ('You reek — uh!'); it's the Greek word for 'I've found it!'

The word is forever linked to the ancient Greek mathematician Archimedes, who's supposed to have exclaimed 'Eureka!' when sitting in his bath one day. Was it because the water was too hot? Had he just located the soap? Not at all. Archimedes had just found the solution to the tricky mathematical problem of how to measure the volume of an irregularly shaped solid. Even stating the problem makes me feel giddy!

While having a relaxing soak Archimedes noticed that after he sat in his tub, the level of the water rose. The clever bit was the realisation that if he stepped out of his bath and placed one of those irregular objects in it, the water would rise again. In other words, he'd found an easy, practical way to measure volumes of objects. Eureka indeed!

New ideas don't come from following routinised methods — powerful though such tools can be in areas where the solutions and strategies are already known.

In this section you can find out why analogies are an essential element in thinking, and why they are often at the heart of creative insights. The explanation involves the very workings of language — in other words I will be trying to use the thing to be explained — to explain it! But bear with me, some of the cleverest people around say that this skill is the gold standard for new and original ideas.

Categorising is an absolutely fundamental human ability — the basis for language and how people divide up the world into bits and make sense of it. But how come people can tell tables and chairs apart, even though they often both have four legs and are made of wood? Or more precisely, quite how do people decide which similarities matter?

Standardised intelligence tests such as the one I present now often try to measure people's ability to categorise, but such tests really only measure a very narrow part of the skill — the logical part. Researchers have found that in real life, categorising is much more complicated than that, involving many judgements and assumptions, most of which people aren't consciously aware.

Think of a category, or 'box', to which all the items in each line of the following list belong:

- ✔ Jupiter, Saturn, Mars, Pluto, Venus
- ✔ Three o'clock, tomorrow, the Stone Age, Wednesday, 1964
- ✔ Mumps, tonsillitis, Asperger's syndrome, acute nasopharyngitis, fractured hip
- ✔ Minim, deed, tenet, God's dog, too hot to hoot

Okay, that was pretty easy. But now try to spot the odd one out each time! You can find the answers in the later, appropriately named section 'Answers To Chapter 5's Box 'Em Up' Exercise'.

Understanding the importance of analogies to creativity

Some researchers looking at the way minds work and how people seem to think place the human ability to see analogies centre stage, and credit it with all the greatest insights and inventions of history.

Anyone who has taken a Critical Thinking test will certainly have been faced with questions like this:

Dog is to rabbit as Cat is to . . . ?

The answer here being 'mouse'. Why? Because mice and rabbits are both furry and cute? Not at all. Because there is an 'important' relationship implied between dogs and rabbits — the former chases the latter. Same thing with cats and mice. It's also the principle being sought in 'missing number' questions like 2, 3, 5, 8, . . . ?

Now Critical Thinking tests recognise the importance of this kind of intuition — the ability to be pick out of a huge range of possible answers the most relevant ideas. The skill is twofold — first of all being able to consider possibilities (which is a skill of the imagination) and secondly the ability to analyse and select. That skill, is the 'librarian' one — the ability to put things into categories.

Watching your language

The great difference between human beings and the rest of nature is that humans have this incredible tool — language — that enables them not only to communicate, but to create and manipulate models of the world in their minds. A Critical Thinker does precisely this whenever he or she tries to tackle an issue. And the building blocks of these conceptual models are words. So to understand and hopefully improve how your mind works, it really is useful to go back a stage and think about how language works. Contrary to popular opinion (reinforced by things such as dictionaries) definitions of words are actually pretty blurry — not so much fixed as fuzzy.

Ordinary words don't just have two or three but an *unlimited* number of meanings. Why then, do people use dictionaries? Well, the fault lies with the philosophers who, ever since Plato, have insisted that every word — whether for grand things such as *beauty* and *truth* or humdrum things like *chairs* and, well, *teapots* — has one very precise meaning, if only humans can find it.

It certainly helps to think about what say, all sofas have in common — is it four legs? Flowery cushions? — and this instinctive ability to put things in the right category requires you to strip away the inessential qualities of things in search of an underlying core. Of course, something could be a sofa even without a flowery cushion. So what is really important to make something a 'sofa'? I can't answer that and 2000 or so years ago Plato flailed about ineffectually too trying to nail the issue. The reality is that words are not used tidily — they are used loosely and allegorically.

People can — and do — use everyday concepts such as *chair*, *teapot* or even *blue*, as well as apparently tightly defined things such as triangles or the number 3, in more than one way.

One word, two jobs

Most words do one job in a sentence — but not all of them. Some words do two! The way some words can modify or govern other words in a sentence illustrates how metaphors and analogies are 'built in' to language.

Here's a good word for Scrabble enthusiasts: *zeugma*. A zeugma is a sentence such as Charles Dickens's remark about Miss Bolo, that she 'went straight home, in a flood of tears and a sedan-chair': one word — 'in' — is made to do two jobs. When a word like 'in' has different shades of meaning, you know you have to look at sentences very, very carefully.

Zeugmas are similar to *anaphora*, another venerable (medieval) term referring to the way words can 'refer back' to terms used earlier. Both of these originally came from Ancient Greece where zeugma meant literally a joining, or a kind of bridge, while anaphora was a clay pot useful for carrying something, say water or wine. (that 'of these' is an anaphora.) The fact that the medieval scholars adapted the terms to talk about how we use words shows just how long the history of the philosophy of language is.

Even the grand daddy (again, he's not *literally* the grand daddy) of the philosophers, Plato, used many analogies, although he sometimes seems to have felt a bit guilty about doing so. (See the nearby box 'Plato arguing about analogies for more examples.) On the other hand, historically, many English and American philosophers have seen their job as eliminating linguistic ambiguities, and to do away with imprecise, 'fuzzy' thinking. Professors tend to see their job like this.

Two great 17th-century English philosophers, John Locke and Thomas Hobbes, prided themselves on the sort of clear, logical thinking that Critical Thinking at its best is all about. They directly blamed imprecise language for much of the world's ills. Hobbes wrote disapprovingly: 'metaphors, and senseless and ambiguous words, are like *ignes fatui;* and reasoning upon them is wandering amongst innumerable absurdities'. (*Ignes fatui* is literally a phosphorescent light that hovers over swampy ground at night, so Hobbes is using an analogy himself!) For Hobbes, the line of reasoning, the 'mental discourse', is true, but problems arise when people try to communicate their ideas, and with the 'translation' of thoughts into words. Not here the recognition that conceptual imprecision allows for grand creative leaps.

As Douglas Hofstadter and Emmanuel Sanders say in a book called *Surfaces and Essences* (Basic, 2013), the history of mathematics and physics consists of a series of 'snowballing analogies'. Snowballing being a metaphor intended to indicate that the use of analogies steadily increases, as old analogies get used to form new and grander ones. They note that the great French mathematician, Henri Poincaré, was a keen thought experimenter and often used analogies to help him along the route towards mathematical discovery.

Seeing how words play tricks

Even when you try to express yourself very simply, you often find that words can confuse and mislead. Sometimes what you mean by a word may not be what someone listening understands by the same word. Take 'happiness' for example. It is such an important idea that it is often claimed to be a human right: 'life, liberty and the pursuit of happiness'. But not all forms of happiness are equally acceptable. You can't claim taking drugs or smashing up bus stops as a 'human right' just because doing so makes you happy. In fact, when people talk about a right to the pursuit of happiness, they mean something more elaborate, something more to do with 'human self-fulfillment'. The point is, even a very ordinary word like 'happiness' which you probably think you know pretty well already, has enough ambiguity in it to cause problems. The key thing for a Critical Thinker is to think about the *context* that words are used in. Who is using the word, who is being talked to? What is the social and scientific context?

There's a huge debate to be had about the extent to which Ancient philosophy is literal — did the Ancient Greek philosopher Thales *really* think that the Earth floated like a beachball in a universe of water? Or was he maybe onto something more subtle, that the Earth is part of an invisible sea of energy? Or was he using water allegorically to mean that which flows and changes? The view you take of analogy can radically change how you read texts. People usually take Thales' words pretty literally, and then chuckle over how simple his ideas were. (You can read more about this in the nearby sidebar 'Philosophers arguing about analogies'.)

Certainly, the history of mathematics and physics consists of a series of ever grander analogies, and remembering this can help you make sense of it. Isaac Newton wrote of what he called 'the Analogy of Nature', giving as one illustration,

Philosophers arguing about analogies

Plato used many analogies but warned his readers that 'likeness is a most slippery tribe'. On the other hand, another great thinker, Immanuel Kant, was emphatically in favour of the technique, describing analogy as the source of creativity. In the 19th century, Friedrich Nietzsche did a bit of 'icon-breaking' by describing truth as 'a mobile army of metaphors'. *Icons* are things, maybe statues or little pictures, that represent something else, and someone who breaks 'em is being iconoclastic. The internet has created new life for the word 'icon' with everyone constantly associated with their own one.

Continental (meaning mainland European) philosophers have historically been more enthusiastic about analogies and metaphors, which fits, because in the world of philosophy, Continentals are all about being mysterious and subtle. By way of a contrast, historically, many English philosophers and American philosophers have seen their job as to eliminate linguistic ambiguities and to do away with imprecise, 'fuzzy' thinking.

possible links between the musical scale and the colours of the spectrum. The great French mathematician, Henri Poincaré, was a keen thought experimenter and often used analogies to help him along the route towards mathematical discovery.

But within science and mathematics, Einstein indisputably wears the hat of the great metaphorical thinker. For more details and how Einstein's famous formula of $E = mc^2$ came to him when he spotted a crucial similarity between two otherwise very different things, check out the nearby sidebar 'Einstein's route to insights'.

One of Einstein's early analogies was of himself as a boy running down a pier with light as a series of waves rolling in from the sea. In this case, the analogy obviously reinforced his view of light as, well, 'waves', the view that he would free himself from only with difficulty later. Similarly, Einstein — like everyone — struggled against the common-sense view of light, which his theory treated as weighing something. Yet how can light 'weigh' something? It's hard to get much lighter than, well, 'light'.

As you can see, word associations in general and analogies in particular can mislead as easily as they can help provide new insights. Fortunately, Einstein had such a love of conceptual similarities and hidden analogies that making one dodgy comparison never stopped his creative process.

The thing with imaginary examples is not to let them take over and start dictating policy (see the nearby sidebar on Darwin), but to remember that they are, well, just imaginary examples.

Einstein's route to insights

Einstein wrote a book describing how his thought experiments helped lead him towards his view of light as being made up of particles rather than waves and the insight that time and space aren't two separate things but one, *Space-Time,* all tangled up. His famous equation $E = mc^2$, that is, *energy = mass times the velocity of light squared,* is itself analogous to a vital, if rather mundane relationship in mechanics that says that kinetic *energy = mass times velocity squared* (albeit with the whole lot divided by two).

Equally, words can confuse and mislead, as the unconventional American anthropologist-cum-insurance man, Benjamin Lee Whorf pointed out as part of his investigations into the workings of language.

One example Whorf gives is of workers in a factory smoking near a drum full of highly flammable petroleum vapours. The workers are ignoring a notice which says: 'DANGER: EMPTY PETROLEUM DRUMS'. But, because everyone associates something being 'empty' with the absence of anything, the warning is ineffective — a bit like a notice which says: 'BEWARE OF NOTHING'! The message really needed was 'DANGER: PETROLEUM DRUMS FULL OF FLAMMABLE VAPOURS'!

Confused Comparisons and Muddled Metaphors

When you start to look, you soon find that lots of people make their points using analogies rather than arguments. Truly, an analogy is worth a thousand words. In Critical Thinking terms an analogy is valid when it identifies a similarity between two different things that sheds light on a particular issue. For example, the premises of an argument are like the foundations of a building. If they are weak or flawed, then the argument will collapse.

But what about analogies that don't really work? In this section I discuss *false analogies,* which are comparisons that mislead rather than shed light. This may be because:

- ✔ The items being compared do not actually have the factual properties attributed to them by the comparison.

- ✔ The comparison actually obscures differences that are more relevant or important than the similarity.

- ✔ The two items just are not similar enough to make the comparison work.

- ✔ There are plausible comparisons and links between two things — but the comparison made simply isn't one of them.

- ✔ The comparison, although not necessarily wrong, excludes important other possibilities.

An example of a good analogy might be that one about the trapping of the sun's heat in the Earth's atmosphere by invisible gases. This physical effect is often compared to the trapping of heat in a greenhouse by the sheets of glass. This analogy is so common that it has become a noun — the 'greenhouse effect'. And it's probably valid as the gases do have a similar effect to sheets of glass.

However, what about a comparison between running a country and running a corner shop? Such comparisons are made, usually to demonstrate that government's must make their activities profitable and not behave like charities 'or else they will go bust'.

This is surely a misleading comparison, as (for example) the aims of governments are to help people, whereas the aim of a corner shop is to make money. Secondly, when a government helps its citizens, for example through spending on education and health, it both saves money later and likely creates money by deepening the pool of skills available for industries and other businesses to draw on.

Seeing false analogies in action

You encounter false analogies repeatedly in everyday life. For example, advertisers often compare their products to quite different things, in the hope of persuading potential customers that in some crucial respect a similarity exists between the two items: driving a car is like flying a fighter jet; eating some chocolate is like lying on a white sandy beach in paradise. The only link offered is the 'feeling' the consumer is supposed to get in the various cases. However, since hardly anyone *really* gets those feelings, the comparison seems a bit false.

Another issue that brings up some dodgy if not downright false analogies is whether or not some kind of plan applies to the universe or whether the world, and everyone on it, just emerged by chance (through the principles of *natural selection,* the principles which ensure certain combinations succeed and spread and others disappear). Nowadays scientists think that they can show 'almost' all the steps to explain how the incredibly complex universe could've emerged from, if not nothing, certainly something very simple.

Whatever the truth of the matter, one thing is clear: the debate about whether or not an all-knowing being is needed to create the universe has produced more than its fair share of ingenious comparisons. Creationists — who think that God created the universe according to a plan — like to point out that the world is made up of many tiny parts that work together with the delicacy and precision of a fine watch. Now a watch, in a sense, is just bits of metal and glass, but to understand what it really is, to appreciate the function of this or that little cog wheel or tiny spring, it does seem true that people need to recognise that it has been 'designed' to tell the time by a watchmaker.

So the claim made by the analogy is that to understand the world around us, we need to see each little bit not as merely 'metal and glass' but as having been designed to serve a certain purpose. Some people then move immediately to suppose that this 'designer' is God. However, there are other ways to end up with a complicated mechanism like the Earth without having to have an incredibly skilled inventor and designer. In fact, biology and geography teachers often use the language of design — or things having particular roles and serving particular purposes — to do this, when they explain, say, bees as being there to pollinate flowers, or earthquakes as the Earth's way of 'relieving pressure' due to the movement of its tectonic plates. So I would say the 'watchmaker' analogy for explaining the world around us is flawed — but not exactly invalid. Flawed as, although not necessarily wrong, it excludes important other possibilities.

Uncovering false analogies

People often use analogies for rhetorical effect, rather than anything more substantial. In other words, analogies are often used to persuade people of a certain point without producing any supporting argument or reasons.

For example, complex issues in bioethics are often distorted by the use of false analogies, with research involving, say, altering the genetic code of human embryos being ferociously condemned as creating 'Frankenstein monsters'. Recall that the original monster was the product of Dr Frankenstein sewing together various bits of dead criminals and bringing it all to life with a massive bolt of electricity from lightning. So the relevant similarity claimed is really the use of science and technology to bring life to organisms that would otherwise not exist with 'unknown consequences'. That's true up to a point, but Frankenstein brings with it all sorts of negative associations.

Or consider another 'old faithful' of an analogy that goes with the watchmaker one in the preceding section. This is the 'Hurricane in the junkyard' comparison that's intended to persuade people that the universe is simply too complex to have emerged by chance. In its simplest form, it says that human beings could no more have arisen by random natural processes than a hurricane bellowing through a junkyard could accidentally assemble a jet airliner out of the scrap metal!

The idea of a violent storm being quite incapable of creating a highly complex machine is certainly persuasive as a piece of rhetoric. However, it doesn't take much time to see that with this analogy, like is not being compared with like. The scientific explanation for the complexity of life isn't that it all arose in one wild 'roll of the dice' but rather that it happened after countless (billions and zillions) of rolls of the dice, with the products of some outcomes being favoured over others.

Dry-eyed scientists quickly point out that the theory of natural selection includes a guiding principle, if not a guiding consciousness, which offers a way for complexity to emerge from chaos that's anything but random.

For example, if rabbits used to have weedy back legs and run quite slowly, a random adaptation that resulted in more powerful legs and helped some rabbits run faster would seem likely to spread through the rabbit population — because the speedy rabbits would have lots of baby bunnies while the slow ones would become dinner for foxes. The guiding principle is . . . *survival of the fastest.*

Analogies are fine things, but be careful if your opponent knows how to ridicule them.

Identifying the link in an analogy can often be the key to seeing if an argument is good — or a stinker. Take this one as an example.

Governments should behave like parents in a family. Parents need to have the ultimate say because they are wiser and their children do not know what is best for themselves.

The idea that the relationship between citizens and governments is like that of children and parents is worth pulling out of many debates and looking at more closely. The supposed link is that parents have authority over children in order to protect them from harm, and that similarly, the state needs to have certain powers over its citizens for similar reasons.

Yet the comparison is misleading in many ways. First of all, government officials may not be wiser than the citizens, whereas parents are — by virtue of their age, and maturity in possession of far more relevant knowledge than (at least) very young children. Teenagers inevitably end up discovering just where parental wisdom runs a bit short! Another way in which the comparison falls short is that parents usually have to 'do', certainly to live with, whatever is decided — whereas governments can carry on very well even after forcing disastrous policies on their citizens. No one made Stalin try out his new farming techniques! Finally, most parents, whatever the wisdom of their views, do love and care for their children, but lawmakers and government officials, alas, don't always have the interests of the common people at heart.

Becoming a Thought Experimenter

Right. Enough theory. Now let's try some practice. The grand claim made for 'thought experiments' is that they are a powerful way to gain knowledge about the world, by means of pure thought, by 'armchair philosophy' only. Indisputably, whether they are called thought experiments or not, the approach has had an important role in not only theoretical philosophy, not only in practical science, but in all areas of thought over the centuries.

In this section you get the chance to observe some famous thought experiments in action.

The term *thought experiments* has no precise, agreed meaning, but it covers a range of techniques from imaginary 'what if' scenarios, to fables and allegories and carefully worked out hypothetical examples, or even *models*.

Discovering thought experiments

Although the term is slightly vague (and people use it in different ways), the first 'thought experimenters' were definitely philosophers. Seeing how they used the method can reveal something about how Critical Thinkers can use it too.

Here's the kind of thought experiment that everyone can make sense of, called 'Schrödinger's Cat', after the physicist who invented it. The issue is from science, and concerns the theory — which is the current consensus — that in the sub-atomic world the existence of particles is affected by whether they are observed or not. Professor Schrödinger thought this was absurd, so he came up with this 'What If?' challenge.

 Imagine there is a cat locked in a box with a radioactive atom and a Geiger counter. If the atom decays, then a particle is released but no one would know. Now — fiendish touch — suppose that the Geiger counter is set up so that if it registers a particle, poison gas is released and the cat dies! (If the atom doesn't decay, no particle, no triggering the Geiger counter and the cat stays alive.)

The point of the experiment is to illustrate the strange consequences of the theory that in the quantum (meaning very, very small) world, subatomic particles both exist and do not exist at the same time.

Professor Schrödinger's imaginary experiment seems to put the cat in the same position, of existing and not-existing — which is ridiculous, and that is his point. He thinks it is ridiculous to suppose that subatomic particles can both exist and not exist at the same time, and are affected by whether anyone is watching them. His experiment links our furry friend's existence to the particle's state, with a mechanism that is practically possible if rather unlikely. He challenges anyone who says 'why yes, subatomic particles can both exist and not exist — no problem' to also say the same thing about cats.

 Does the thought experiment work — or mislead? See the 'Answers' section at the end of this chapter for one objection.

The great advantage of a thought experiment over say, practical research, is ease. Anyone can come up with a thought experiment, and the evidence it provides is free.

Take a question like one that might come up in sociology — whether people are fundamentally good, but are pushed towards bad behaviour by circumstances. Well, one way to investigate it might be to look at lots of prison records and see the backgrounds and experiences of criminals. But another way would be to imagine some extreme examples, and then, simply by using informed guesses or intuition, imagine what would happen next. Plato's imaginary story of a shepherd who finds a magic ring seems as good a way to investigate human nature. as cataloging any number of 'real life' cases would be — and it's certainly a lot easier to do!

On the other hand, magic rings, like many thought experiments are well, impossible. Can reliable conclusions be drawn from arguments that start with impossible assumptions? Strictly speaking they cannot — as the rule for valid arguments is that the premises must be true. If the premise is impossible, it can't be true. I'm not going to try to solve that problem though for the technique here — suffice to say that plenty of very practical issues — in economics, in physics, in mathematics — have been explored with thought experiments that include within them completely impossible assumptions. In a way, that seems to be another powerful feature of the technique!

At its simplest, a thought experiment is a simple imaginary example, a 'what if'. You probably use this kind of example yourself all the time without noticing. Certainly teachers use it in schools, usually to tell children off. 'What do you think would happen if everyone walked on the flowerbeds?' 'What if I decided I wanted to not come to school but to carry on playing football with my friends?'

Another powerful-but-simple thought experiment technique simply involves substituting one element in an argument for another. For example, suppose someone says that it must be wrong to eat dogs as they are often kept as pets. In that case, you can test their claim by swapping the animal in question for another — perhaps 'horses'. Horses are often kept as pets but are still eaten in much of Europe and even as delicacies in certain posh restaurants. Now this argument doesn't prove eating horses is 'right' — but it does highlight a weakness with the supposed rule.

Dropping Galileo's famous balls: Critical Thinking in action

As well as being one of the most famous thought experiments of them all, Galileo's Balls is also one of the simplest.

This experiment is the classic example of a skill that all Critical Thinkers must have. The matter being investigated was whether heavier objects fall faster than lighter objects — the kind of question that you might well suppose called for some practical — not thought — experiments. But Galileo (the Italian philosopher mathematician and astronomer) proved just by 'thinking things through', that we have all the information we need already– without needing to start dropping lead weights or so on.

The thought experiment demonstrates the power of the technique for much more important things than mere physics! If you can make sense of why this one 'works' then you can really get a 'Eureka' moment and insight into the whole notion of reasoning by analogy.

The example of Galileo's Famous Balls also illustrates several crucial features of Thought Experiments. One is that they all follow the Critical Thinking pattern of presenting a series of assumptions. Another is that there is no attempt to turn the starting assumptions in reality — they are just imaginary starting points. You might say, but why not start with facts? The point is that the focus in a thought experiment is on the argument and reasoning — not on the premises. Galileo's thought experiment — used to prove one of the most important ideas in physics — is a good way to illustrate this. That's right, this thought experiment really does *prove* something and that something really is useful.

The experiment (but it's imaginary remember!) starts with Galileo climbing the leaning tower of Pisa, leaning over the parapet and dropping two metal balls — a large 'heavy' one and a smaller 'lighter' one, and watching to see which hits the ground first. Galileo was thinking of one of Aristotle's laws, which said that the rate at which an object would move depends on how heavy it is — and rather tidily too. If one weight falls a certain distance in a certain time, then

Aristotle said that a half-as-heavy weight would take twice as long to fall.

But Galileo didn't want to think of feathers and hammers. Instead, he was thinking balls (no sniggering at the back). Which ball do you suppose would reach the ground first? According to Aristotle the large ball would hurtle twice as fast to the ground as the light one. Well . . . maybe. But now here comes the power of the thought experiment technique: imagine that you tie a piece of string between the two balls. *Then, what do you suppose would happen?*

Here's where the Critical Thinking process starts. First of all assume that heavy objects *do* fall faster than light ones. In that case, the heavier weight falls as in Figure 5-1, with the lighter weight acting, as it were, a bit like a parachute. Thus the two balls together fall more slowly than the heavy weight would on its own.

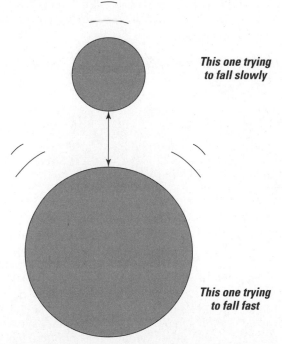

This one trying to fall slowly

This one trying to fall fast

Figure 5-1: The clever bit is when Galileo asks us to imagine a string is tied between the two lead weights

On the other hand, when the two weights are tied together and held out over the parapet with the string pulled tight, they've effectively combined their weights, becoming one greater weight. Imagine holding the little weight, with the big one dangling beneath it — now as the little weight falls it's surely going to be pulled down even faster by its big companion!

So, seemingly, putting a cord between the two weights together *must* make them fall both more slowly and yet, equally, *must* make them fall faster than when they were released separately. Now, philosophers love a contradiction, which in this case can only be avoided in one way: to assume that the heavy and light weights fall at the same speed.

So, does the experiment work? Yes, physicists know the principle that it established, that all bodies fall with the same acceleration irrespective of their mass and composition, as the Principle of Equivalence. It led directly to Einstein's General Theory of Relativity, which explains gravity by saying that when the Earth orbits the Sun, it's 'falling' through curved space-time. How about that for the power of thinking!

Splitting brains in half with philosophy

Many thought experiments force you to rethink — critically — assumptions that you had originally taken for granted. This happens even though the experiments themselves may be, a little ridiculous. Remember, that is because it is not the 'facts' that are deciding the case, but the reasons used to draw conclusions from them.

A great way to see how thought experiments can test assumptions is to consider a gory one involving cutting brains up. In fact, tinkering with the human body has often appealed to thought experimenters. Typical is an experiment proposed by the American 20th-century philosopher Derek Parfit. Imagine, he says, a surgeon carefully removes someone's brain and then reinserts it into someone else's body, in such a way that the original person's memories and personal psychological characteristics were intact enough for people to feel it really was 'them' afterwards (only in a new body). Okay?

Now imagine (a fiendish touch) *that half a brain* turns out to be enough to do this? Surely not an impossible supposition. Yet, in that case, potentially you can make two new people — say two new Derek Parfits — out of one!

Therefore, saying which 'person' is the 'real' Professor Parfit would be impossible. As with the Galileo example (in the preceding section), the result is a contradiction. The idea that one person can become two (or maybe three or four, as neuroscience and surgical techniques improve!) is unacceptable to other firmly held beliefs. The experiment thus forces people to rethink — critically — their assumptions.

Answers To Chapter 5's Exercise

Here are the answers to this chapter's earlier 'Box 'em up!' exercise. How did you get on?

The categories are fairly uncontroversial:

- ✓ Jupiter, Saturn, Mars, Pluto, Venus are all **planets.**

- ✓ Three o'clock, tomorrow, the Stone Age, Wednesday, 1964 are all to do with **time.**

- ✓ Mumps, tonsillitis, Asperger's syndrome, acute nasophrn-gitis, fractured hip are all **illnesses.**

- ✓ Minim, deed, tenet, God's dog, too hot to hoot are all **palindromes** — words or phrases that read the same backwards as they do forwards.

But deciding on the odd word out is much more subjective than tests often allow and many answers are possible. (In fact, you can often identify more than one category for some lists too):

- ✓ **Pluto** was recently reclassified as a 'minor' planet, on account of it being little more than a large rock with an irregular orbit around the sun.

- ✓ **Tomorrow** is the only measure of time that's 'relative'. Tomorrow will be a different day in a week.

✔ **Asperger's syndrome** isn't really an 'illness'. (Did I say it was? You should have challenged me!) It's considered a psychological disorder, characterised by difficulties in social interaction and communication. But an equally valid distinction would be that the fractured hip is the only *trauma* (injury).

✔ **God's dog** is the only palindrome with an apostrophe. Admittedly that seems pretty arbitrary, but it's still a fact.

Schrödinger's Cat

One objection would be that cats are conscious too! Maybe they cannot talk, but they can surely tell if they are being poisoned, so that means that if (inside the box) the chain of events was started with the release of the particle by the atom, the cat would not be in a suspended state of being both alive and not-alive anyway — the implausible state that the experiment is supposed to mock.

Chapter 6

Thinking in Circles: The Power of Recursion

· ·

In This Chapter

▶ Refining your thinking to make it more powerful

▶ Dialling into dialectical thinking

▶ Taking practical ideas from design philosophies

▶ Spotting the important points in an argument

· ·

> *The transition from data to theory requires creative imagination. Scientific hypotheses are not derived from observed facts but invented in order to account for them. They constitute guesses at . . . uniformities and patterns that might underlie the occurrence. 'Happy guesses' of this kind require great ingenuity.*
>
> —Carl Hempel (Philosophy of Natural Science, Prentice-Hall 1966, p. 15)

*T*he quote above from Carl Hempel, a 20th- century American physicist, points at one of the great circles of science — that theories don't appear in a puff of smoke, but emerge out of a chain of events, starting with guesses about patterns that may or may not be there in the data. The guess then influences the selection of data, and that in turn affects the exact nature of the scientific theory. Science is actually a kind of a 'chicken and the egg' situation — which comes first, the theory or the observation? And like the chicken and the egg, really it doesn't make much sense to try to answer that, the one affects and requires the other — in a perpetual circle.

At school and college, however, children and students are encouraged, to think in straight lines: to start at the beginning, work their way through the middle and then stop at the end. But in the big, wide world, things are more complicated than that. Nature is all about cycles — and circles. Hardly surprising then that Critical Thinking encompasses all shapes and sizes of thinking, by which I mean not only the linear logic of informal arguments, with their sequence of steps from premises to conclusions, but also powerful techniques of thinking with their roots in many different areas of life.

In this chapter I start by looking at some of the powerful — techniques that lie behind computer science, and also at some of the great ideas from design philosophies, used across a broad swathe of practical subjects. Both approaches emphasise the idea of repeating processes to refine an argument in order to progress. And in between, I take a look at a powerful, circular idea from philosophy — dialectical thinking.

One of the great tips from design thinking is to generally avoid 'yes/no' language and questions, and interact with other people in a non-linear, less 'directive' way. Instead of questions and answers, which are like a series of straight lines, sometimes it is better to go for stories — which are like shapes. And so, to finish this chapter you can test your skills out on a real story, which contains within it a 'real argument', as a practical exercise. Then you may want to return to the start and read this introduction again!

Thinking Like a Computer Programmer

If you find the potential implication behind this heading scary, let me reassure you. When I advise thinking like a computer programmer, I don't mean the following type of yikes-inducing thing:

x = 3 GOTO line 24. STOP! Next y. Repeat until 'bedtime' is TRUE. Hello World!

No. The things to admire about computer programming are much less to do with mathematics and much more to do with communication, language and arguments. First of all, software designers have to work out exactly what the problem is before they can work out how to program a computer to do it. There's no chance that a computer will guess what a programmer *meant* to say, so programmers have to be very clear in their own minds, and able to communicate their message without ambiguity. This skill is just as important for Critical Thinkers.

A second powerful technique for Critical Thinkers used every day in computer science is recursion. What's that then? Going round in circles. Far from being a set list of steps, computer programs endlessly refer back to themselves, one section (or 'procedure') calling up another section which in turn calls up another which maybe checks back with the first. Only this time with new information to process.

The key idea to grasp here is that a circle in computer programming means a series of steps repeated, and repeating things is not bad! The ability to continually repeat steps isn't a weakness or an admission of defeat but a central strength of programs.

Another principle of computer science worth borrowing is that of modularity. Instead of having one great long text with everything in it, you have a series of short discrete sections. Books like this one have taken a leaf out of computer science — because the material is arranged so that it does not have to be read in one long linear sequence, but so you can 'dip in and out' of it and create your own sequence of reading to suit your precise needs.

Taking tips on clarity from programmers

The first thing computer programmers have to discover is how to express themselves clearly. The machine doesn't 'guess' what you mean . . . computers just follow instructions, with one step following another. In fact, the most dangerous step a computer can take is the one that starts a circle. When your computer stops working in the middle of an operation it is usually because the programme is following a circular sequence of instructions that will never end. It is not for nothing that the jokers of Apple named their posh California HQ 'No. 1 Infinite Loop'.

Now you may think that expressing yourself clearly sounds like something you're already pretty good at. But try explaining how to tie a shoelace to a 5-year-old without demonstrating the method physically:

> *Take a lace. Pull it tight. Take the other lace. Pull it tight. Pull the first lace so that it's under the second lace and then twist it so that it makes a kind of circle. Oh dear. . . . Place it under the other lace and. . . .*

In fact, explaining laces has always been considered a tricky problem to describe, and computers are usually given simpler tasks. But whatever the job, long before the programmer gets down to the basics of 'coding' – the 'if $x = 2$ then $y – y + 1$' sort of stuff – someone has analysed the task and come up with an algorithm to solve it.

Thinking methodically with algorithms

Algorithms sounds like a type of jazz-funk music – al-go-rhythms! – but the word really means a sequence of steps taken to solve a problem, a methodical strategy for solving problems in a systematic manner. This type of approach is integral to Critical Thinking, particularly Critical Writing.

Here the sequence of steps in an essay or book is crucial. The more complex the arguments the more you need to have a clear plan, and what is more, to communicate the strategy to the reader. Readers need to know how the parts of the argument connect to each other, to be given 'signposts' and summaries. Stripped down to their essence, these kinds of structural considerations constitute an algorithm.

Approaching the chaos

At first sight problems can look chaotic: they need to be analysed and 'broken down'. But how do programmers — or indeed anyone — move from chaos to order? The bottom line is that no explicit way exists of devising an algorithm for a new problem. Instead, this part remains rooted in creative insight. In other words, to be good at solving problems you need to be able to think divergently — to think about lots of possible solutions. Sometimes, faced with an issue, this kind of thinking is done without you even being aware of it — and when the answer occurs to you it seems to pop up out of nowhere.

Here's a 'real world' problem to solve ('The Maze Flow Chart'), which shows you how to express a problem in a precise and unambiguous form. In so doing, you may find that your under-standing of what is required is not quite as clear as you thought!

A group of tourists have to find their way through a maze of streets from the town gate to the café (check out Figure 6-1). Think about how a computer programmer may set about writing an algorithm to help tackle this issue.

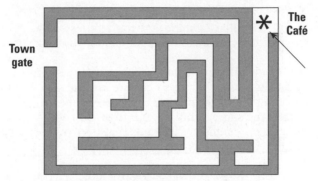

Figure 6-1: The old town's streets are a bit of a maze!

Looking at the figure, I expect you can see that one answer could consist of a series of very precise instructions, the sort you'd get from a knowledgeable local:

1. **Enter the old town through the town gate.**

2. **Turn right.**

3. **Take the first left.**

4. **Turn left at the end of that street.**

5. **Turn right at the end of that street.**

6. **Turn left at the end of that street.**

7. **Turn right at the end of that street.**

8. **Keep the houses always on your left and just keep walking; the café will be there!**

Now that's the kind of algorithm that I can come up with! It has a few weaknesses, however, notably that it applies only to one very particular problem, one particular walk from one particular starting point through one particular maze of streets. And what if no one knows the town well enough to give this sort of turn-by-turn guidance?

Can you produce an alternative set of instructions that not only gets the tourists safely to their lattes and cappuccinos, but also works in lots of similar town-like mazes?

Flip to the later section 'Answers To Chapter 6's Exercises' for an answer (notice I say 'an' not 'the'!).

Producing a solution

If you think like a computer programmer you have no trouble coming up with an alternative plan for the maze problem.

To begin with, you make sure that you know the starting conditions, which in this case means that you insist on always entering the town through the gate (as shown on the map). That's the same as before, but then the rules are different; they're *systematic* in the sense that they provide a system for dealing with all possible similar situations:

- ✔ **Rule 1:** Always walk forwards unless a row of houses blocks you, you face a choice of paths or (of course) you find the café.

- ✔ **Rule 2:** Whenever you encounter a choice of paths, choose the right-hand turn.

- ✔ **Rule 3:** Whenever the path is blocked, turn around and walk back to the last place with an unexplored choice of path and take the left-hand one instead.

This solution isn't brilliant, because in most cases the tourists end up walking most of the town before they find the café. But it will get them there — and computers don't mind trying out lots of options, because they can do it so quickly. As before, the tourists just have to follow the instructions; they don't need to worry about never getting lost because the system is all they need.

Notice that the maze 'program' contains circles. That's easier to see if you represent the three steps in a diagram. Even if you're not used to thinking diagrammatically, have a go! Trying to put things into a diagram is great for concentrating the mind.

Distinguishing between semantics and syntax

 To express yourself clearly and effectively in writing or speech, try being more like a computer and less like Shakespeare. Construct your sentences so that the meaning is unambiguous and listeners or readers can easily follow your line of reasoning, instead of leaving them to imagine alternative arguments you've never dreamt of.

 A useful distinction in computer programming in this regard is between semantics and syntax. In ordinary language:

- **Semantics:** Covers questions about the meaning of words or phrases.

- **Syntax:** Concerns putting the words and phrases together correctly (grammatically) and considering their positions and relations to each other.

Trainee programmers regularly get that awful message — SYNTAX ERROR — but computers never, ever, complain about semantics, because they aren't interested in the meaning of words — or even of numbers. They're symbol processing machines that just move 0s and 1s around very fast. In contrast, natural languages, such as English, are hugely complicated in terms of syntax. Take a phrase like 'turn off'; it can have many meanings in English. You can turn off a light, turn off a road or turn off studying! In this sense the English language is very flexible, which makes it tricky, but in other ways it is inflexible — which also makes using it hard! For example, unlike other languages, English has strict rules governing the structure of sentences. One is that you usually have to use a subject-verb-object pattern — for example:

The students [Subject] study [Verb] the rules of thinking [Object].

If you write, say, *Study the rules of thinking students* or *The rules of thinking study students,* you will run into problems!

A computer program pretty much defines its own rules for how to handle the content — in other words, defines for itself the syntax that controls which words the computer understands, which combinations of words are allowed and the punctuation that must be used too.

Critical Thinking is about avoiding ambiguity and confusion, so leave poetic flourishes to others and become a lover instead of correct syntax.

The rules of syntax for natural languages aren't completely defined and many forms (words, claims, phrases, sentences) are ambiguous. Take even that most serious verb 'to die', for instance. Most of the time, this verb's meaning is pretty well fixed — but you'd be silly to be too worried if you were told that your friend had 'died' when selected to sing Madonna's 'Like a Virgin' at the office Christmas party.

The nearby sidebar 'Playing at semantics' has more on such complications.

Playing at semantics

Here's some snippets of conversaton that you might overhear in a bar. Uneducated folk, obviously. But uneducated or not, one phrase you are extremely unlikely to hear — can you spot it?

I like drinking beer! I like men to drink beer. I like women to drink wine.

I don't like drinking beer! I don't like men to drink beer. I dislike women to drink wine.

Oops! Syntax error! Although saying 'I like to do' such and such is a very useful standby in English, you can't really say 'I dislike to do such and such'. Nonetheless, if someone did say it, the meaning would still be quite clear. The expression is semantically okay but syntactically incorrect.

The other side of the coin is when sentences are semantically confusing, but syntactically perfectly correct. For example, the question: Why can't journalists in Russia take pictures of people with wooden legs? The answer? Because you need cameras to take pictures.

Almost every word has another sense, as standup comedians know very well. (In a pub, a man orders a double entendre. 'Sure,' says the bartender. 'You want a large one?') Normally, however, people hardly notice the ambiguity of language, because they're so good at 'guessing' the meaning from the context. Computers — even today — are lousy at this.

If you can't explain your approach to a problem in a form that can be turned later into a computer program – you probably aren't being quite clear enough.

Combining the Thinking Spheres

The thinking sphere is a buzzword in Critical Thinking that's taken from philosophy. One use made of it is to emphasise two very different modes of thinking, two distinct 'spheres' — a thinking one and a feeling one .

In the West, people normally assume that thoughts are an inner, silent language in their brains. But there are plenty of other philosophical and cultural traditions that think about thinking as a much broader process, encompassing not only thoughts as a kind of inner dialogue, but also feelings and emotions, sensations and perceptions, and even a feeling of a sort of inner awareness. I'm talking meditation now!

The term *the thinking sphere* seems to go back to the German philosopher, Georg Hegel who warns, in an obscure book called *Lectures on the Philosophy of Religion* (developed in four versions from 1821 to 1831) that 'If the thinking sphere empties itself,' then the brain can no longer makes sense of any of the information the senses provide, 'in the same way that I cannot use my eyes without a light source if the light is taken away'.

Even though Hegel seems not to have used the phrase again, it has often been used to emphasise a supposed split in the various possible ways of experiencing the world.

Actually, Hegel tended to split *everything* into two opposed extremes, which he then predicted would always 'fight it out' until a new *third force* emerged combining the best of the previous ones. For example, he supposed that, in the distant past, human beings had split into the two groups of masters and slaves and the necessary result was an all-powerful state. This is an example of what he described (rather grandly) as a new and unprecedented way of thinking and named *dialectical*.

Hegel was very proud of his idea, which he saw as entirely novel and very powerful. I'm not sure it is either really, but Hegel has touched upon something important for Critical Thinking which is that it often does help to 'deconstruct' issues by identifying two opposed views or perspectives and then trying to find a way to combine or reconcile them. This new view would need to combine elements of both and super-cede them, and would then offer a more complete perspective on the issue than could have been obtained if you tried to avoid the conflict in the first place.

Another 'circular' characteristic of Hegel's new way of thinking is that the new view inevitably creates its own 'contradiction' as he puts it, that is to say, every new idea produces an opposed critique (or at the very least refinement) of the idea. Sure enough, these two views eventually have to battle it out too.

Hegel says that his new dialectical form of thinking is superior to the old ways (the structured thinking kind and the intuitive or emotional kind) because it includes already within it mul-tiple perspectives and seemingly contradictory information and positions. He sums up this idea of continually bringing together opposites under new headings by saying that phi-losophy 'resembles a circle of circles'.

Sort, Select, Amplify, Generate: Using Design Skills to See New Solutions

You may be sceptical to hear that design philosophies can offer you a powerful set of tools for thinking. But these design skills aren't about constructing items from wood or fabric in the workshop. Instead they draw on ideas and experience from design and engineering, as well as social science, busi-ness and computer studies.

Powers of Ten

Here's a great idea from design for Critical Thinkers: a strategy called *Powers of Ten* (sometimes called a *reframing technique*). Basically, the method is to exaggerate everything and take it 'to the extreme'. If you're, say, designing a play area for children on a budget of £1,000, you may ask 'what if the budget is only £10 – or what if it's £1 million? If the area is likely to fit in a classroom, you may ask what if it's just 1 metre square — or what if it's the size of the playing field?

Just as a picture can look very different if you put it in a different frame, reframing issues and problems that you are tackling can bring about a surprisingly big shift in how you think — and feel — about them.

The philosophy of design is very old and pre-dates engineering. One of its most characteristic parts, and the most useful for Critical Thinking, is that it puts the human factor at the heart of its solutions. For an example, see the nearby sidebar 'Powers of Ten'.

This section is all about how to treat data — or in a broader sense, how to refine ideas. The language — 'Sort, Select, Amplify, Generate' — is that of computer science, but the concepts are universal: Critical Thinkers need to organize their thoughts, weed out the irrelevant aspects, expand on the key issues and hopefully emerge with something new and original at the end.

Specifically in this section I examine 'Check all the Angles', which is a simple way to reveal contradictions and conflicting views that may be blocking the finding of solutions; an important idea in software design called 'State-gather-analyse' which is about how to handle information, and then it's back to circles again — or at least loops. The section 'Look close, look away, look back loops' and the box on 'Why questions' will give you some practical tips that will help you both to generate insights and to help them grow.

Check all the angles

Checking all the angles is a standard tool from design skills that's elementary, but efficient, and incredibly simple to do. It's used for 'unpacking' contradictions and highlighting possible conflicts, always a useful skill in Critical Thinking.

Here's how it works. Take a sheet of paper and draw a square on it with a question (or problem or issue) at the top. Split the square into quadrants that indicate the following:

- **First quadrant:** Concerns the what and the how of the issue. Put your observationas and experiences here.

- **Second quadrant:** Examines who and why — who gains and who loses? Try to guess what is motivating everyone too.

- **Third quadrant:** Relates to values — whether it's a good wheeze and why just maybe it's a bad one. Think about the overall aims and context here.

- **Fourth quadrant:** Looks at the practicalities — the when and the where, but how and who may come in to it again too.

If the question was 'How can I get a job as a radio presenter', then the sort of things that you might put in the four quadrants might be:

- **First quadrant:** I want to be on a big, national station, not just a little one. Definitely not hospital radio!

- **Second quadrant:** I suppose I want to feel important and be popular! Plus it's a great way to hear music and meet cool people.

- **Third quadrant:** Maybe I need to get out more — make some new friends. Plus I used to want to be a doctor and help cure people.

- **Fourth quadrant:** I should try finding out a bit about how all the famous DJs got their jobs, and maybe go to my local radio station and ask if they offer any work experience. I have to get some experience first on (maybe) hospital radio.

Don't get hung up on which point goes where. There is a lot of overlap in the potential interpretations of the quadrants. The point is really to trigger ideas and encourage people to step back slightly from an issue in the hope that this brings a new perspective. It can be a great way to get a new take on a student assignment, for example.

The idea is that insights emerge from contradictions (like the hospital radio one!) within a quadrant or from two different quadrants.

The unpacking method is similar to the idea of having a critical reading checklist. David Larabee of the Stanford School of Education developed the original checklist tool and noting what he had in mind is useful. He says that people should always ask themselves questions in four basic areas about their point of view, which I summarise as follows:

✔ What's your aim? What's your perspective or framework? Is it user-centred, needs-based or insight-driven?

✔ Who says? How 'valid' is your point of view? Is your position supported by evidence and experience?

✔ What's new? What's significant?

✔ Why does your point of view matter anyway? Who cares? How will it make a difference?

These questions correspond to the four quadrants. But the important thing isn't to put points in the correct corners; it's to think through issues from all the angles.

State the problem, gather relevant information and analyse the implications

Solving a problem involves several stages, but the most difficult part is knowing how to pose it. In fact, before you can state the problem effectively you need to clarify its nature and have some idea about the sort of answer you're looking for. Only when you have a working notion of these aspects can you formulate questions and start to gather information systematically.

So formulating questions is not only the necessary first step but part of the second and third steps. Once again, the Critical

Thinker needs to be prepared to think in circles by being prepared to go back to stage one after refining ideas as part of stages two and three.

As you gather info for these purposes, you need to collate and organise it, in the process condensing and summarising the information.

Analysing the material should enable you to make better sense of the original problem — so you may want to go back to where you started and fine-tune the questions you started with. There's a long tradition of that too — the philosopher credited with bringing in scientific thinking, René Descartes advised his readers (in what is in many ways a foundation text in 'Critical Thinking', the *Discourse on the Method,* published way back in 1637!) something similar: 'to divide each of the difficulties under examination into as many parts as possible, and as might be necessary for its adequate solution'. You may also want to break the problem down into smaller, more manageable parts, each with its own information-gathering procedures.

Practise your skills by investigating this rather tricky poser, which I call 'Help me!' Stating the problem is easy – but do you also need to gather and/or analyse?

Joanna's mother has had three children — all girls. The first child she named April. The second child she named May. Got all that? Now, what do you think was the third child's name? (The closing section 'Answers To Chapter 6's Exercises' has the answer.)

Look close, look away, look back

Where others look for clarity and precision before starting, design skills encourages ambiguity and vagueness! It suggests that you start with a vague impression of the whole and then take a series of ever-closer looks at the issue. These are called *look close, look away, look back loops* and ideas emerge and take shape during these stages:

> ✔ **Loop 1: Ask why.** Designers use lots of brainstorming techniques that often boil down to the simple skill of asking yourself questions. Even when you think you know the answer, ask people why they do or say things. The answers may surprise you.

Obviously don't annoy everyone by simply repeating 'why' like a mantra, but pick up elements of what others have said and then press for new information and insights. The nearby sidebar 'Why ask why?' contains a couple of examples

✔ **Loop 2: Test your Idea.** In a design context, the testing may be by making a physical prototype or just by imagining something. The key thing is to suppose an action, think about what effects and consequences may follow and then take those insights back to your starting idea to see whether you can improve it. This process is often called *iteration*. The key idea is that the more times you go round the cycle – the better!

Why ask why?

As a general rule, asking why leads to ever more general, abstract replies. These abstract statements are often more meaningful when not as directly applicable as the first answers. Take for example these short interrogations:

ME: Cats should have to wear bells around their necks.

YOU: (loop 1 – just ask why) Why?

ME: To stop them killing little songbirds.

YOU: (loop 2 – testing) Why is that important?

ME: Because we need biodiversity.

Or this one.

TAXI DRIVER: The police should not be allowed to just stop lawmaking people at random.

YOU: (loop 1 – just ask why) Why?

TAXI DRIVER: Because it wastes valuable time and is annoying.

YOU: (loop 2 – testing) But why do you find it annoying; don't you like helping the police?

TAXI DRIVER: But it's not like you're helping them; they give you the impression that you're a kind of criminal.

As a practical tool, or a group activity, why questions and responses can be visualised as a rising ladder — the first statement is the bottom rung and the aim is to ascend upwards to get the general overview, sometimes called *Why-How Laddering*.

Try to avoid facts

Another way to get new and broader insights when talking about issues and problems with other people is to avoid factual exchanges.

For example, if you're talking about gardening or landscaping, don't ask, 'When is the best time of year to plant trees?', but rather, 'Tell me about your successes and failures in planting trees'. The first kind of question gets a pretty short answer ('in the autumn'), whereas the second kind may produce unexpected extra information.

Design thinking encourages storytelling. This goes against many prejudices you may have from school — stories aren't reliable, aren't 'true'. But whether or not the stories are true is irrelevant; they reveal how people think about the world.

Storytelling is a deeper form of communication than the mere exchange of facts and when people draw on more profound insights you're likely to spot more inconsistencies. But don't criticise and tell them to think harder! In design thinking, inconsistencies are much-valued paths to interesting insights.

Observing the difference between what people say and what they do is worth any number of facts in terms of understanding processes. Inconsistencies are precious clues giving access to the most profound insights.

Ordering Yourself a Nice, Fresh Argument! (Exercise)

In this section I've come up with the kind of exercise that students regularly use in Critical Thinking courses. To explain: they are given an extract from a published source, often it is less fun that this one, but the principle is the same, and asked to identify elements of the 'argument'. A sizeable proportion not only of conventional Critical Thinking courses but generalized intelligence testing is devoted to this kind of stripping down of texts for the core structure and argument. I have used the story of Frankenstein to give you a more light-hearted opportunity to practice a very business-like skill.

The extract is from Mary Shelley's classic novel *Frankenstein,* which is the name of the mad professor, by the way, not the large and ugly creature he creates out of bits and pieces of bodies robbed from the local churchyard. Anyway, near the beginning of the story, before he goes rampaging around, the monster tries to insist on his right to have a companion in life.

Your task is to help Dr Frankenstein's monster by putting his assumptions upfront, along with evidence to support them, all in short bullet points. Also aim to pin down the argument that will persuade anyone who accepts the monster's premises to also accept his conclusion.

So jot your ideas down and then see the next section for my take on the answer.

> THE BEING finished speaking, and fixed his looks upon me in expectation of a reply. But I was bewildered, perplexed, and unable to arrange my ideas sufficiently to understand the full extent of his proposition. He continued:
>
> 'You must create a female for me, with whom I can live in the interchange of those sympathies necessary for my being. This you alone can do; and I demand it of you as a right which you must not refuse to concede.'
>
> The latter part of his tale had kindled anew in me the anger that had died away while he narrated his peaceful life among the cottagers, and, as he said this, I could no longer suppress the rage that burned within me.
>
> 'I do refuse it,' I replied; 'and no torture shall ever extort a consent from me. You may render me the most miserable of men, but you shall never make me base in my own eyes. Shall I create another like yourself, whose joint wickedness might desolate the world! Begone! I have answered you; you may torture me, but I will never consent.'
>
> 'You are in the wrong,' replied the fiend; 'and, instead of threatening, I am content to reason with you. I am malicious because I am miserable. Am I not shunned and hated by all mankind? You, my creator, would tear me to pieces, and triumph; remember that, and tell me why I should pity man more than he pities me? You would not call it murder if you could precipitate me into one of those ice-rifts, and destroy my frame, the work of your own hands. Shall I respect man when he condemns me? Let him live with me in the interchange of kindness; and, instead of injury, I

would bestow every benefit upon him with tears of gratitude at his acceptance. But that cannot be; the human senses are insurmountable barriers to our union. Yet mine shall not be the submission of abject slavery. I will revenge my injuries: if I cannot inspire love, I will cause fear; and chiefly towards you my arch-enemy, because my creator, do I swear inextinguishable hatred. Have a care: I will work at your destruction, nor finish until I desolate your heart, so that you shall curse the hour of your birth.'

A fiendish rage animated him as he said this; his face was wrinkled into contortions too horrible for human eyes to behold; but presently he calmed himself and proceeded —

'I intended to reason. This passion is detrimental to me; for you do not reflect that you are the cause of its excess. If any being felt emotions of benevolence towards me, should return them an hundred and an hundred fold; for that one creature's sake, I would make peace with the whole kind! But I now indulge in dreams of bliss that cannot be realised. What I ask of you is reasonable and moderate; I demand a creature of another sex, but as hideous as myself; the gratification is small, but it is all that I can receive, and it shall content me. It is true we shall be monsters, cut off from all the world; but on that account we shall be more attached to one another. Our lives will not be happy, but they will be harmless, and free from the misery I now feel. Oh! my creator, make me happy; let me feel gratitude towards you for one benefit! Let me see that I excite the sympathy of some existing thing; do not deny me my request!'

I was moved. I shuddered when I thought of the possible consequences of my consent; but I felt that there was some justice in his argument.

Mary Shelley (Frankenstein, 1818)

Answers To Chapter 6's Exercises

Here are the answers to this chapter's earlier exercises.

The Maze Flow Chart

Take a look at Figure 6-2 for one approach to addressing this problem.

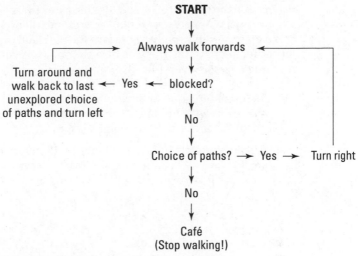

Figure 6-2: One way a computer may tackle the maze problem.

'Help me!'

The skill needed is definitely information-gathering — no deep analytical skills at all are needed! The girl is called 'Joanna'. Be careful that your assumptions, perhaps about the progression on months, don't blind you to solutions.

The Monster's Argument

As with many real arguments, the monster's conclusion is put first, before the evidence and before the argument:

You must create a female for me.

He claims it as a 'right', and a crucial part to note is his claim for a right to companionship:

✔ *Everyone* has a right to companionship. (Premise 1)

✔ The only possible companion he can have is another monster. (Premise 2)

✔ Therefore, Dr Frankenstein must make him a companion. (Conclusion)

Also as in many real arguments, the monster includes some supporting 'evidence', expressed as statements of 'fact'. These claims aren't really necessary for his main argument, but rather seem to be pressing his case to be considered on the same basis as everyone else:

✔ The monster's bad behaviour is only because he's miserable, otherwise he'd be a creature of good character and return kindness shown to him a hundred fold.

✔ He's miserable because he's lonely and shunned by everyone, he says: 'if I cannot inspire love, I will cause fear'.

Chapter 7

Drawing on Graphical (and Other) Tools for Thinking

. . . .

In This Chapter

▶ Mapping ideas with charts

▶ Seeing graphical tools in action

▶ Discovering powerful tools for thinking

. . . .

> *Reason makes things which are hard to define, difficult to comprehend.*
>
> —*Pete Smee (UK professor)*

*I*t's lucky that there are more ways to try to understand things than by using reason alone. The human mind is actually very good at grasping complex relationships expressed in pictures and diagrams, for example. But how do you get an issue usually addressed in words and sentences to become one expressed graphically? This chapter is about how to do exactly that — and draw upon maybe unsuspected powers lurking within you!

Mind maps and other kinds of concept charts extract ideas from your head and turn them into something visible and structured. Sounds good, right? Well, they are, but here's the catch: although you can dash off the simplest charts fairly effortlessly, the more useful ones require a lot of thinking. Not only that, they require a lot of *different* kinds of thinking.

Hence the huge difference between a good chart, a useful chart and a bad one that sheds no light at all.

In this chapter, you not only find out how to use graphical elements in a Critical Thinking context (which *everyone* seems to be doing nowadays), but also how to do so meaningfully, which is rather rarer. Think of this chapter as the 'art' one of the book . . . your chance to use different colour pens, browse clip art and maybe try out some computer design packages.

But the pictures or, more accurately, the diagrams you end up with aren't just pretty illustrations. They're ways of coming to deeper insights and more sophisticated understandings of issues and processes.

And in this chapter I'll also look at some other tools that can do this, including several different ways of brainstorming, the art of summarising and a variety of approaches to the technique known as triangulation. Sounds complicated? They're not, and I'll explain why.

Discovering Graphical Tools: Mind Mapping and Making Concept Charts

In this section I introduce some graphical tools that Critical Thinkers can use to gain insights into complex conceptual relationships and clarify issues. I call them all 'concept charts' but you can find plenty of other names being used, such as mind maps, flow diagrams — or even word trees. Don't get hung up on the terminology in this new and evolving area — the key thing is to see which ideas and techniques work for you. Indeed, you can (and should) just 'pick'n'mix' techniques if it seems useful.

The process of constructing mind maps and other kinds of concept chart, hinges on using *nodes* and *links*. The nodes are represented as circles or squares or other shapes and stand for ideas and information. The lines connecting the nodes are the links and these are the defining relationships.

By connecting information like this, you are actually making knowledge explicit — in other words, knowledge is dragged from the subconscious and put on paper in plain black and white (or gorgeous colours). When you create concept charts, you not only become aware of what you already know, but are also able, as a result, to modify and build upon it.

Professors take the term nodes from maths, where a node is a point in a network at which lines intersect, branch or terminate. Concept charts are networks made up of those nodes and links.

To discover the history of producing concept charts, check out the nearby sidebar 'How it all got started'. The crucial point to bear in mind is that two nodes plus a connecting link represent a true statement. Remember that and you can't go wrong.

How it all got started

Joseph D Novak, a Professor of Education and Biological Sciences at Cornell University in the 1970s, developed the idea of concept charts as a means of representing scientific issues with his students, but always claimed that the approach has its roots in a broader philosophy known as *constructivism* — very simply, the idea that people actively construct their understandings of the world. A very important related idea is that in constructing their theories, people have to build upon what they know, or at least think that they know already.

Joe Novak taught students as young as 6 years old to make concept charts. One he liked particularly involved the question: 'What is water?' and another was 'What causes the seasons?' My concept chart for water (see the later Figure 7-3) is a simplified version of his one, which was, supposedly, used with primary school children. But if so, I don't think the children had much input into the making of the chart — it includes links indicating that the movement of molecules explain the different 'physical states' of water. No one seems to have noticed that at age 6 children don't really understand the molecular structure of matter. Another oddity, which I have accurately reflected in simplifying from his original chart, is that the concept 'water' is both at the top of the hierarchy and at the

(continued)

(continued)

bottom! (When the founding father of the technique contradicts himself like that, you know that you don't need to take any expert's word on the 'correct way to do concept charts' too literally.)

Novak's book argues the following:

The most important single factor influencing learning is what the learner already knows.

—David Ausubel (US professor)

For almost a century, educational theory and practice have been influenced by the view of behavioural psychologists that learning is synonymous with behaviour change. In this book, the authors argue for the practical importance of an alternate view, that learning is synonymous with a change in the meaning of experience. They develop their theory of the conceptual nature of knowledge and describe classroom-tested strategies for helping students to construct new and more powerful meanings and to integrate thinking, feeling, and acting. In their research, they have found consistently that standard educational practices that do not lead learners to grasp the meaning of tasks usually fail to give them confidence in their abilities. It is necessary to understand why and how new information is related to what one already knows.

—Joe Novak (Learning how to Learn, 1984)

Minding out for mind maps

A mind map is a particular kind of concept chart that usually (but as I say, people use the term pretty fluidly) has one term or concept as its focus. The aim is to literally map out your thoughts, using associations, connections and triggers to stimulate further ideas.

But how do schematics like these ones work? Most of the time, whether speaking or writing, people present information in a linear sequence. They have to because people can't read or listen to two things at once — the competing information becomes a jumble. But in diagrams, the rules change. Suddenly information can be presented in ways that are much more in tune with the way the brain functions — by making multiple connections and comparisons simultaneously.

In a mind map, for example, information is structured in a radiant rather than linear manner, as Figure 7-1 shows. The core idea 'transport' generates four sub-divisions, which in turn prompt a whole range of specific examples.

Researchers have long known that the brain likes to work on the basis of association and it connects every idea, memory or piece of information to tens, hundreds and even thousands of other ideas and concepts. Mind maps are said to reflect the way the brain is 'wired' to automatically associate words and concepts with one another, or a new experience with a recent experience.

Counting on concept charts

Concept charts (sometimes also called *concept maps*) have a slightly different aim to mind maps. As you may guess from the name, these diagrams depict suggested relationships between concepts. As such, they prove useful in the 'soft' social sciences, for marketing experts' presentations, for hard-nosed designers, engineers and technical writers, and for countless other tasks, to present, organise and structure factual information. And that's not even to get into the notion of the way information *flows* around the charts (see the next section). Don't let the seemingly obscure distinctions that

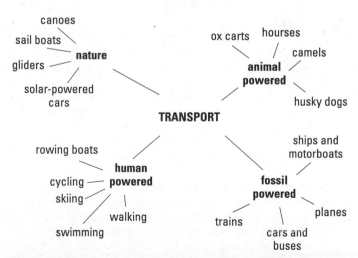

Figure 7-1: A mind map on the core theme of 'transport'. This is the kind of thing that a brainstorming session may produce.

When is a concept not a concept?

Don't worry about the term 'concept chart'. After all, what is a concept? Is 'water' a concept? Is 'learning' a concept? You can see that most of the distinctions offered by all the different kinds of diagrams used to illustrate or represent processes and ideas are supplying spurious precision in an area that is actually pretty vague. Indeed, often the definitions are contradictory! Just choose the style that suits you best, or pick elements out from the range of charts available, and use them wherever and whenever they seem to you to be useful — and definitely not otherwise! The chart is a tool for developing and communicating ideas, not an end in itself.

the different names imply intimidate you into not using the tools as you like (and check out the nearby sidebar 'When is a concept not a concept?').

Following links and going with the flow

By convention. Mind maps and other kinds of concept chart usually represent ideas and information in little boxes or circles (or even little 'thought clouds'), which are connected by lines indicating the links. Sometimes these linking lines can be represented as arrows, reflecting the supposed direction of causation, the 'flow' of the process being represented.

To see what I mean, look at my 'Roads are Evil' concept chart (in Figure 7-2), of the kind green activists may create at protest camps. Here the arrows tell a causal story: building the road led to the pollution and to the car accidents, which led to cyclists deciding to drive to work instead.

Notice how the arrows in the figure serve to make an 'argument', but also that a chart maker could choose to direct them very differently. In fact, a more accurate flow chart would be one showing all the feedback effects of certain decisions in transport policy — for example, how more cars being used also means more roads are built. This aspect could be shown with a bi-directional arrow, or by not using an arrow at all, just a line.

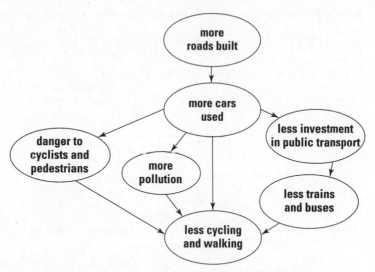

Figure 7-2: A flow chart that seeks to demonstrate (argue) a particular point: how and why building roads is bad.

On the other hand (to the extent that fewer buses would be wheezing round the streets and so on) less public transport could mean 'less pollution' and more walking! But arrows for this possibility aren't included. Diagrams soon get hard to follow if too many factors are included.

In practice, a flow chart requires a lot of careful selection of which elements to represent. In this sense, the charts aren't seeking to show the whole truth, just to argue a point or theory.

Yet, curiously, people tend to believe charts more readily than mere words! Therefore, Critical Thinkers need to be as sceptical of charts and diagrams as of any other form of communication.

Take a look at the concept chart for water in Figure 7-3.

Since water is in all living things Figure 7-3 shows a nice solid line connecting the two. However, no plant cells grow in animals, and so there is no line between these two nodes (animal cells and plant cells). Simple but effective!

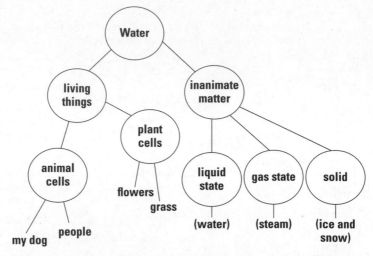

Figure 7-3: Water concept chart. A simplified version of one of Joe Novak's original concept charts (see the earlier sidebar 'How it all got started').

Putting Graphical Tools To Use

At the start of this chapter I promise to show you how to put graphical tools to meaningful use in a Critical Thinking context. Well, this is that practical, get-your-hands-dirty, section.

Choosing the right chart arrangement

You can select from three main kinds of concept maps, but remember, don't get too hung up on the distinctions, let alone the names:

- ✔ **Spider:** This chart is the easiest one to draw. It starts with the core concept at the centre with other ideas and connections radiating out (see Figure 7-1). Mind maps are essentially spider charts.

- ✔ **Hierarchical diagrams:** These often also branch out, but with a lot of categories at the bottom and just the one at the top (see Figure 7-3 on water).

✔ **Various kinds of flow charts:**, The key characteristic of these is that information 'flows' around the chart, with the focus often more on this flow than on the concepts in the nodes (check out the later section 'Drawing flow charts'). Some flow charts specify where things start — *inputs* into the system — and where they can end — the *outputs*. Others may have no start or end points but describe the flow in terms of self-contained cycles (see Figure 7-2 on roads for an example).

You can rough out concept maps using those sticky yellow notes. Then you can easily reorder the material as your ideas about its proper arrangement develop.

Some people think that labelling the links — the lines — between the concepts is very important. But I'm not so sure, and it's certainly not universally agreed. Some maps use labels such as 'includes' or 'with'. For example, in a map looking at geology, you may be told 'metal' *includes* 'gold' and *includes* 'silver', which seems to distract from the way the map is supposed to reflect the brain's architecture, and to have lost the good, original principle that instead of thinking only in words, people should try to visualise multiple relationships and connections. Add to which, labelling the lines requires people to go back to thinking 'linearly'.

If, however, your chart *is* pretty formal, perhaps representing a process, with only one correct way possible to read it, the labels are useful; indeed they're an essential part of the chart's information.

A similar 'you win some, you lose some' consideration comes with the notion of organising concept charts so as to have the more general, abstract concepts at the top of the page (or whiteboard), and more specific, less inclusive concepts at the bottom — like the hierarchical charts I introduced at the start of this section. Joe Novak, who popularised the technique originally, thought this arrangement was very important (see the earlier sidebar 'How it all got started').

Developing simple concept charts

Basically, all concept charts represent statements, just like a written description does. In particular two nodes plus a

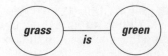

Figure 7-4: A one-line concept chart.

connecting line represent a proposition, a statement that's supposed to be true. For example, the concept chart in Figure 7-4 is one way to represent the sentence 'grass is green'.

But a more complex and more useful example is to try to represent a sentence such as: 'Red berries are yummy'. This process of adding new factors is well represented here (see Figure 7-5).

Now red berries — like strawberries — are yummy. Raspberries are yummy. Hawthorn berries can be used in jams and wines. But other kinds of red berries, such as yew and holly, aren't yummy.

These maps help both teachers and students to focus on the key ideas (concepts) needed in any given area of enquiry. Like how not to get poisoned when out on nature rambles!

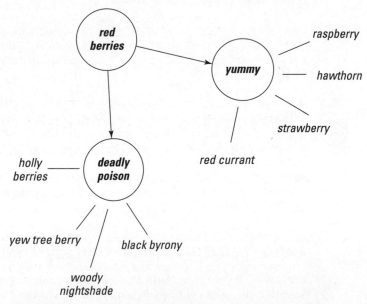

Figure 7-5: A simple chart that begins to do some conceptual work.

Using maps and charts in the real world

Concept maps have their roots in the sciences, and are widely used today in fields such as software design or engineering, but they're also used in many business and (of course) educational contexts. Some charts are really too personal and idiosyncratic to say very much to anyone except the person who designed them — but others are precise and unambiguous blueprints. Such a wide spectrum of charts and maps exist that finding any features that they all share is difficult.

One useful distinction, certainly one that's often claimed, is that a well-made concept chart grows within a context frame, typically an implied argument or question, whereas a mind map often has only branches radiating out from a central word, or picture (your chance to use some clip-art!), representing an idea or concept.

Because concept charts are constructed to reflect organisation of the *declarative memory system,* a technical term used to describe things such as facts and knowledge that can be actively recalled and, well, 'declared' (such as 'Paris *is* the capital of France!'). they're often claimed to facilitate analysis and evaluation of information people already have. The other kind of memory is called *non-declarative* or *procedural memory,* and refers to unconscious memories. Things such as skills like, for example, riding a bicycle, or how to construct sentences correctly.

Appreciating the different styles of concept charts and mind maps

When you're producing mind maps and concept charts, you need to be aware of how different graphical techniques suit the different issues, questions or problems.

Concept maps and topic maps (to add another term for something very similar) both allow people to connect concepts or topics via a graphical representation, and both can be contrasted with the particular idea of mind mapping, which is often restricted to radial hierarchies (those spider diagrams) and tree structures. Topic maps are intended to be easily navigated and quickly indicate information — like a well-designed index at the back of a book. But out of all the various schema and techniques for visualising ideas, processes, organisations, concept mapping is unique in its philosophical basis. Which, according to its inventor, Joe Novak, 'makes concepts, and propositions composed of concepts, the central elements in the structure of knowledge and construction of meaning'.

Another contrast between the more formal kinds of concept mapping and mind mapping is the speed and spontaneity possible when creating the latter. A mind map typically reflects what people think about a single topic, which can focus group brainstorming (something I discuss further in the later section 'Conjuring up ideas with brainstorming'). The more formal kind of concept chart is rather harder to create, but when done, it can provide more insights. It's a true map, in the sense of something that tells you how things relate and how one thing connects to another. It provides a system view, of a real or an abstract concept.

Graphically, concept charts can become complicated and cease to follow any obvious spatial logic as multiple hubs and clusters are created. For example, one part may be unimportant but take up a lot of space, and another important element may be represented by just a single word or image. In this sense, Mind maps, which fix on a single conceptual centre and then radiate out, have a nice kind of visual logic built in.

Concept mapping can be a first step in constructing a framework for organising knowledge — a process sometimes given the fancy name *ontology-building* — or used to represent formal (as in 'formally expressed') arguments in logic. As such, you'll find concept charts particularly useful in education and business contexts. You might also consider creating formalised concept charts using special software.

Adding movement to your diagrams by drawing flow charts

A common type of technical diagram is a flow chart — which in the broad sense is a concept map. However, the term usually means a pretty precise kind of schematic representation of a sequence of operations, as in a manufacturing process or computer program.

You can see the similarities between these kinds of technical diagrams and rather more free-spirited efforts in the social sciences when you consider the ways that technical flow charts are used. These usually include:

- ✔ Defining and analysing a process.
- ✔ Providing a step-by-step picture of a process for later analysis, discussion or communication.
- ✔ Defining or standardising a process.
- ✔ Looking for ways to improve processes.

Most flow charts are made up of three main types of symbol:

- ✔ **Elongated circles:** Signify the start or end of a process.
- ✔ **Rectangles:** Show instructions or actions.
- ✔ **Diamonds:** Show decisions that must be made.

Within each symbol, you write down what the symbol represents: the start or finish of the process, the action to be taken or the decision to be made. Finally, symbols are connected one to the other by arrows, showing the flow of the process:

Why not practice with a simple chart on, say, 'Reading a book'?

1. **Start the flow chart by drawing a circle shape and labelling it 'Start'.**

2. **Move to the first action or question, and draw a rectangle or diamond depending on whether a decision is required at this stage or not.**

3. **Write the action or question inside it, and draw an arrow from the start symbol to this shape.**

4. **Work through your whole process, showing actions and decisions appropriately in the order they occur, and linking these together using arrows to show the flow of the process.**

   Where a decision needs to be made, draw arrows allowing for every possible outcome from the decision diamond. These arrows are usually labelled with the outcome. At the end of the process is a circle labeled 'Finish'.

5. **Test-run your flow chart, working from step to step asking yourself if you have correctly represented the sequence of actions and decisions involved in the process.** And then (if you're looking to improve the process) think about whether work is duplicated, or whether other stages should be added.

Flow charts can quickly become so complicated that you can't show them on one piece of paper. Instead, you can use *connectors* (shown as numbered circles) where the flow moves off one page, and where it moves onto another. By using the same number for the off-page connector and the on-page connector, you show that the flow is moving from one page to the next.

The process of physically splitting up your diagram can also imply a way to mentally split up a complex issue or process, enabling you (or the people you are sharing the idea with) to concentrate on particular parts of it better.

Considering Other Thinking Tools

The graphical tools I discuss in the preceding section aren't the only ones available to you. Here I cover dump lists, summarising, brainstorming, meta-thinking and triangulation. You can think of these tools as organizational strategies for the contents of your brain!

Dump lists is a way of organizing information in your head, summarizing and meta-thinking are about making sense of things you read or hear, and triangulation is about checking the quality of what you have come up with. Brainstorming is primarily a tool for generating ideas but can also be used to help sort and analyse information.

Emptying your head with a dump list

The truth is that coming up with material is much easier than analysing and selecting the key ideas within it.

Dump lists are a powerful but neglected tool in thinking. Basically, you just empty on to a page everything swirling around your head (on a particular topic or issue).

Say that you're wondering about a practical problem that presumably has a practical solution, such as why all the plants in your house always die, but you've not yet been able to find the answer. Try a bit of Critical Thinking.

Start by dumping all the thoughts in your head that seem like they might be relevant even if, at the moment, you're not sure how or why. In my houseplants scenario, the dump might look like this:

- ✔ Lots of my house plants dry out.
- ✔ Nothing seems to grow.
- ✔ The leaves of my plants go brown and then drop off.
- ✔ Even the cactus has a kind of white fungus.
- ✔ Maybe I should water my plants more.
- ✔ Maybe my plants need plant food.
- ✔ Maybe the rooms are too draughty.
- ✔ Maybe the plants aren't getting enough sun.

The next step is to do some sifting, sorting and maybe simplifying of the list. Could some of the points usefully be grouped together as concerning the same sort of thing? Is there any one step that would solve the problem. Perhaps you can get rid of things that are easy to solve: for example, the problem 'the soil has dried out' implies the solution 'I should water the plants'. On the other hand the problem 'Even the cactus has a kind of white fungus' seems to indicate that maybe too little water is not the problem. So beware crossing out things too soon on your list, as oversimplification of an issue can lead to errors later.

A safer approach with a dump list is to add priority numbers — a simple way to arrange your jumble of thoughts into a hierarchy with the most urgent steps (say), or the most practical ones, given a higher priority.

Sifting for gold: Summarising

Summarising is such a useful skill! It involves separating the wheat from the chaff, the golden nuggets from the heaps of spoil, the key words and phrases from the blah, blah blah. Put more simply, summarising is a key life tool that enables you to organise and make sense of the world around you. Here's some simple techniques that can help you do it effectively. Plus, it's a great chance to use those highlighter pens that come in so many more shades than fluorescent yellow.

All you do is use your favourite highlighter to mark up the key points in a piece of text. If you find you've marked up several paragraphs, maybe you aren't being quite critical enough — not summarising but, well, highlighting. So be strict with yourself: only mark up the key idea in any paragraph, and only highlight elements from the most important paragraphs.

A simple exercise this one: summarise that last paragraph.

Summarising is about capturing the main ideas of a text or lecture in a greatly reduced space. Academic study is all about making use of the ideas of other people — not their words! Summaries help you to do the former and not the latter.

But when you do find a phrase in the original text that's particularly striking, and really can't be summed up without losing something, do use the author's exact words. Highlight them! If you make a note, make sure that you put quotation marks around the words and indicate the source — otherwise that fine phrase may turn up, rather disgracefully, unattributed in your work.

In theory, a well-structured essay or document already contains the key ideas in a summary, but don't believe that a passage is a summary just because someone writes the word in big letters above it. After all, alas, the skills of summary writing are by no means universal. Plus, what that person is interested in may not be what you're interested in. Summaries reflect his or her interests, not yours.

You can also organise your notes in new ways on little cards (or these days, as computer files, or even on computer sites such as 'wikis', that let you easily create and organise pages), perhaps providing an overview of a topic on one and subtopics on others, maybe using colours to aid categorising.

Conjuring up ideas with brainstorming

Brainstorming is the name given to the fairly obvious technique of quickly jotting lots of ideas down in response to a question — or even simply a concept. You can brainstorm on your own, but the real advantages of the technique come when you're in a group, because that's where other people's ideas can spark new ones among other members of the group.

The claim of the method's supporters is that brainstorming allows a group to think collectively and build on each other's ideas. Conducting a group brainstorm can also create a buzz, something that can be absent when you work on your own. But brainstorming can be a bit of a 'lowest common denominator' exercise too — by which I mean that the idea that everyone likes is not the best one but only the one that everyone shares. Worse! The group may not recognize a good idea just because it is a bit different or novel. So how you brainstorm is important.

Brainstorm, mind-monsoon, cranial blizzard!

Brainstorming was popularised by Alex Faickney Osborn in a 1953 book called *Applied Imagination: Principles and Procedures of Creative Problem Solving*. He got the idea from where he worked, which was an advertising agency. You can imagine how the executives sat around a whiteboard while someone wrote up a word such as 'coffee', and everyone shouted out word associations: 'aroma', 'Brazil', 'going to work in the early morning'.

No one censored the suggestions: instead they were taken as was, noted on the board, and only arranged, highlighted or deleted later.

Groups use many different ways to capture the ideas of a brainstorming session, but here are two of the biggies, both of which are led by a co-ordinator:

✔ **Scribe:** Co-ordinators (the scribes) not so much write (which can be a cumbersome and inefficient process) but rather 'capture' on the board all the ideas that team members call out. They try to sum up the idea in an appropriate way, regardless of their own feelings about the merits or demerits of the idea.

✔ **All-in:** During these sessions, team members can write on the board their ideas just as they come, or perhaps instead verbally share them with the group. The ever-useful yellow sticky notes can be brought out, so that everyone can write their ideas down and then stick them on the board.

The attitude and abilities of the co-ordinators are vital to a successful brainstorm — and although not everyone automatically has the 'right stuff', some principles certainly can be adopted. The person leading the brainstorm needs to be enthusiastic and encouraging. Adding 'fun' constraints can help spark new ideas — for example, if a group is wondering about, say, how to revitalise inner cities (perhaps a bit of a downer for an early morning session), the co-ordinators can constrain the issue by asking instead: 'If you had to improve life for people in inner-city Liverpool with just one big project — what would it be?'

Now 'harvest that brainstorm'! At a session act as the co-ordinator and focus on the ideas that the people seem most excited, amused or intrigued by. Don't judge things by thinking that they aren't practical. An impractical idea may still have within it something useable. And remember to involve groups, of course, in the weeding. One way of increasing participation in this stage is by voting. Hey! Sticky notes prove their usefulness yet again.

Ascending the heights: Meta-thinking

Concept charts require the higher skills in Bloom's famous taxonomy, from mere recall at level one to complex evaluation at level six (check out Chapter 8 for details). In fact, Joe Novak (see the earlier sidebar 'How it all got started') says it requires students to use *all* the levels at once!

But *Meta* means 'above' or 'higher', and so *meta-thinking* indicates taking an overview (view from above) *and* represents a higher (more critical) level of thinking skill. To be critical often requires a move from ground-level to meta-level thinking.

The meta-level understanding asks why such a particular strategy is the one to use. Without this, learning new strategies is useless, because you don't know when they're appropriate. The contemporary thinking skills guru, Edward de Bono, who invented the term 'lateral thinking' and wrote a book called *Six Thinking Hats*, calls meta-thinking 'Blue Hat' thinking — summing it up as 'thinking about thinking'.

In his terms, Blue Hat thinking focuses on how to manage the thinking process, checking its focus, setting out the next steps, creating action plans. For instance, if a football team is discussing how to win the next game, the coach likely automatically adopts the Blue Hat style, reminding the players that:

✔ The focus is how to win the next game against the Brickworks Eleven.

✔ The agreed next steps the team has identified include practising penalties (because the Brickworks team commit a lot of fouls and maybe will give a penalty away).

✔ The longer-term aim is how to build on the expected victory over the Brickworks Eleven and get the team promotion to the Grimsby West League!

Trying out triangulation

Or 'How to triangulate the data to stop the roof falling in' (that's a metaphor, by the way, which seemed appropriate to me because most roofs contain wooden triangles, which literally stop them falling in).

Triangles are very strong structures and perhaps this is the best way to think of the activity that academics have in mind when they use the term *triangulation* to describe a methodological tool used when constructing essays and arguments across all areas of knowledge (instead of the mathematical sense, used for many purposes including surveying, navigation, metrology, astrometry and so on.

The use of triangles to estimate distances goes back a long time, certainly to the 6th century BC when the Greek philosopher Thales is said to have used 'triangulation' to calculate the height of the pyramids. In Critical Thinking, however, where triangulation is about running a check on your work and strengthening conclusions, the term was only introduced in academia in the 1960s.

An argument is much more convincing if three people have independently reached the same conclusion by different routes. The same reasoning applies when just one person — you — demonstrates a point using three different approaches. But despite what the song says, nothing is magic about the number three: Two arguments for a point (or different perspectives on an issue) are better than one, and four or five are good too.

Both qualitative and quantitative researchers use the triangulation method and get different things from it:

- ✔ **Qualitative researchers:** People whose research involves judgements more than mere measurements often use it as a kind of double check on their background assumptions. When triangulation throws up inconsistencies, these researchers (who are concerned with human perspectives) often see the differences as an opportunity to uncover deeper meaning in their data.

- ✔ **Quantitative researchers:** These more 'scientific' number-crunching researchers may be more interested in spotting flaws in their methodology and usually just want all their studies to arrive at the same figures. They're inclined to consider differences as very bad news, as 'weakening the evidence'.

Different kinds of triangles

Social scientists use various methods of triangulation, but they all ultimately aim to do the same thing: to make research conclusions more persuasive:

✔ **Data triangulation:** The most common kind is the technique of using different sources of information in a study. In the case of an investigation into a new town square, for example, getting the opinions of all the stakeholder groups is obviously a good idea: the views of tourists, of local residents, of local shopkeepers. During the analysis stage, feedback from these stakeholder groups would be compared not only to establish areas of agreement but also to reveal areas of divergence.

✔ **Investigator triangulation:** Simply means involving several different observers, interviewers or data analysts. Take economic statistics for example — you can easily find three economists who draw very different conclusions from the same data.

✔ **Environmental triangulation:** Suppose you want to see whether cycle lanes have a significant effect on people's use of bicycles in a holiday resort. You produce a more compelling study if you triangulate the data by taking your measurements or interviewing your participants or whatever at several times of the year — not just in the middle of winter, not just at peak holiday season.

✔ **Theory triangulation:** When expert opinion on a matter is known to be grouped into warring camps, it makes good sense to offer the data to someone from each school to see what they make of it. Again, taking economics, suppose you're interested in looking at the effects of high interest rates on business investment. You may find differences between the views of the Marxists and Free Marketers, or between Keynesian and Chicago Schoolers — or whatever. Note that to some extent one researcher could try to adopt these different perspectives alone without necessarily needing to find different people.

✔ **Methodological triangulation:** This approach is very important and involves using several *methods* to study a question. For example, results from surveys, focus groups and interviews can be compared to see whether similar results are being found. If the conclusions from each of the methods are the same, validity is established.

In my own experience, as a researcher into an educational policy (on the using of computers more

(continued)

(continued)

in schools), I used interviews with teachers and children, classroom observation, and analysis of official documents to assess the changes. These are all qualitative measures — but I also gathered quantitative data using questionnaires and doubtless I could have used figures from things such as actual exam results or even classroom attendance levels. When all the findings from all the methods point at similar conclusions, the methodological triangulation has helped to 'establish the validity' of the research.

Real-life triangles

One example of the correct use of triangulation, in this case methodological triangulation (see the nearby sidebar 'Different kinds of triangles' for an explanation), comes from research looking at the needs and experiences of relatives when a loved one is very ill or dying in hospital.

Gayle Burr found that two very different impressions of family needs came about depending on whether the relatives were interviewed in person or merely filled out questionnaires. The relatives who were interviewed found talking to the researcher about their experiences therapeutic, and thus were inclined to be positive, but those who only filled out questionnaires used them to communicate their frustrations. Thus, using both research techniques (interviews and questionnaires) added an extra level of insight to the results, making them not only more 'valid' in an abstract sense but much more useful in a practical sense too.

A nice way to visualise triangulation is given in a well-known book on research methods by Matthew Miles and Michael Huberman. They say that doctors, detectives and even your local garage mechanic automatically use the technique in order to increase the likelihood that their diagnosis, be it concerning an in illness, a burglary or a broken-down car, is right.

When the detective amasses fingerprints, hair samples, alibis, eyewitness accounts and the like, a case is being made that presumably fits one suspect far better than others. Diagnosis of engine failure or chest pain follows a similar pattern. All the signs presumably point to the same conclusion. Note the importance of having different kinds of measurement, which provide repeated verification.

—*Matthew Miles and Michael Huberman*
(Qualitative Data Analysis:
An Expanded Sourcebook (2nd Edition),
Sage Publications 1994)

Denzin's three-sided methods

Norman Denzin wrote two books about alcoholics and hospitals that some people in the sociological research business think are hugely underrated classics on a par with the writings of the 19th-century sociologist, Emile Durkheim. Whether Denzin's really is a 'great' or not shouldn't matter to Critical Thinkers, but his books certainly contain important messages about a profound social malaise in America, which he attributes to a 'white male culture'.

Denzin's study follows in the footsteps of Durkheim, whose research into the thinking of people who committed suicide gave insights into the role of social groupings in society, and also the work of German philosopher Max Weber, whose investigation of the links between the protestant religion and business, suggested that religions were shaped by economic priorities.

Denzin argues that the story of alcohol is intricately connected to the story of American society, because alcohol is a key link between individuals and the social structure. Alcoholics, he says, use alcohol to try to assert their place in the word, and to 'control' the world. Of course, in extreme cases, they're the ones who lose control — to alcohol.

Now because Denzin is interested in the inner world of the alcoholic and in the social structures and the 'real world' surrounding them, he asks the reader to think of two researchers studying someone who's suffering mental illness and is in hospital. Each of the researchers chooses different methods: one opts for a survey while the other uses participant observation. These methods lead to differences in the questions they ask and the observations they make.

Crystallising ideas

The notion of triangulation has been popular in social and educational research for decades. Over the years, however, the term has been used in so many different ways that it no longer seems to have a specific meaning and use: many studies claiming to use triangulation share little resemblance. Margarete Sandelowski, a professor of health science, has even complained that 'having too much meaning, the word triangulation has no meaning at all'.

Seeing this, some researchers have proposed that in the social sciences at least, the term 'triangulation' should be replaced by 'crystallisation', on the grounds that crystals are a better metaphor for what's really going on. In the words of two sociologists, Laurel Richardson and Elizabeth Adams St Pierre, because a triangle is a 'rigid, fixed, two-dimensional object' the term implies a certain attempt to impose rigid two-dimensional meanings on complex issues. Much better, they argue, to use crystals because these are 'prisms that reflect externalities and refract within themselves, creating different colors, patterns, and arrays casting off in different directions. What we see depends on our angle of repose — not triangulation but crystallisation.'

Certainly, if you intend to use triangulation to make your arguments more persuasive, you have to be clear about which form you're using, and why and how you intend to do so.

In addition, the findings are coloured by the researchers' different personalities, biographies and biases, which influence the nature of their interactions with the social world. Each uncovers different aspects of what takes place in the hospital but neither can reveal it all. Therefore, Denzin concludes, to get as full and as accurate a picture as possible, researchers must use more than one strategy.

Answers to Chapter 7's Exercises

Check out the following answers to this chapter's exercises.

The Plant Problem

Here's my approach to addressing this problem:

- ✔ **Problems:** Plants dry out. Leaves go brown and then drop off.
- ✔ **Solution:** More water.
- ✔ **The cactus:** A special case! Separate it out.

Summarising the paragraph

The key idea here is: 'use your favourite highlighter to mark up the key points in a piece of text'.

Chapter 8

Constructing Knowledge: Information Hierarchies

In This Chapter

▶ Seeing how people handle new information

▶ Thinking deeper about the knowledge pyramid

▶ Resisting the temptation to give up learning

> *Information is not knowledge. The only source of knowledge is experience.*
>
> —*Anon.*

*S*ome people attribute this piece of wisdom to Einstein, but no one seems to be able to trace it to anything specific. It's certainly the sort of thing he'd say, being a scientist, but then it's also the sort of thing that lots of philosophers have said (such as John Dewey, who guest stars in this chapter). I start with this quote, because it reflects a central theme of this chapter: that many stages of information processing lie behind every piece of knowledge.

To illustrate the process of building knowledge, this chapter uses the analogy of constructing a pyramid. I describe climbing the knowledge pyramid by checking out the building blocks of knowledge: *data* and *information*. I also discuss the elegant and definitely pyramid-shaped ideas of Benjamin Bloom as well as another American professor, Calvin Taylor, who extended Bloom's ideas to emphasise the importance of creativity. In addition I look at how to get and keep yourself motivated on that climb to the top of the thinking pyramid.

Although some of this chapter may seem a bit theoretical and abstract, bear with me. These ideas are in fact highly practical in terms of developing your Critical-Thinking skills. So put on stout boots, pack some sarnies and fill a water bottle, because you have a steep but rewarding climb ahead!

Building the Knowledge Pyramid with Data and Information Blocks

Philosophy starts with the question 'What is knowledge?', but this section trumps that by going back a stage and asking 'What is data?' Or maybe even something like 'What do we mean by data? This extra step is definitely useful, because knowledge is constructed from smaller building blocks, called data or, sometimes, information.

In this section I pin down the three crucial terms of 'data', 'information' and 'knowledge' and describe how they're related. I discuss them in relation to education and learning and warn about when they can cause problems.

One of the key insights of this chapter is that *what* you know is less important than *how* you know it. That sounds a bit cryptic but boils down to the difference between two types of thinking:

  ✔ **Low-level, concrete thinking:** Concerns simple observations and facts and figures, and is the foundation of the next, more elaborate, type of thinking.

  ✔ **High-level, abstract thinking:** Concerns relationships and things that don't exist (yet). This type of thinking can't take place without the first type.

Now I know that anything hierarchical sounds rather snooty, but it doesn't have to be that way. People certainly need both types and the hierarchy isn't one of value. But nature first makes people experts in practical, concrete thinking, and because you have to train your mind before you can do the abstract kind, a premium applies to the ability to think at the higher level.

Viewing the connections of data and information

Part of the difficulty in this area is the lack of apparent agreement on the meaning of the terms *data*, *information* and *knowledge*. Some dictionaries say that knowledge is the same thing as information, but that data is quite different, whereas others say that data is the same thing as information, but that knowledge is quite different. That such fundamental notions can be so loosely defined is pretty amazing. Critical Thinkers, of course, can't afford to be so lax.

Even professors and other experts often use the words interchangeably, as if they're the same thing. In fact, they're quite different. Their relationship is hierarchical and the arrangement is like a pyramid:

- ✔ **Data:** At the bottom of the hierarchy. Data consists of facts and figures.

- ✔ **Information:** In the middle of the hierarchy. Information comprises data that has been organised to a greater or lesser extent.

- ✔ **Knowledge:** At the top of the hierarchy. Knowledge is certainly like information but rather purer, grander and certainly rather harder to find.

Another way of looking at the relationship between information and data is that the key factor is the degree to which items of data are interlinked. Take a look at Figure 8-1.

In the left hand panel, data consists of dots, showing each bit of data in splendid isolation. But in the middle panel, the data has been made 'sense of' and connected up. This network of connections is information. Finally, a possible view of knowledge as information further organised within collective, socially constructed linked structures.

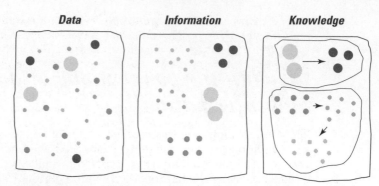

Figure 8-1: Constructing knowledge: A visualisation of the relationship of data to information and knowledge.

Joining the (data) dots to create information

John Dewey, a professor of education in the United States — and something of a progressive — created his Recipe for Education, which concerns the importance of the relationship between facts (data) and how people turn them into information.

Read through and then test your skills of comprehension on the following argument from Professor Dewey on democratic education. Try to reduce it to just one line, and then compare what you extract to my note at the end of this chapter (you can read the whole article at http://www.the-philosopher. co.uk/dewey.htm):

> 1. The human mind does not learn in a vacuum; the facts presented for learning, to be grasped, must have some relation to the previous experience of the individual or to his present needs; learning proceeds from the concrete to the general, not from the general to the particular.

> 2. Every individual is a little different from every other individual, not alone in his general capacity and character; the differences extend to rather minute abilities and characteristics, and no amount of discipline will eradicate them. The obvious conclusion of this is that uniform methods cannot possibly produce uniform results in education, that the more we wish to come to making every one alike the more varied and individualised must the methods be.

3. Individual effort is impossible without individual interest. There can be no such thing as a subject which in and by itself will furnish training for every mind. If work is not in itself interesting to the individual he cannot put his best efforts into it. However hard he may work at it, the effort does not go into the accomplishment of the work but is largely dissipated in a moral and emotional struggle to keep the attention where it is not held.

—*John Dewey (in The Philosopher, 1934)*

Another question to ask yourself is what would this argument mean in practice? In his book, *Democracy and Education,* Dewey gives an example of a man entering a shop showroom full of different chairs. He says that the man's past experiences will help him choose the chair that best suits him. And the more experience he has with various chairs, the better prepared he will be for selecting the correct one.

Everything he knows about chairs comes from the connections that he's created in his mind in the past, such as how comfortable they are to sit on, how difficult to clean, how strong and so on. These connections form the content of his knowledge about chairs. This kind of content is what enables people to make the new connections needed in new situations.

We respond to its [the new experience's] connections and not simply to the immediate occurrence. Thus our attitude to it is much freer. We may approach it, so to speak, from any one of the angles provided by its connections. We can bring into play, as we deem wise, any one of the habits appropriate to any one of the connected objects. Thus we get at a new event indirectly instead of immediately— by invention, ingenuity, resourcefulness. An ideally perfect knowledge would represent such a network of interconnections that any past experience would offer a point of advantage from which to get at the problem presented in a new experience.

—*John Dewey (Democracy and Education, 1923)*

So Dewey says that information, let alone items of knowledge, can't really be considered in isolation. Nonetheless, there is some sort of difference worth making. The following simple example illustrates the distinction in a nice, simple case.

Suppose that I measure rainfall in my garden for two years and write the figures into a notebook. The list of figures comprises the data. I then make a chart out of the data and send it to my local paper along with a letter explaining that my research shows that it has been a very wet summer. Both the chart and the view expressed in the letter are kinds of information — ways of processing the data.

Data just 'is'. Data is 'facts' that can't be argued about, although (to extend my example) my rain gauge may be faulty. Nonetheless, the list of readings I have is my data — for better or worse.

As soon as I turn them into a chart — that is, organise the data — put it under a heading and make it 'send' a message, the data becomes information. (That's also what Carl Hempel means when he says that the transition from data to theory requires a bit of creative imagination — see Chapter 6.) Information is built up out of data, from facts. The facts don't have to be statistical ones like rain measurements, of course. They can come from all kinds of experience from listening to music to watching the sunset. (*Qualitative* data is descriptive information.)

Watching for errors and biases

Alas, the transition from data to information brings with it the possibility of error and bias.

In the measuring rainfall scenario in the preceding section, for example, I could easily introduce distortions through the decisions I take for things such as which readings to include (and which to leave out), the scales used for the axes on my chart or maybe even my choice of measuring equipment. Perhaps, to strengthen my point, I might have been tempted to start the readings a bit later than I originally intended to avoid a dry period in the spring!

For reasons such as these, someone seeing my chart could reasonably dismiss it as only my opinion (my letter to the paper certainly is), yet not, I think, the underlying data. They constitute raw and brute facts about my garden *as recorded by my gauge*.

Here's a question for you to mull over: When I say 'it's been an exceptionally wet summer' — is that a statement of fact or merely an opinion? Flip to the end of this chapter, and compare your view with my take on this problem.

Turning the Knowledge Hierarchy Upside Down

Several thinkers have adopted and adapted the knowledge hierarchy described in the preceding section, adding extra layers with particular functions to it, such as the intellectual stages of comprehension, analysis and synthesis — and some have even inverted it!

Here I describe the key aspects of this important revising work, particularly that of Benjamin Bloom, who despite his name isn't one of Batman's fantastical foes.

Thinking critically with Benjamin Bloom

Benjamin Bloom was one of a group of educational psychologists in the US who devised a pyramid model that they said represented different ways of learning. They made it a pyramid to show that the highest form of learning, which for them was evaluating information, was ultimately based on a much broader level of information that had just been, well, learned.

Meeting Bloom's Taxonomy

Bloom wanted to promote higher forms of Critical Thinking in education, such as the use of analysis and evaluation of material, away from teachers just drilling people into remembering facts and rote learning. His system is now half a century old — yet still looks pretty 'progressive' in educational terms, which tells you something about how stuck-in-the-mud schools and colleges are as regards learning.

Unlike in the 'no frills, economy class system' dissected in the preceding section, which places knowledge at the top, Bloom's *Taxonomy* — nothing to do with creepy stuffed animals, thankfully, but a system for classifying or arranging things or concepts — starts by placing knowledge at the bottom of the heap (see Figure 8-2). The pyramid then rises upwards through six levels. Here they are, with examples of each one:

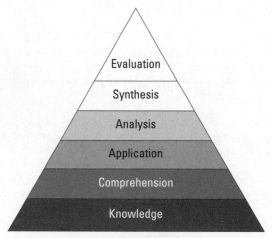

Figure 8-2: Bloom's original triangle.

- ✔ **Level 1 – Knowledge:** Normally people think of knowledge as something wonderful, even powerful. But Bloom defines 'knowledge' simply as the remembering of previously learned material. Nothing very grand about that, which is why he puts it right at the bottom of his hierarchy of learning. An example is recalling data or information, such as knowing the names of different kinds of trees.

- ✔ **Level 2 – Comprehension:** The next rung up, comprehension, is the ability to grasp the meaning of material. But this kind of understanding is low-level stuff too. An example is understanding texts, instructions and problems, such as being able to restate something in your own words.

- ✔ **Level 3 – Application:** This stage is a step up the hierarchy, because it requires the ability to apply, to use, the 'learned material' in new situations. An example would be the practical use of concepts or skills: someone who has studied the difference between facts and inferences is able to apply this skill to certain texts in his examination of arguments.

But if you just rote learn how to apply something that you've been told about (as many people remember being drilled to do in classes), this is still learning at Level 1.

✔ **Level 4 – Analysis:** Only with analysis (a word which means to take things apart) does learning require an understanding of the material. You can't rote learn how to analyse things, though I suppose you can rote learn certain steps that may help you to do it. Analysing is, say, splitting up a text into its component parts to better see and understand its structure — perhaps to spot certain logical fallacies in someone's reasoning.

✔ **Level 5 – Synthesis:** Follows analysis because it refers to the ability to put information and ideas together to create something new. Creativity is involved. For example, the skills of synthesis are needed when constructing a new structure from diverse elements or reassembling parts to create a new meaning or interpretation: such as writing an original essay using multiple sources, or designing a garden choosing from a range of possible tools and approaches.

✔ **Level 6 – Evaluation:** This, the top level of the Taxonomy, is defined as the ability to assess the value (or perhaps the 'usefulness') of the knowledge comprehended, applied, analysed and synthesised at the earlier levels. Evaluation is really the stuff teachers wax long on (Benjamin Bloom was a professor!) about the value of ideas or materials, whether arguments work and even about the merits, skills and abilities of people. A typical example could be choosing the best book when preparing to study a new subject.

Bloom's Taxonomy was primarily created for academic education, but it's relevant to all kinds of learning.

Making knowledge flow upwards

Water can't do it, but knowledge does, or at least, that's the implication of Bloom's hierarchy — the upper levels draw on the lower levels but the lower levels can't call upon the higher levels.

Revising that Bloomin' taxonomy

During the 1990s a new group of academics who rebranded themselves as 'cognitive psychologists', despite evidently doing much the same thing as Bloom, including Lorin Anderson (one of Bloom's former students), updated Bloom's pyramid to, or so they said, reflect new 21st-century insights into how people think. The key changes were:

✔ Changing the names of the six categories from plain-speaking nouns to gerunds at each level. (*Gerunds* are verbs turned into active nouns by adding the 'ing' ending. You can see them in section headings throughout *For Dummies* books.)

✔ Rearranging the hierarchy. The biggest 'change' (see Figure 8-3) is that 'Creating' is now top of the pyramid — a skill that Bloom didn't even mention. The other changes seem to be more or less changing the style more than the substance.

Other new models have also come along. One of the most interesting, proposed by two Australians, a psychologist and novelist John Biggs and Kevin Collis, a business consultant with an interest in lateral thinking, is called the Structure of Observed Learning Outcome (SOLO) taxonomy. This one consists of five levels:

✔ **Missing the point — Pre-structural:** These learners don't understand the lesson or subject. (I've been there!)

✔ **Single point — Uni-structural:** These learners have a basic insight into the subject, but only focus on one relevant aspect.

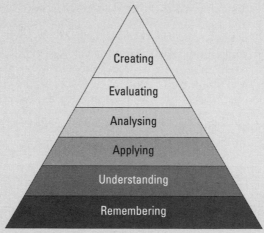

Creating

Evaluating

Analysing

Applying

Understanding

Remembering

Figure 8-3: The new Bloom triangle.

✔ **Multiple unrelated points — Multi-structural:** These learners now focus on several relevant aspects but these are all treated in isolation; the insights are disconnected.

✔ **Intermediate — Relational:** At last the different insights have become integrated. These learners have mastered their subject by being able to join all the parts together. This is where most learning stops.

✔ **Logically related — Extended abstract:** Some learners may go one step further and be able to create new ideas based on their complete understanding of the subject.

Don't mistake this talk about different levels for something hopelessly abstract: it's all highly practical. For example, if all someone is able to do by way of research is (say) to read about something in Wikipedia and edit down to the sections that seem immediately relevant, that person has a way to go before creating something new. The person who wants to do that must at least be able to combine several sources, which requires the high-level thinking skills of synthesis. Plus only people who can evaluate material can judge whether what they've produced is any good. In other words, only people at the top of the knowledge pyramid can write good essays — let alone mark them!

Thinking that requires all the skills in Bloom's pyramid is 'better' than thinking that requires less of them. Creativity that has a practical outcome (in other words, inventing) is supposed to exemplify this kind of 'everything' thinking, because it draws on the four highest levels of learning: application, analysis, synthesis and evaluation, in addition to the core skills of knowledge and comprehension.

For more recent developments see the nearby sidebar 'A 21st-century triangle'

Thinking creatively with Calvin Taylor

An American Professor of Psychology, called Calvin Taylor, is an important figure in the study of human creativity. His key idea was that many different kinds of skills and abilities exist

Creativity goes into space

During the mid-1950s, in response to the Sputnik launch and other Cold War pressures, the United States government began to devote increased funding to the development of scientific talent. One beneficiary was Calvin Taylor's own Institute for Behavioral Research in Creativity which held many summer creativity workshops for teachers. NASA funded studies there as part of a bid to find the ingredients that might indicate a future successful scientist or engineer. The research findings indicated a consistent pattern of independent thinking and working — and lots of self-confidence.

and that people who're gifted at one thing may not be much good at many others.

Taylor claimed that typical intelligence tests measure only a small fraction of talents that have been identified: 10 per cent at most. So he proposed that multiple talents should be evaluated in the classroom instead. He came up with nine 'talent areas' that he said were often sidelined by the emphasis on traditional measures of talent and ability: productive thinking, planning, communicating, forecasting, decision-making, implementing, human relations and discerning opportunities.

Great news! Many people rated as low performers by the traditional measures rise to at least 'average' level in one or other of the new talent areas. Taylor claimed that one third of students would probably be highly gifted in at least one of the new talent areas. This new rating would thus increase their motivation, and also allow efforts to be directed more constructively towards 'what people are good at' instead of uselessly at what people aren't good at.

Maintaining Motivation: Knowledge, Skills and Mindsets

The importance of maintaining a positive attitude in order to succeed while studying is well known. One study found that two-thirds of students who dropped out of school cited lack of motivation as a factor. Worse still, many of the one third who remained in school were also demotivated!

This section is about how *mindsets* (psychological attitudes) can determine levels of skill and even abilities. I hope that this section helps you to get and keep yourself motivated on that climb to the top of the thinking pyramid, because it's up there that the most interesting things are happening.

But being motivated is not quite as simple as it's sometimes made out to be — say by P.E. teachers chasing stragglers on a cross-country run. It's not enough to always be keen to do something, or even to make yourself do something — you have to be a realistic judge of your own abilities, and most importantly, about how to build upon them.

Feeling your way to academic success!

So, plenty of research suggests that motivation is crucial to success, but this sort of evidence points at a problem.

Pause a moment to put your Critical Thinking hat on and jot down some possible weaknesses in the argument that boosting motivation is the key to success. (You can read what I come up with at the end of this chapter.)

Nonetheless, solid research shows that motivation is a key indicator not only of school or academic success but also for achievement in all areas of life. Hardly a surprise, of course. But motivation isn't something that gets taught at school or college — though a bit is trialled as in-service training in the workplace.

Instead most educational activity is firmly focused on 'delivering the curriculum' and *pedagogy* (teaching methods). This approach is despite the fact that much research shows that psychological factors (such as motivation) often matter far more than so-called cognitive factors (such as verbal skills or even general intelligence) in terms of eventual results. Feelings matter! Feelings, say, about a student's own worth, towards the school or college, or beliefs about job prospects.

Perusing the paradoxical nature of praise

In the 1990s, as part of what was later called the *self-esteem movement,* some teachers attempted to instill more positive beliefs in their flocks by concentrating on making them 'feel good about themselves' and their abilities — and their prospects of success. Unfortunately, the strategy intended to improve students thinking rested on flawed thinking. The self-esteem movement assumed that assuring students that they were exceptional people, clever and talented and so on, would not only make people feel positive about themselves, but also increase their motivation to work and do well too. In fact, it had the opposite effect.

Praising students for their ability tends to produce a defensive response — afterwards students want to 'rest on their laurels', so to speak. The study found that students who were praised like this were more likely afterwards to try to avoid starting hard problems — because such problems seemed to carry a risk of failure (a risk of losing their 'laurels'!).

Praising abilities makes recipients think that they have a fixed level of intelligence, instead of them seeing learning as something they can nourish, and developing and increasing their intelligence.

Developing the necessary mindset

The reality is that in all areas of life, learning and achievement are about the willingness to explore new areas, and to work persistently, steadily and conscientiously. The paradox of praising someone's intelligence or skill levels is that it can discourage that person from progressing. (Which is not to say that plenty of other ways exist to discourage people too — such as calling them stupid and useless.)

The mindset needed to achieve and be successful has two essential ingredients:

  ✔ A willingness to take on challenging tasks that provide opportunities to learn new things, instead of settling for easier tasks in your comfort zone.

Would you pass the Marshmallow Test?

Walter Mischel and colleagues at Stanford University in the US conducted a famous study in the 1970s to investigate the relationship of 'self-control' to later academic achievement.

Very young children from the University nursery school were asked to wait for 15 minutes in a room with a little bell in it. In an apparently nice gesture, they were told that they could have marshmallows. But here's the catch: if they rang the bell to ask for their marshmallow, researchers would bring just one, albeit immediately. On the other hand, if they were patient and waited for the researcher to arrive, they'd be given two marshmallows!

Children's responses varied greatly. Some rang the bell only seconds after the experimenter had left the room, while others waited the full 15 minutes.

The second part of the study compared the achievements of the patient children some years later with the 'instant gratification' children. The researchers used the results of the standard school-leaving test as their measure and claimed that there was a striking correlation between the ability to wait for marshmallows at age 4 and the ability to solve verbal reasoning problems at age 11.

The moral is: psychological self-control is an essential tool for later achievement. The good news is: most people can do something about it!

> ✔ The psychological skills of persistence and self-control, instead of being the person who delivers a half-done project because the deadline clashed with a favourite TV show or last week's hot weather and fresh air seemed too enticing. Check out the nearby sidebar 'Would you pass the Marshmallow Test?' for research in this area.

Answers to Chapter 8's Exercises

Here are the answers to this chapter's exercises.

Dewey's recipe for education

My quick note would be: knowledge is all about connections. The rest of the material is interesting, but this is the key idea.

'It's been an exceptionally wet summer'

I have the rainfall measurements, but the statement is still definitely my opinion. Consider the background context of the claim: with which other towns or areas do I compare my figures and over what time periods? Plenty of value judgements are lurking behind even this simple claim.

Research on the problems of demotivation

I can see at least three things that should ring alarm bells for a Critical Reader with this kind of research:

- ✓ **The claim that low motivation explains students dropping out from school.** The significant finding to support this view would be low motivation among dropouts and high motivation among those who see their courses through. However, perhaps in their zeal to see low motivation everywhere, the researchers also identified evidence of low morale among those who stay in school, which undermines the idea that motivation is the key factor in whether a student stays on or drops out.

- ✓ **A 'cause and effect' law applies to this kind of claimed relationship.** Students who struggle academically may become demoralised and drop-out, instead of vice versa.

- ✓ **The evidence offered is too vague to be persuasive.** The researchers offer no names or dates for the survey, which is essentially a bit of hearsay, or these days, 'something read on the Internet'. Such research wouldn't stand up in a court of law — it doesn't really stand up in an essay!

Part III
Applying Critical Thinking in Practice

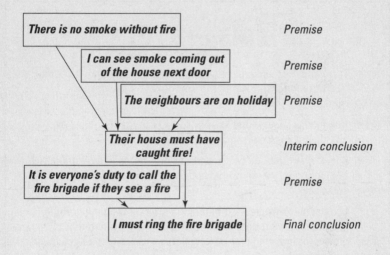

There is no smoke without fire	Premise
I can see smoke coming out of the house next door	Premise
The neighbours are on holiday	Premise
Their house must have caught fire!	Interim conclusion
It is everyone's duty to call the fire brigade if they see a fire	Premise
I must ring the fire brigade	Final conclusion

In this part . . .

✔ Turn yourself from a passive sponge of a reader into an active 'author-eating' shark with the low-down on critical reading.

✔ Make your own writing shark-proof, by respecting the key principles of good writing.

✔ Raise the curtain on two grand performances where speech predominates — the formal lecture and the college seminar.

✔ Look at the ingredients that make a presentation memorable, dissecting the group dynamics and learning particular techniques for listening and making notes — plus how to get your point across.

Chapter 9

Getting to the Heart of the (Reading) Matter

· ·

· ·

Reading furnishes the mind only with materials of knowledge; it is thinking that makes what we read ours.

John Locke *(As quoted in 'Hand Book: Caution and Counsels' in The Common School Journal Vol. 5, No. 24 (1843) by Horace Mann)*

Critical Thinking is fed and nurtured by great books, which firmly places Critical Reading skills at the heart of good learning. Critical Readers do not accept passively what they read — they read actively, constantly weighing up the strengths and weaknesses of the author's case. As I explain in this chapter, they move beyond meekly bowing down before presented facts and instead question and assess all the evidence, whether it's stated openly or submerged deeply within.

Of course, Critical Reading is about discovering ideas and information — but that's no use if you can't remember much of what you've read afterwards, if you have trouble getting your hands on the specific bits you need or you're short of time. For this reason, I offer some practical tips on note-taking and skim-reading to finish off the development of your Critical Reading skills.

Appreciating Critical Reading as a Practical Skill

In some contexts, being an uncritical reader is sufficient: in fact most education encourages this approach. The main skill that schools develop is the ability to summarise rather than select; while challenging or disputing sources — be they other books or teachers — is actively discouraged. Colleges are no better.

This may be because education operates in a bit of a sealed bubble. The exam board tells the teacher what to teach; the teacher tells school students what to learn; and the exam board checks only 'how much' the children remember. Critical Thinking doesn't come into it! Put another way, a college course can be badly designed, out-of-date and irrelevant, but if the people who teach and mark it are happy with it, that's the course you have to succeed in.

This focus may lead you to think that Critical Reading isn't a necessity. But don't make this mistake! Instead, look on it as an investment for later life.

Take healthcare, for example. Professionals of all kinds are responsible directly to their clients and reading that a particular new approach is effective isn't enough if people using it find that it makes the situation worse. Doctors are deluged with medical studies that argue persuasively for new treatments, which some years later turn out to be ineffectual or even harmful. A careful, Critical Reading of the claims made for the treatment may reveal early on that the evidence advanced for them is weak. So, having Critical Reading skills can be a matter of life or death!

Reading between the Lines

Wouldn't life be much easier if you could assume that what you read is a straightforward account and that — by and large — authors are truthful. Yet people can be wrong and texts can be misleading — and for many more reasons than authors simply being mendacious (I swear it's true, honest!). They may be misinformed, out-of-date or simply incompetent; or mixed up, muddled or just lazy. Or all of them!

So you need to be a sceptical reader. In this section I describe a number of mental checks to run on any piece of writing that you're reading critically, to help assess the soundness of its content. You may be surprised just how much information you can glean from a few fairly basic quality controls.

Checking the publisher's standing

If an article or book is from an academic journal or an academic publishing house, you can assume that several people with relevant knowledge of the themes and topics it covers have checked it. They should have knocked out sloppy writing full of basic errors. Plus, you can be sure that if it's from a respectable source, you can quote safely from it without risking looking silly.

But, despite what even some Critical Thinking experts say(!), all topics in scholarly life contain a range of diametrically opposed opinions. Therefore, this academic type of check is far from a guarantee that the text isn't making more sophisticated and significant mistakes, that it isn't partisan, or indeed that the work's whole approach isn't wrong.

Academics tend to hunt in packs, and so authors and reviewers can easily find experts to back up — or rubbish! — adopted positions. Real life features plenty of examples of mainstream views being wrong and minority views being right, and (last time I looked) academics are part of this real world.

Cross-examining the author

Ask yourself whether what you're reading is an academic study, a news report, an expert's opinion or an anonymous website. If one or more authors are named, what's their background, their area of expertise and experience? In other words, consider what qualifications they have to write on the subject.

Perhaps you've asked yourself what qualifications I have to write on Critical Thinking. You should have! Well, to put your mind at rest, I do have relevant degrees and I researched and co-authored a report on the subject for the UK government. *For Dummies* guides also require a popular touch, and so it's relevant that I've written many books for general readers too.

Being aware of potential author bias

Critical Thinking professor, Richard Northedge, when writing advice for students on sources, praises an article by an academic called Richard Layard on social inequality. He counts in favour of the article the fact that Professor Layard is an advisor to the UK government and had been, as it were, 'commended, for his services by being made a Lord.

To me though, this fact indicates that Professor Layard's views could be (I'm not saying they are, just that they *could* be) influenced by what's politically desirable or useful to say, as well as by what's academically important to say. Richard Layard is at the top of the social pyramid in the UK, very much part of the 'establishment'. and his perspective on the British government's efforts to help disadvantaged folk might seem to be a little bit too cozy.

Authors having first-hand, relevant experience makes their books more credible. But look out for authors whose experience may indicate that they have a bias — it's an easy mistake to make. For a possible example, see the nearby sidebar 'Being aware of potential author bias'.

Considering why the text was written

Ask yourself whether the writing is supposed to serve a particular purpose, perhaps to record an event, or whether it's intended to find a large paying audience (and make the author money), or maybe to obtain a qualification. (The nearby sidebar 'Being aware of potential author bias' *may* indicate a text with a hidden function.)

Publishers need to sell books and even academic writing is a product of fashion — authors are more likely to write such texts if they're part of a live debate going on within the field. A *live debate* may be one with recent discoveries and developments — or where a lot of money is being spent on new research! In all such cases, try to put the book into a wider social and scientific context.

Appraising how a text is written and presented

Consider whether the text is presented as a factual report or as a logical argument. Or is it part of a campaign, even a piece of propaganda or advertising? If it's a piece of research, 'how well' has it been done?

Judging this last point is by no means straightforward. Evaluating research is a special process, involving consideration of several factors as I describe in the nearby box 'Checking the methodology'! Even so, a Critical Reader should at least consider this issue.

Checking the methodology

When authors write books, conduct studies or investigate a topic, they operate within a *research paradigm* (a theoretical framework) that affects how they view and investigate the subject. In formal academic studies, authors discuss the research paradigm upfront, and so that's straightforward. But more often, they leave the nature of the chosen paradigm in the background — as a given. So the Critical Reader has to make a specific effort to work it out — and consider how the choice may skew the information reported.

Here are some useful questions to ask when looking at reports and research findings in the broad area of social science:

✔ *Theoretical or empirical:* Is the text primarily concerned with ideas and theories or primarily based on observations and measurements? Most texts mix the two approaches, but Critical Readers need to identify which element should be the primary focus — even if the author seems confused!

✔ *Nomothetic or idiographic:* These grand terms originate from Ancient Greek (*nomos* means law and *idios* means own or private) and refer to laws or rules that apply in general in contrast to ones that relate to individuals. Most social research is concerned with the *nomothetic* — the general case — because even when studying individuals researchers usually hope to generalise the findings to everyone else. Always bear in mind the extent to which entirely valid observations about a particular case can safely be generalised.

(continued)

(continued)

✔ *Cause or correlation:* So many people mix up these terms that the error has its own special name — *cum hoc ergo propter hoc* (Latin for 'with this, therefore because of this'). In other words, putting things together whose connection is unproven. Take a medical example. A recent study of over a million women with breast cancer checked how many were cured by operations to remove suspected cancerous cells. It found that two thirds were still alive ten years later. It might seem natural to assume that the survival was due to the treatment, but the study also found that a control group of women given a mock operation (involving no removal of any cells) had an identical survival rate — plus greatly reduced risks or ill-effects from the procedures. Be aware that in experimental studies, there is a built-in bias exists to see causation even when, maybe, none exists.

✔ *Statistical answers or ideological hypotheses:* A lot of research is based on probabilities. But working them out is something that even experienced researchers get wrong — perhaps applying the wrong statistical procedure to their data and generally overestimating the significance of their findings. Statistics aren't simple plain-as-a-pikestaff facts; they're created, misunderstood and manipulated, which is why politicians and businesses sometimes seize on them in order to present a partial picture.

Taking into account when a text is written

If a text is presented as a factual report or as research, the date when it was written can be crucial. The 'when' is a vital bit of the context.

First of all, facts keep changing — new discoveries are made, old discoveries are revisited and found to have been mistaken. Astronomers only recently discovered that calculations and assumptions about the universe in the twentieth century were way out and that it now seems that 95 per cent of the universe consists of so-called dark matter and dark energy, which is basically invisible. Views in many areas of science and indeed the arts are similarly in constant site of refinement and modification. And then there's 'context'. Huge events change perspectives long after. Something written in the politically optimistic years prior to World War I is going to be quite different to something written afterwards. Likewise, the political background of the idealistic (hippy) 1960s, the decade which ended with Man on the Moon, compared to the late 1980s, the decade which ended with the collapse of the communist dreams of the Soviet Union, has a profound and maybe underappreciated influence on books, the pervading artistic climate and culture.

Judging the evidence

Offering evidence for a position is surprisingly easy — the real question is how you decide what counts as good evidence. For example, is a book with ten pages of sources at the back better than one with no sources offered (like this one)?

I'll stick my head out a bit here and say (contrary to much academic practice) that the key thing is the main text. A source looks grand and fine, but the question of 'who says that and why' is really just being passed on — it doesn't go away. Where did the author of the book used as a source get *their* info from? Authors should give as much evidence as readers need to make an independent assessment of an issue in the main body of the book. As a reader, you shouldn't be obliged to either take things on trust or to check up yourself on all the footnotes and sources offered in a library!

 The important thing is to give enough information to readers at the point they need it. Be suspicious of texts that are long on assertion and short on detail.

A connected issue is the question of whether a book argues just one perspective or several. As I explain in Chapter 10, a good book needs to have the feel of a debate carefully guided by a strong chairperson. For the Critical Reader, even if not for the general public, a book that presents opinions as facts and fails to indicate other views and approaches to the matter reduces its own credibility.

Assessing your reasons for reading the text

It's amazing how many different responses people can have to the same text. So it's important for Critical Readers not only to think about the author's reasons for writing something, but their own reasons for reading it!

Ask yourself how you first encountered the book or article. Did you just happen to come across it, were you directed or referred to it, or did it appear at the top of a systematic search (say by putting keywords into an Internet search engine)? Is your source for the text anecdotal information, summaries of published works (for example, on Amazon) or a newly minted academic reading list?

The answers to these questions matter because, say, if your source is something you just happened to come across, it may not be representative of the consensus of opinion on the subject. It may be the point of a view of a small, activist minority — or just someone who doesn't really know their stuff. It's human nature to seek out views that reinforce ones we already hold, so beware 'uncritical' reading of articles and books you chose just because you liked the look of them. On the other hand, suppose that your source is a book that has been recommended to you by someone else, in such cases the recommendation is only as good as their judgement. If they are a professor in the subject, yes, that's normally a good start because they will surely have a good grasp of the general context (it's their job to), but equally they may have quite narrow, fixed views. You may be being steered towards a standard view at the expense of other, less conventional but maybe more fruitful ones. The point is to always be aware that you could — and maybe should — *be reading something else!*

Playing Detective: Examining the Evidence

The Internet makes 'fact checking' any document incredibly quick and easy — although there are a lot of wonky websites and you may make a worse mistake if you prefer a web page to a carefully researched book. But in any case, you need to look for several kinds of evidence when reading, of which 'facts' are only the most superficial layer.

Uncritical readers usually think that evidence is about 'facts' — but Critical Readers go a lot further. They don't read simply to discover facts; like good philosophers, they know that the 'truth' is anything but simple and that any number of possible facts exist. So instead they aim to critically evaluate ideas and arguments, aware that the important decisions in writing come in the author's selection and arrangement of the facts.

Weighing up primary and secondary sources

In this section I describe the detective work that Critical Readers carry out to uncover the hidden premises or chains of reasoning in a text — that is, the implied but not stated assumptions.

✔ **Primary sources:** Primary sources are a researcher's gold dust. They are original materials from the time period involved that have not been filtered through interpretation or evaluation. Primary sources present original thinking, present and report discoveries, or share new ideas or information.

✔ **Secondary sources:** A piece of journalism or a book about someone else's opinions, research or writings. They are interpretations and evaluations written in hindsight, but — don't let's be snotty about this — hindsight is pretty powerful too!

Think about the Global Warming controversy and just how many facts exist on both sides in the debate. If you look at different websites, arguing over exactly the same piece of news (say, that the Greenland ice sheet has been reported as shrinking) you can find two authoritative and equally factual explanations that come to completely opposed conclusions.

In this debate, as in many others, the selection of facts is what's important. That's why the Critical Reader doesn't just examine the evidence but looks 'behind the facts' too. Check out the earlier section 'Reading Between the Lines' for a more detailed look at this.

When reading a primary source, a short quote provides you with gold-plated evidence for your argument — as well as being more interesting to read. For example, if you are waiting for an author to prove to you that a newspaper called the *Daily Wail* once warned that polar bears were in danger of dying out, then a quote from the paper itself doing just this is much better than anything else and certainly worth any number of experts recalling or remembering hearing that the *Wail* did do such things. The *Daily Wail* would be, in this case, the primary source.

However, to take the same article as proof that researchers believe that polar bears are dying out (let alone that they really are) would be to use the newspaper as a secondary source. The problem with secondary sources is simple: What you read is no longer what someone said or (more subtly) the meaning may be different in the original context. The longer the chain of sources, the more likely distortions are to appear (as in a game of Chinese Whispers).

If you're reading someone's views of someone else's views, which is what almost all writing does come down to, count the author as being the authority instead of trusting him or her to have accurately conveyed anyone else's words. For that reason, select the text that you use very carefully — very critically.

How long before the coral reefs disappear?

To believe the *Times*, the answer to the above question is a few decades. In 2009, the paper devoted a supplement to warning against the rapid disappearance of coral reefs, which it attributed to the use of fossil fuels and the related emissions of carbon dioxide. The supplement contained an impressive range of graphs and glossy photographs of reefs 'prior' to their destruction. The central argument was that the almost mind-bogglingly huge reserve of water comprising the Earth's oceans had become more acidic in the last two hundred or so years, as a result of industrialisation, and was about to become much more so, poisoning the reefs.

First, Critical Readers would note that the *Times* is acting only as a secondary source and communicating research by other people.

Second, as a newspaper the *Times* may well have a political interest that affects its reporting. In this case, the editor in charge of the supplement admits elsewhere to feeling a duty to alert the world to the dangers of Global Warming: having considered the range of effects anticipated, the editor identified the threat to the oceans as the one with most resonance. In other words, the supplement was propaganda for a political position (to persuade governments to do more to reduce carbon dioxide emissions).

As far as the science goes, coral reefs have been around about 500 million years, during which time the oceans' temperatures, acidity and salinity have varied significantly. Many scientists argue quite different positions to that advanced (apparently dispassionately and authoritatively) by the *Times*. Critical Readers have to be suspicious of all claims, no matter how glossily and imposingly presented. Check the sources, cross-reference facts and actively look for contrary reports. Then, whatever your eventual decision, it's much more solidly grounded.

I'm interested in coral reefs and gave a paper to a conference in Queensland, Australia, on the topic of the Great Barrier Reef off Australia (which featured in the *Times* report). The reef was certainly in danger and suffering, but not from Global Warming. The cause was fairly obviously as a result of fertiliser (which contains nitrogen) run-off from the huge farms in Queensland. Explanations for the damage that spoke of worldwide emissions of carbon dioxide (particularly by the Chinese) were politically convenient, whereas satellite images showing nitrates swirling out of the river estuaries towards dead and dying parts of the reefs were definitely not!

Following chains of thought

Another way to be a Critical Reader is to strip texts down to their argumentative skeleton. What do I mean? Well, as I explain in more detail in Chapter 11, non-fiction texts consist of two sorts of arguments:

✔ **Explicit arguments:** Signposted clearly in the text by discussing competing views and giving reasons why such-and-such is right or wrong. Explicit arguments often end up with marker terms such as 'In conclusion', 'Therefore' and 'Thus it can be seen'.

✔ **Implicit arguments:** Just as important and, as the name . . . er . . . implies, a lot harder to spot. There's many different ways to imply something, so these arguments come in many shapes and forms. For example, an account of the meltdown of the nuclear reactor at Chernobyl might include an implicit argument that nuclear energy is a bad idea. A newspaper story describing how famous pop singers cheat on their boyfriends or girlfriends might constitute an implicit argument that pop singers are all empty-headed people with no morals. Or, on the other hand, it might be written in such a way that the implied argument is that 'free love' is fun and normal.

All arguments — not just dodgy ones — are based on more assumptions than meet the eye. Check out the nearby sidebar 'Breaking the argument chain' for an example.

Breaking the argument chain

Euclid's axioms are rules for geometry saying things such as 'Parallel lines never meet' or 'Things that are equal to the same thing are also equal to one another'. Euclid believed that his axioms were 'self-evident' statements about physical reality, meaning that you can see that they must be true by thinking about it. In fact they can be faulted for containing hidden assumptions. For example, the one about parallel lines assumes that space is flat, as parallel lines certainly do meet if you draw them on a sphere (try drawing two parallel lines on a football!). Behind his rules are assumptions like the one that space is *homogeneous* (the same everywhere) and

unbounded, which are necessary to ensure that any point can be transformed into another point by some mathematical operation, but not in themselves proven.

Einstein (whose theory of relativity significantly modified Euclid's view) was a great Critical Thinker, and part of the reason why is that he was prepared to throw out so many of the assumptions of his time. And yet his own theory contains lots of hidden assumptions — such as that one about space being homogeneous. (The more powerful telescopes get, the less this seems to be true too — the matter in the universe seems to be distributed unevenly.)

Read me! Testing your critical reading skills

Here's a longish extract for you to use to practise your reading skills. Try to identify the important features and write your own brief notes on it, including a summary of the argument (turn to the later section 'Summarising with effective note-taking' for some tips). State whether the argument is persuasive and any other textual features you think need noting, such as dodgy argumentative techniques or hidden premises. Flip to the answers at the end of the chapter for my take on the piece.

Philosophy has long had a dislike of astrology. It is, after all, irrational. And one of the most surprising, some would say alarming, facts about Ronald Reagan is that, as soon as he became the President of the United States, he appointed a personal astrologer to help him take decisions. But then, for thousands of years, all the Kings and Queens had their personal astrologers to do much the same thing. These were experts that they consulted on important state matters, such as when to invade the neighbouring country, when to harvest the crops — or how best to bring up baby.

Reagan had acquired the habit of consulting an expert in the Occult Arts when he was but a humble actor in California, doubtless the process helped him decide which role in which film he should accept — and we know where that ended: Breakfast with Bonzo (1951). But once he took high office, the role of astrology became even more in important.

Reagan consulted his personal astrologer, Joan Quigley, about the personality and inclinations of other world leaders, and used these insights to help him assess the prospects of meetings succeeding. It seems, for example, that the stars looked favourably upon one Mikhail Gorbachev, the then leader of the otherwise Evil Empire, and hence Reagan was encouraged to attempt the rapprochement that in due course led to the end of the Cold War. In fact, the timings of all policy initiatives had to be squared with the movements of the cosmos, and White House staff were instructed to liaise with her in all their plans. She was responsible, in short, for the success of all that Reagan did. And these days, Reagan is counted as a pretty successful President, although that judgement is itself by no means necessarily a very scientific one.

Of course, Ronald Reagan came in for a bit of stick for consulting astrologers. Just as more generally scientists and attached pundits love nothing better that to mock more humble folk who follow their forecasts in the newspapers and magazines. For many educated people, nothing better illustrates the gullibility and foolishness of the masses, and the need for the lead of a scientific elite than the continued activities of 'unlicensed' specialists in the influence of the stars and planets on human affairs. They don't seem to remember, or want to be told, that for a thousand years, Universities taught astrology as one of the core subjects, and that it was part of a sophisticated system of medical knowledge involving the different parts of the body and different herbs.

Even if that founding figure of sensible science, Isaac Newton, was brought up on a diet of esoteric knowledge, in which astrology ranked as one of the great studies of mankind, even if astronomy profited from the mystical approach of Pythagoras, even if the best of modern medicine is borrowed from herbalism and chemistry is a side-shoot of alchemy. Even if, in short, in Paul Feyerabend's words, everywhere science is enriched and sustained by unscientific methods and unscientific results, today astrology is firmly fallen out of favour with philosophers, let alone scientists. Little remains of the subject other than the superficial popular and psychological forms, yet astrology, like many of the now much derided esoteric studies of the distant past, still has the potential to inform and underpin our understandings of the universe. Because thousands of years of thinking are contained in those ancient astrological myths and legends. Science is just a blip in this long history. . .

Spotting the hidden assumptions

Here's an argument that I adapt from Sam Harris, writer, commentator, and co-founder and chief executive of *Project Reason*, which says that it seeks to encourage Critical Thinking. Sam is convinced that science holds the answers to everything — including matters of right and wrong — and what's more, he thinks that he can prove it. (He was so pleased with this argument he offered a cash prize for anyone who could find a hole in it!)

I summarise his argument below, with my own clarifications:

✔ **First premise:** Notions of right and wrong and human values in general all depend on the existence of conscious minds, because only conscious minds can experience pleasure and pain.

(In other words, morality is rooted in awareness of pain and pleasure, which are brain states.)

✔ **Second premise:** Conscious minds are natural phenomena, and so they must be fully explained and constrained (limited) by the physical laws of the universe (whatever these turn out to be in the end).

(In other words, consciousness is reducible to physical states, such as electrical signals or chemical changes in brains.)

Now Sam draws speedily to his knock-out conclusion.

✔ **Therefore:** All questions concerning human values must have objectively right and wrong answers, and these answers can be obtained through the techniques of natural science.

Sam adds that he means this 'in principle', if not in practice.

Okay, that's the argument. Now what assumptions do you think are present that ought to be brought out into the light and checked? Answers at the end of this chapter.

Filtering out Irrelevant Material

If only as much effort went into reducing words and arguments to their essentials, as goes into producing and expanding on them! The world would be a less wordy place, communication would be enhanced and knowledge would flourish like a well-pruned tree.

Alas, the world isn't like this, and you need to be quite ruthless in hacking away at all the verbiage. In this section, you can find out how — and why — to make your notes effective, and strategies to get your reading done in a fraction of the time you've been taught to do it in.

Ignoring irrelevant material saves you time and effort and improves the quality of your work, because it allows you to focus your efforts on what's genuinely useful. I discuss two tools in this section: effective note-making and skim-reading.

Summarising with effective note-taking

Note-taking requires you to use several key Critical Thinking skills: comprehension and analysis, synthesis, and writing and communication skills. Summarising is the ability to make use of information, and it helps you to make sense of material.

In practice, Summarising often involves:

- ✔ Reading a text, or listening to a lecture. Yes, that's right, you can't avoid it!

- ✔ Identifying the elements that are *most important* or *most relevant* for you.

- ✔ Noting down these points in your own words.

- ✔ Organising your notes clearly and effectively.

The art of summarising is in that last sentence. Anyone can write a summary: writing a *useful* one is much harder.

Summary tips

Never let taking notes slow down your thinking or get in the way of your own ideas — let alone start to destroy your interest in the subject. Instead, actively follow debates and make any notes later. With books, you may well be better off reading the whole thing, or at least the chapter, and then whizzing back to jot a few notes. Wonderful thing the brain — you find at once that most of what you may have noted before you can now see isn't worth noting after all!

The things that most cry out for summaries are books. If most books on Critical Thinking are careful to include chapter summaries and so on — many, mainstream academic books don't do that. Instead you have to read from *Chapter 1* to *Chapter Zzzz* — and maybe the index and footnotes too to find out the author's point. That's not good.

My own experience reading philosophy is that even the great works contain only one or two small ideas worth noting. I'm not making it up! After I read these books — or a rather skim-read them (see the next section) I usually find it requires just a few hundred words to sum up all the key points in a book of about 100,000 words. A few hundred words is a lot easier to write down, a lot easier to remember and a lot easier to develop and take forward for your own purposes later. But don't be too dogmatic — if something is full of important ideas, your summary is going to get a bit longer.

In cases where there is a lot of detail you really want to note, I recommend writing down an umbrella sentence to indicate what there is (and where — the page number, even the paragraph number), instead of specifying it. For example, if a book contains a series of biographies of famous scientists, write down that fact, with maybe a few of the names, but don't note any of the details — unless you won't have access to the source again.

The key thing in summaries is that what you put in depends on what you want out. Don't summarise just for the sake of so-called completeness! You're almost certainly wasting your time, and what's worse, making it harder for you to develop the information later.

Remember, while you're making notes you can also be engaging purposefully and creatively with the topic, connecting up your own thoughts with the views of the author on the subjects.

Research shows that in higher level work involving ideas and concepts, actively thinking about what you are reading or hearing, and then paraphrasing the information — putting it in your own words, rather than writing it all down verbatim — makes it easier to recall later (say in an exam). And though they may seem scruffy and old-fashioned, *handwritten notes* are much easier and more likely to be paraphrased than those typed directly into a computer or laptop.

Actually, as I explain in Chapter 7, even informal jottings frequently help you to find thoughts that previously you weren't aware of! When taking notes is done correctly, it is not a desperate effort to get down an accurate record of what's in the book or what the lecturer is saying — it is a much more constructive and personal activity. In effect, you 'discover' your own ideas through the apparently reverse activity of writing down someone else's.

P.S. Use abbrev.!

The importance of factual notes

Okay, okay, I know taking notes is boring. Much better to hope your brain remembers everything important and sorts out the information later subconsciously.

Dream on! Unless you're very unusual, your brain forgets 98 per cent of what you've carefully read and mangles the remaining 2 per cent. That's where factual notes come in. Look on them not as a chore, but as a powerful thinking tool. A note acts as a safe-deposit box that doesn't disappear over-night — and a page of notes is an organised store too.

Notes should never be simply an abbreviated copy of the original text; they should be an attempt to pick out particular insights in the text. They're your signposts to the key ideas in what you've been reading.

Using your time wisely: Skim-reading

Skim-reading is such a powerful technique — strange that it isn't taught more. Indeed, teachers and professors usually insist that if they set a chapter to read, you better read every last word of it! But Critical Readers are an unconventional lot and can afford to risk the odd frown of disapproval.

When *skim-reading* you read just the first one or two lines of each paragraph on the first page of any chapter. (A website is a bit like a chapter in a book, and a web page is a bit like a paragraph.) If none of what you read seems tempting, jump to the next chapter. If any of the paragraphs seem worth investi-gating further, keep reading at least until the next paragraph, and then check out the first lines of the following few para-graphs too.

Only read sections of books that seem useful — and of course you don't need to read them all either. As I say, usually you can see whether a paragraph is useful to you by just reading the first line. As long as material seems relevant and useful, you keep reading, because you've 'struck gold'. As soon as you sense the material isn't right for you, skim the first lines of the next few paragraphs and if (to quote Mick Jagger) you still 'can't get no satisfaction', start flicking pages until you get to the next marked out section. (And certainly pause at a new chapter).

When you seem to be in a useful part of the book, look more closely at the text than if you seem to be wading though irrelevant text. If (after about two minutes of skimming) the whole book seems a bit dull — stop and ask yourself, hey, why am I reading this? Maybe you could spend your time better.

Target your reading for the information you're after. For example, if an article's abstract provides what you need, skim the rest. If all you want to know is a study's research outcomes, you don't need to read the methodology and context.

Answers to Chapter 10's Exercises

Here I provide my thoughts on this chapter's two exercises.

Read me! Testing your critical reading skills

I'm sure that you can find many things to say, but here are my notes.

The piece is an informal argument. The author argues that something useful may reside in astrology and that it's too often dismissed. To back this assertion up she gives a number of examples. The first one is that of Ronald Reagan, who it seems relied on astrological advice for all his key policy decisions. A specific example is given: Reagan's decision to work with the Russian president to end the Cold War was based on advice from his astrologer that this would be a good policy.

Another more general defence of astrology is that 'for a thousand years, Universities taught astrology as one of the core subjects'. The hidden assumption, or *implied premise,* is that if something is taught at university it must be useful and important. The author adds that astrology was historically part of 'a sophisticated system of medical knowledge involving the different parts of the body and different herbs'.

The point isn't made explicit but seems to be that astrology has aided the development of medical knowledge in general and herbalism in particular. But no evidence is offered for 'how' astrological notions aided and guided herbalism, and so this seems to be *argument by positive association* — sometimes called *the association fallacy.* Similarly, the reference to Isaac Newton seems to be included more to associate a great scientist with astrology rather than to demonstrate anything more substantial about astrology's scientific usefulness.

Here's one factual mistake in the piece that I spotted. The film referred to as *Breakfast with Bonzo* is actually *Bedtime for Bonzo.* This is a small mistake but does cast doubt on the author's other factual claims. In summary, the piece presents itself as a factual argument but seems to rest on subjective opinions.

Spotting hidden assumptions

I think the argument is basically that morality is reducible to calculations of the total amount of human 'pleasure' as opposed to the amount of human 'pain', and that these sensations are also reducible to physical states, such as electrical signals or chemical changes in brains. Therefore, it seems reasonable to conclude that scientists can objectively measure and investigate such physical states.

So what are the hidden assumptions or implied premises? For starters:

> ✔ *[Implied premise]* **Answers are 'right or wrong' in science.** This assumption is pretty large, because science is a lot more complicated than this. Scientists, for example, tend to agree on a particular interpretation of data, out of a range of possible interpretations. The agreements do not hold long! As one recent book puts it, surprisingly little of what experts held to be true even 20

years ago is still thought to be true today — and likely much of what's considered to be settled fact today will be adjusted in the next 20 years. Instead of giving 'right or wrong' answers, science provides working hypotheses that are open to rebuttal later.

✔ *[Implied premise]* **Minds equal brains.** An ongoing debate exists about whether minds and thoughts are the same thing as brains and chemical states. Clearly a link is present — but one theory is that thought is a social phenomenon: what people think depends in subtle ways on what other people around them think, and on *all* the physical sensations that they're having and have ever had.

✔ *[Implied premise]* **Morality is simply a matter of maximising pleasure and minimising pain.** This assumption barely fits any simple ethical test! Imagine, for example, a nasty neighbour who locks her family in her house and proposes to shoot her children one by one unless you agree to shoot yourself first. Sam would say that not only the scientifically right, but also the morally right, thing is for you to do just that. (One dead person is less bad than two.) I'd say you are under no moral obligation to do so.

No doubt plenty more hidden assumptions exist, so don't necessarily count yourself wrong if you have a different list!

Chapter 10

Cultivating Your Critical Writing Skills

> *Explanations exist; they have existed for all time; there is always a well-known solution to every human problem — neat, plausible, and wrong.*
>
> —HL Mencken ('The Divine Afflatus', New York Evening Mail, 1917)

*T*his chapter is all about applying Critical Thinking skills where they belong best — in writing. You get an overview of how to write effectively and also an 'inside view', as I explain the sorts of things that help to make writing, especially academic writing, clear, concise and successful. In the process, you really get into the nuts and bolts of Critical Thinking.

In this chapter, you can find out how to structure your writing to make its points clearer as well as about the 'who, what and where' factors that are vital to guiding your arguments. I dish up some tasty tips on preparation and research, and describe how to home in quickly on the textual clues in writing — by being aware of the key terms and words.

Finally (and that's a straightforward textual clue to flag the end of these introductory paragraphs!), you have an opportunity to develop your argumentation skills by deconstructing a passage into its constituent, logical parts, and specifically, its intermediate conclusions. *Intermediate whats?* It sounds like jargon, I know, (indeed, it is jargon) but the concept is useful and intermediate conclusions matter. You can find out all about them in this chapter.

Structuring Your Thoughts on the Page

By definition, a solid structure provides support for your piece of writing and gives readers the best chance of grasping your point or argument. In this section I cover the basics, show how to handle evidence and how to make sure that you really answer the question in an exam or assignment. All sprinkled with some essential tips on structure from an expert in the Critical Writing field.

Indentifying the basics of structure

What are the ingredients of a well-structured piece of writing? Well, writing first things first is a great start.

You confuse readers when you don't tell them your overall position early on and upfront. I know that keeping a few tricks up your sleeve is more exciting — or even better (like a detective story) subtly leading readers into believing something that's the opposite of what turns out, in a dramatic final paragraph, to be the case! — but it *is* confusing.

Also, in the context of factual writing, revealing your position at the outset is more honest, because then readers can critically evaluate your arguments. For instance, if you're going to present an argument that Shakespeare was an Eskimo, say so early on and then readers can be duly sceptical of any incidental details your essay starts to dwell on regarding textual evidence of Shakespeare's deep interest in snow and ice.

Another part of structuring your writing is to keep related information together. Suppose that you're discussing the health effects of pollution and you have three points about the ways that cars create dangerous fumes. At the very least consider whether to group the points together. (Sometimes. of course, you may have good reasons for keeping them separate.)

A book's index often reveals how methodical and organised the author really is, and how well he (or she) has grouped connected material together. If key topics in the index are revealed as *page sweeps* (such as 34–41), this is a better sign than if the same specific theme turns up in 10 or 20 different locations in the book.

View an index as a kind of X-ray of a book that reveals its hidden structure. Try indexing some of your own longer pieces of writing; you may be surprised to see how scattered your thoughts are! Even easier and quicker if you're word-processing is to search your document for certain words. Do you keep mentioning 'paradigm', for example, or have too many 'buts' and 'howevers'? X-ray your own work by checking for key terms. Sometimes the check reveals problems!

What about layout and graphics? After all, isn't a picture worth a thousand words? Well, maybe for writing holiday news, but not in Critical Writing. No, no, no! Don't use graphics to *prove* your arguments. Critical Writing isn't marketing. Use graphics only to illustrate ideas that you've presented first in the main text. Similarly, don't rely on headings or snazzy fonts and text styles to make your points. But you can use all these things to highlight ideas and signpost things to the reader. That's after all, what a *For Dummies* book is doing all the time. Look at the next heading — doesn't it help you quickly navigate the text?

Presenting the evidence and setting out the argument

In Critical Writing the emphasis is on producing reasons to support or (equally importantly) to discredit a position. Evidence is crucial for both kinds of activity, although clearly you need to produce more evidence for controversial claims than for common sense assertions that your readers may reasonably be expected not to need convincing of.

Leave background information, anecdotes or jokes, useful as they are for reaching word-targets, to Internet chat rooms! Likewise, statements of personal opinion don't fit in with the central idea of Critical Writing, which is to persuade through argument.

Writing comes in all shapes and sizes, but the essay format is often the way in which colleges demand it and so I concentrate on that style here. Academic essays are supposed to argue a certain position and provide reasons that support a conclusion. Thus they are 'critical thinking' in capsule form.

But, like life, an essay is more complicated than that. In Critical Writing you need to make a particular effort to identify conflicting positions and to acknowledge different views. A more sophisticated essay shows how the main conclusions follow from the evidence provided, but may also explore issues and arguments related to the question that *don't* support the eventual conclusions. In this important sense, a good essay consists of several arguments, some of which are in competition with each other.

I hear you saying, 'hold on there!' Surely the aim is to write only what's strictly relevant and right? But remember that interpretation is the key in Critical Writing. You don't need to show you can either rote learn or reinvent the wheel. In most cases your job is to examine other people's ideas and select from them the elements you need to argue your case.

And don't be dogmatic (I say dogmatically). Respect different views and approaches and display a spirit of negotiation in your Critical Writing.

Let everyone have their say

In essence, your job in Critical Writing is to allow a real debate and properly air views — for and against — issues; it's not to settle the issue once and for all. Even Einstein in writing his famous Theory of Relativity didn't seek to shut the debate down. He recognised that what he was producing might be flawed, and invited his readers to keep testing and exploring the issues. Indeed some of them spotted key errors in his maths — the part that's normally supposed to be pretty 'black and white'. Einstein had to revise his equations many, many times.

Checking out the key principles of well-structured writing

Writing well requires three things — knowledge of your topic, organisation and communication skills. The last one is the Cinderella skill — not invited to the party — in many academic contexts. In this section, you can learn how to make all three elements come to you as naturally as breathing.

Lecturer Andrew Northedge is an expert in this area and here, to get you started, are some of his most useful points for his students.

Knowing what you're writing about

Andrew Northedge is a lecturer in the Open University in the UK. He specialises in writing guides for students, which include lots of ideas relevant to Critical Thinking.

The Open University is different from other universities in that its students are a mix of ages and backgrounds, often studying part time, and the courses have to be delivered, not in person, but at a distance, often via the Internet. Getting students to think critically is thus a particular concern of the Open University. Northedge urges students to spend a bit of time *before* they start writing to ask themselves just what they're meant to write. In other words, to try to identify the topics, information and ideas that a tutor — or more generally, future readers of the essay — will be looking for.

This may seem obvious, perhaps, but as Northedge says, writing is a particularly private activity — people retreat into a quiet corner on their own to do it. And if students spend a lot of time thinking about their own writing, and a bit of time thinking about the feedback later from tutors, most students never see what anyone else has written during their course. They live in a bubble and their writing is sealed off from public view. So make a special point of peering out!

Doing initial research

Carry out some broad-brush, preliminary research before you write. Don't just look up a few bits you need and plonk them in the writing. Instead search for background material that allows for thinking and reflection. Yes, I know it takes up valuable time, but (just like painting a wall) if you spend half an hour preparing you often save several hours later — or at least that half an hour!

Preparing before writing means:

✔ Reading about your subject.

✔ Thinking about the issues.

✔ Making notes and perhaps doodling some ideas (check out Chapters 9 and 11 for more on this invaluable skill).

All this work improves your writing — and makes your arguments more effective — when you commit your ideas to paper.

Taking lessons from others

Talk about the subject of your essay with other people, specifically those doing similar subjects: perhaps ask to look at some of their writing for ideas on style.

Of course, if you're a student doing an assignment, maybe don't look at essays on exactly your topic, or if you do so, make sure that it's after all the essays — your one and those you might be looking at — have been marked! (Otherwise, you're in danger of looking like you're copying ideas.) However, if your pieces of writing are regularly criticised for lacking clarity and structure — which is a vague sort of criticism and hard to act upon — comparing your efforts to those of someone whose writings have been praised for just these sorts of features can give insights.

Then, when you start writing, aim for simplicity and elegance over grandiose constructions intended to be huge and imposing. As Andrew Northedge sums it up:

> *There's no great mystery about what is good writing and what is not. Good writing is easy to read and makes sense. Poor writing is unclear and confusing; it keeps making you stop to try to work out what it's saying and where it's going.*

> —*Andrew Northedge (The Good Study Guide, 2005)*

Re-working that first draft

When you've written your first draft, you arrive at the often neglected after-writing stage. No, not turning the TV on, putting your feet up and getting the beer out! It's now the real work begins.

Lecturer Andrew Northedge's tip for this stage is to spend time on *improving the flow*. He means mainly ensuring that the paragraphs follow (flow) in a smooth sequence. He recommends adding in extra text at key points that helps readers by tipping them off in advance where the argument is heading. Check out the later section 'Spotting and using keywords' for more details.

But just *saying* what the next paragraph is about isn't enough: you need to have a reason for your choice of content too — a sensible plan guiding the writing overall. The topics need to follow on from each other coherently and logically.

To make sure that this happens, you need either to be very good at writing 'off the top of your head' (what's sometimes called 'steam of consciousness' writing — the optimistic idea that your subconscious does all the work for you) or you need to have a pretty detailed and careful draft outline to guide your writing. You won't be surprised that for most people, a separate plan — one that delivers a sequence of points for the essay — together with links that connect them one to the next, works best in practice.

Linking can seem a subtle concept, but it's not difficult. It simply involves using certain words to connect your paragraphs. Suppose that you're writing an essay on the prospects of a manned base on Mars in the next decade, and your paragraph ends with the observation that the Mars base will require protection from meteorites. Then the next paragraph really needs to follow up this issue, perhaps by talking about meteorite proof domes or about other problems. When the essay changes direction, you can start the new paragraph with a few *link words,* such as 'Another practical issue for any future interplanetary base may be . . .'.

Such writing tricks are so easy that people often take them for granted. Yet they can make all the difference between readability — and indigestibility.

Most people can always identify good writing because only good writing is interesting, effective and informative. For this reason, a vital part of Critical *Writing* is Critical *Reading*, because you have to be able to read and re-read your drafts with a critical eye before you're going to be able to improve them.

Deconstructing the question

Essay titles and assignment questions matter. Think of them as introducing you to an audience with a very particular interest. Imagine, for example, people who have paid to hear a talk on how to grow tomatoes — they're not going to be happy with one about the merits of ketchup over brown sauce!

The Critical Thinker's first job when writing is to think through exactly what that interest is — all the implications of the essay title or question. Don't tell the audience what *you're* interested in — tell readers only about what they want to know. The title or question is your indispensable guide to that.

Critical Thinking involves close examination of texts. Yet students often spend surprising little time on the very short and easily underestimated line or two that comes in the form of the question or assignment. Yet if you settle for a general impression of this short text, and charge off in the wrong direction, you can waste a lot of time and effort. Much better to *deconstruct* the question carefully, noting the choice and special significance of the words and assumptions behind it.

In the academic context, the need to 'answer the question' is paramount. As Andrew Northedge, the Open University lecturer stresses, *everything* in an essay should relate to the question, and what's more, you need to make clear that this is the case. Northedge sees successful essays as featuring one long argument with every paragraph leading inexorably to, and supporting, the conclusion. Although that could be that there are no simple answers.

Producing effective conclusions

A crucial part of structuring an academic essay is ensuring that your conclusion is effective.

Don't just answer the question, *make clear* that you've answered it. And the 'it' must be the original question. Yes, this advice sounds obvious, but in colleges anyway, the answer is only right if it matches the original question. Often it doesn't matter whether you agree or disagree with the question under examination or in the title, or if you conclude that there's no answer or that it all 'depends'. But absolutely without exception you have to make clear and unambiguously that your conclusion follows from the evidence you've presented and deals with the point you set out originally to explore.

So, when you write the conclusion, don't worry about insulting the reader's intelligence — just go right ahead and spell things out. The same applies for all your earlier, subsidiary points too — your *intermediate conclusions* that build up to your final one (more on these in the later 'Using intermediate conclusions' section).

Choosing the Appropriate Style of Writing

Critical Writing requires keeping your audience in mind constantly. Therefore, you need to select the right information for them and present it in a way that's appropriate for them, avoiding unnecessary technicality or jargon.

Keeping your audience in mind

It's only common sense that different kinds of writing are aimed at different kinds of readers, and for sure, Critical Writing is expecting Critical Reading later. But it's important to realise that this readership is essentially imaginary. Be careful not to aim at too narrow an audience. What you *don't* do, for example, if you're a student asked to write an essay entitled 'What's the root of the world's problems today?' is produce an essay arguing in favour of a radical redistribution of wealth and against cruelty to animals, just because your teacher is a sandal-wearing vegetarian who hates rich people.

Noooo, not at all! You address not your supervisor but (at the very least) all the people the supervisor would expect your essay to need to convince too. For a student, rather obviously and literally, this would be examiners, but examiners too stand in for a wider audience. On a topic like this they'd judge an essay to be convincing and persuasive only if it would persuade any educated and reasonable person.

That said, the judgement about audience, however, is far from being as simple as just writing for some perfectly 'wise person'. You need to consider the whole range of particular factors. For example, if you're writing a student dissertation for a supervisor in China or India or Saudi Arabia, you shouldn't assume the same shared base of political opinions as you maybe can when writing within the UK, or indeed, Western Europe.

Considering the detail required

Any question set by an exam board or a tutor comes with certain expectations of the 'level of detail' wanted and about background knowledge within a certain subject domain — plus important assumptions about the style of writing. I know from personal experience that writing an interesting and highly creative narrative on a topic is pointless if the examiner wants a demonstration of knowledge of certain particular points. Dull, maybe, but that's how it is, and Critical Writers are nothing if not realistic.

To work out the relevant 'domain of expertise', to use a flowery phrase, ask yourself: what's the practical context? For example, if you're writing an essay on 'What role can organic farming have in feeding the world?', you need to identify the appropriate framework: is the context a course on economics, farming technology or social psychology? Or perhaps it's not a course at all, but an assignment for a company making, say, organic ice cream.

The topics and evidence you look at in most detail depend on the key audience you're writing for (see the nearby sidebar 'Types of audiences' for more information).

Student essays aren't exactly journal articles, let alone full-blown dissertations (thank goodness), but they're a highly structured kind of writing that must focus on developing an argument.

A good way to road-test your writing is to write your conclusion down — and then write the opposite! Now, can you quickly find in your piece of writing the key points that you can read out to dissuade anyone arguing this 'opposite position'?

Types of audiences

Here are some general approaches for particular types of writing aimed at specific audiences:

✔ **Academic studies and report writing:** A summary usually starts this kind of writing and the main body of the report usually follows a set pattern: a section outlining the problem, a section that explains what people have already said about it and the all-important research methods section. This latter section is where the author explains why he's chosen to go about exploring the issue, whatever it may be, in a certain way. The bulk of the report then concerns an account of 'what was found out' using this method, and the final sections concern the conclusions being drawn from this research.

✔ **Journal articles:** Usually begin with a separate summary called the *synopsis* and the main body starts off by looking at the context of the issue and examining several possible positions, all taken with very detailed referencing. The final paragraph may well be called 'Conclusion' and that's what it is — drawing together the threads of what has been discussed earlier. The synopsis and the conclusion of many aca-demic journal articles are very similar.

✔ **Magazine article:** May well start with a little story, or a teas-ing question, which is followed by a discussion that gets more detailed as you read on — and may well end up with a surprise at the end!

✔ **Newspaper article:** At least conventionally, these start off by stating all the key points in the first line! The second paragraph then expands on this opening, and the article itself consists of the same again in more detail. Newspapers articles don't save the best bit until last, because for practical production rea-sons, the end of the article is the first bit cut if space is a bit tight. Old-school journalists used to be told always to structure sto-ries the same way: to say *who, what, when, where, why, how,* in that order.

Don't dismiss journalistic writ-ing! It *is* structured, and it shares one important feature with aca-demic writing — the search for impartiality.

'What you see is news, what you know is background, what you feel is opinion', as American journalist Lester Markel said.

Getting Down to the Specifics of Critical Writing

At the start of this chapter I promised to cover the nuts and bolts of the Critical Writing skills and so now here they are. It all hinges on strategies for straightforwardness, keywords, evidence, signposts and conclusions.

Understanding that only gardens should be flowery

Rule number one of Critical Wiring is keep sentences short and simple. Doing so is easy and it's a mystery why many people seem to prefer writing long complicated sentences that introduce ambiguity and are tiring for readers to follow. They oblige readers to retain in their memory, at least briefly, one part of the sentence while they struggle to process the next bit — or the bit after that!

Rule 2 is avoid specialist terms and technical language where possible, and where you do need them clearly introduce and explain them. Similarly, flag up non-specialist terms that can be used in more than one way as ambiguous and define them for the purposes of the essay.

A good way to road check the comprehensibility of your writing, or at least of certain phrases, is to read it aloud. Remember, you don't have to appear to be a know-all. So simplify wherever possible.

Spotting and using keywords

Keywords emphasise or indicate the focus or intentions of the writer. They ask the readers to think in a particular way, specifically to anticipate what's about to happen next. The use of appropriate keywords makes your writing much more effective.

Okay, so keywords are worth using. But which ones are they? Not all words are equal! Part of writing effectively is certainly to use a relatively small number of powerful words, in the sense that they help to shape your argument and guide readers through it.

Between you and me, quite a bit of nonsense is sometimes written about Critical Thinking keywords, which in no way fits with real language and the kinds of things that people read and write. For example, when you read a journal article, you're unlikely to find a phrase such as 'I will start by arguing . . .', but many Critical Thinking guides call this an excellent syntactical device! Similarly, some lecturers forbid their students from writing 'Finally, in conclusion', but some Critical Thinking guides earnestly assure their readers that this is part of constructing a good essay.

No, the truth is a bit more subtle. A lot of the navigation of writing is implied: the first paragraph is probably going to introduce the topic, for example, and the last one is probably the conclusion.

With that cautionary note in mind, here are some patterns in writing that you need to be aware of:

- ✔ Keywords flagging up another argument in support of a view: *Similarly, equally, again, another, in the same way, likewise.*

- ✔ Keywords flagging up alternative perspectives and arguments: *On the other hand (that's one of my favourites!), yet, however, but.*

- ✔ Keywords rowing back against a criticism just advanced, in support of an earlier view: *Nonetheless, even so, however, but* (yes, keywords can serve different purposes).

- ✔ Keywords to tell the reader that you're about to draw some conclusions (get ready!): *Therefore, thus, for this reason, because of this, it seems that.*

Presenting the evidence and setting out the argument

Particularly in the academic context, where issues are complex and approaches can differ widely, a written essay is like a spoken debate, with several speakers who present their positions, and have to justify them too. Your role, as the author of the piece of Critical Writing, is to 'chair the debate' — asking searching questions, and (most exciting of all!) ruling on whether the speaker has met the objection or is starting to digress.

A skilled Critical Writer (like a good chairperson in a meeting), always tries to get all the important issues at least aired, and also knows how much space to give to each position, not forgetting when to rein people in — to 'keep them to the point'.

Critical Writers need to argue one thing one moment — then another contrary thing — and at any point change their tone and 'their mind'. They have to think for several people all at once — it requires them to become almost schizophrenic! Plus, they continually try to judge the whole situation as reflected in what they've just written!

Thus, a danger always exists that a piece of Critical Writing can degenerate into a babble of different opinions, all competing for the reader's attention and appearing not to relate to each other. At worse, such writing becomes an unstructured mess.

Avoiding commitment with weasel words

You may be surprised to discover that weasel words aren't always a bad thing: they have a good side too. Critical Writing recognises more than one explanation for everything — correction! for *most things* — and so introducing a little bit of flexibility into your writing avoids committing yourself unnecessarily to more sweeping opinions than necessary. For example:

✔ **Write 'in many cases' instead of 'every':** Don't say 'every cloud has a silver lining' but argue that 'often, a cloud has a silver lining'.

✔ **Never write 'never'! Use 'rarely':** Don't insist that an earthquake has never happened in the UK, just argue that there have rarely been any large earthquakes in the UK. The word 'large' is also a way of finessing the claim.

In general, don't try to prove your point, just tentatively offer it. So, instead of writing 'this proves' or 'I have proved', write 'this indicates' or 'the evidence presented here suggests'.

As in a debate, the key thing in Critical Writing is to have a good chairperson . Someone has to be in charge and you, the writer, are the all-important chair of the debate. Happily, as with a real debate, in Critical Writing one position can 'triumph' over another — by producing a killer fact, for example, or by demonstrating a contradiction in the opponent's logic. Rule on those points for the reader.

Signposting to keep readers on course

Give directions! Use signpost words to guide your readers:

- ✔ **To introduce a new idea:** Write phrases such as 'first of all' or 'some recent research shows'.

- ✔ **To back up something already mentioned:** Use words such as 'similarly' or ' indeed'.

- ✔ **To indicate a change of direction and introduce alternative perspectives on an issue:** Use phrases such as 'on the other hand' or words like 'equally' and 'nonetheless'.

Paragraphs are another great tool to help readers navigate your writing. Ensure that each paragraph deals only with one idea, and in a similar spirit aim to give each idea its own paragraph.

Some ideas of course require several paragraphs, but in this case, each paragraph represents a slightly different aspect of the discussion:

- ✔ Deal with each idea in its own paragraph.

- ✔ Use the first line to signpost the contents of the paragraph.

- ✔ Arrange the paragraphs in a logical sequence.

Using intermediate conclusions

Many arguments contain within them smaller arguments — *sub-arguments*. When the conclusion of this sub-argument is needed for the following, larger argument, they're called *intermediate conclusions* (see Figure 10-1).

Providing sources with references

Here's some good reasons why you should use references in your writing:

✔ **Honesty:** You don't want to steal anyone else's ideas. Give credit where credit is due.

✔ **Helpful:** Readers may want to follow up what you're saying. The reference points them the right way.

✔ **Scientific:** The reference provides more detail on what you're claiming is the case. People can then check whether you're putting the position accurately and — much more than that — they can check the arguments offered by your source.

References are useful to writers too, because they remind you where certain ideas came from. They can even help you to avoid common pitfalls in writing, such as committing yourself to out-of-date or plain wrong positions, as well as providing a quick way to check or expand on things you've written about.

But be critical about your own sources, and demonstrate that you're doing so in your writing. Who are these other authors anyway? Why should readers take their word for anything?

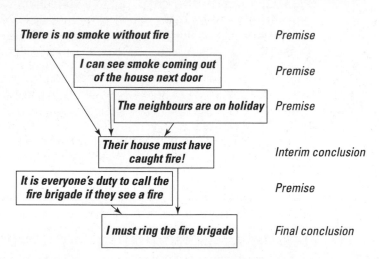

There is no smoke without fire	Premise
I can see smoke coming out of the house next door	Premise
The neighbours are on holiday	Premise
Their house must have caught fire!	Interim conclusion
It is everyone's duty to call the fire brigade if they see a fire	Premise
I must ring the fire brigade	Final conclusion

Fig 10-1: A simple argument with one intermediate conclusion.

So, intermediate conclusions are (surprise, surprise) a kind of conclusion — but they're also *propositions* (the series of claims in an essay about the world — about facts or logical relationships). In romantic novels, a proposition is usually a man asking for a woman's hand in marriage, but Critical Thinkers aren't interested in that kind of proposition!

Often a proposition is the length of a sentence, but propositions and sentences don't necessarily correspond. A sentence can easily contain several propositions. For example, the sentence 'Eating sugar makes children fat and rots their teeth' is really two propositions. (Consider, for example, that eating fried foods will make children fat but not rot their teeth.) On the other hand, some propositions may be spread over several sentences.

In an essay arguing for a particular point of view, the author will often simply assert at least one but, more usually, two or three) propositions which together make up — the *premises* or starting assumptions — and provide another proposition as the conclusion.

In between, however, the piece of writing may contain several intermediate conclusions that are derived, directly or indirectly, from the premises. These intermediate conclusions have a special character — they're supported by reasons and themselves lend support (acting as a reason) for the main conclusion. Intermediate conclusions are both the premises for a new argument and the conclusions of an earlier one. They're like stepping stones to the main conclusion.

In fact, you can strip down a successful essay to just the propositions (P), intermediate conclusions (IC) and final conclusion (FC) (identified perhaps P1, P2, P3, IC1, IC2, FC), even if this means throwing out everything that made the essay colourful, readable and fun. As far as the logic goes, it wouldn't matter.

This exercise (which I call Intermediate Conclusions on the Moon) makes this point clearer. Strip the following short passage down to its premises, intermediate conclusions and final conclusion (answers at the end of the chapter):

> *If humankind is to be survive an all out nuclear war on Earth, then people must be prepared to create colonies on the Moon. However, the Moon is a hostile environment. For a start, it contains very little water and there is no breathable atmosphere. It may be possible to import from*

Earth a certain amount of material to create a base but from then on the base must be self-sufficient and able to continually recycle everything humans need to survive.

Unfortunately, experiments with sealed communities in the desert on Earth have shown that there is always a degradation and loss of minerals and nutrients in such biospheres. Therefore the only way for a long-term Moon base to survive is for the astronauts to mine the surrounding rocks for minerals and water.

Recent measurements by orbiting satellites indicate that the Moon likely has adequate reserves of everything that a Moon Base may require, and so, the dream of 'Man on the Moon' is perhaps not so far-fetched after all.

Answers to Chapter 10's Exercise

Here are my answers to the Intermediate Conclusions on the Moon exercise.

If the exercise was presented as a question it would be something like: 'Is a Moon Base a realistic proposition?' Then the structure of the argument seems to be as follows:

✔ **Premise:** People may need to create colonies on the Moon.

✔ **Premise:** The Moon contains very little water and has no breathable atmosphere.

✔ **Intermediate conclusion:** Therefore, the base must be self-sufficient and able continually to recycle everything humans need to survive.

✔ **Premise:** Experiments show that biospheres always feature a degradation of resources.

✔ **Intermediate conclusion:** Therefore the only way a Moon Base can survive is by mining the surrounding rocks for minerals and water.

✔ **Premise:** The Moon has adequate reserves of everything that a Moon Base may require.

✔ **Final conclusion:** A Moon Base is possible.

Chapter 11

Speaking and Listening Critically: Effective Learning

● ●

In This Chapter

▶ Loving lectures and succeeding in seminars

▶ Taking effective notes

▶ Doodling for success

● ●

The growth of knowledge depends entirely on disagreement.

—Karl Popper

Critical Thinking is an active, questioning activity that inevitably involves speaking and listening critically. In order to communicate your own ideas and views effectively, and to appreciate and analyse those of others, you need to interact with people, hearing what they're saying and responding clearly.

In this chapter I suggest ways to make lectures, seminars, discussions and meetings, all kinds of activity where speech predominates, more productive. I discuss the pros and cons of formal lectures versus less structured methods of learning.

Despite my reservations about lectures, I include some practical strategies for getting more out of seminars and lectures and ways to extend Critical Thinking from not only what you read and write but to what you hear and even what you say.

I show how note-taking and doodling can provide the crucial missing interactive element. And don't forget, as this chapter has a polemical edge you can practise your Critical Thinking skills by weighing up the arguments I present.

Getting the Most from Formal Talks

When you're reading or indeed when you are writing, you can at least take a little time to be properly analytical and organized. Not so when you are talking! Or indeed when you are trying to keep up with what someone else is saying. This section is all about how to get straight to the heart of issues in 'real time' — that is, how to keep up with live arguments and debates. In the academic context of seminars and lectures. It will give you some insights into how to deal more effectively with the ideas and information presented.

Whether you're a student or teacher, an employee or a boss, you will sometimes need both to take in detailed information delivered verbally, and to explain things on your own behalf to others — perhaps individually, perhaps in groups. Most people will have been brought up with really just one model of communication — the lecture style — the one which dominates education from age five onwards. And I mean *onwards*, because even PhD students spend most of their time passively taking in information delivered by specialists. However, formal lectures are a very inefficient way to convey information and ideas. In the world of business, the assumption is often that if someone has been paid to give a talk, then they better do just that — and share as much of their expertise as possible in the time available (and many professors seems to think the same way). When they're essentially delivering the kind of information that the listeners can read for themselves (and where the audience is earnestly trying to put down on paper the lecturer's words) the approach becomes pretty absurd.

But the formal talk or lecture does have its role, which is when the talk goes beyond a written document. The most important way to achieve this goal is to be interactive and responsive.

Good lecturers are like actors on a stage, totally aware of their audience. I've known some lecturers who even managed to perform like standup comedians, which I know sounds rather frivolous, but a lot of information can be conveyed using humour. Don't underestimate it — *For Dummies* critics who think that books which adopt a light tone are less informative than the ones that just plod monotonously on are wrong!

Of course, multimedia tools can boost the formal talk's usefulness. But really, the only way to keep the attention of audience members is to have a genuine interaction between them and the speaker.

Teachers often complain that their students fail to remember what they've been taught from one week to another, that they forget what was in chapter one by the time they are at chapter three and so on. More sophisticated professors may bemoan the inability of students to transfer what they've studied from one context (or problem) to another.

Why do students do this? In fact, the fault may lie more with the teachers than the students. Most learning follows a hier-archical model where knowledge is delivered by an expert to students who're supposed to record it passively on paper and ideally commit it to memory later (certainly before the exam!).

Yet here's a paradoxical thing. *Rote learning*, that is passive learning, is inefficient learning, because the brain hates disassociated information. Facts and ideas are best digested when they can immediately be put to use, which is why a well-chosen question in a lecture can help listeners to sort out what they think and both organise and retain it better. It is this ability to sort information, to create mental links between different things already learned and, most of all, to have the kind of brain ready to see new links and possibilities that Critical Thinking encourages, and for very practical reasons. Plenty of, although, to be fair, certainly not all, research studies find that lots of high-achieving students who just soak up facts and figures on no matter what, and thus excel at exams are duffers when faced with real-life issues and problems in their working lives because they have not developed the more important 'metaskills' of actively processing information.

Suppose that you have to give a 5-minute presentation on the topic 'Effective Communication', in the context of leading a student seminar. Obviously, you'll need to practice what you preach! So what would be a nice entertaining way to start off the presentation?

Hint: you might start with a question — but what would be a good one? Or you might start with a joke or personal story — but again, what sort of joke or story would fit the context?

Participating in Seminars and Small Groups

The latest research on teaching emphasises that the best teachers say the least — though you'd hardly know it: the model of a subject expert giving a lecture is pretty hard to uproot. Thank goodness for that alternative way of learning — seminars.

A successful seminar is one in which the leader prepares the environment for everyone else to enter into real discussions. The only role of the group leader is maybe to ask questions — but these are open-ended questions, not ones with preconceived right or wrong answers. The leader may act also as a little bit of a facilitator, perhaps dampening down the over-enthusiastic tendencies of some students to dominate and gently ensuring as wide a range of contributions as possible.

A smart tip for making the most of academic seminars is to participate in the pre-seminar activities — nothing too racy mind, more like reading the set texts or researching the topic. Remember the Scout motto: be prepared! So how do you get the most out of a seminar or similar small group discussion? Of course, the short answer is to be prepared, but quite what preparation is, depends entirely on the context. However, some general advice I have for seminars would be:

✔ Really do any specific preparation asked for — it's only polite!

✔ Make a list of questions that you might expect the seminar to help you answer.

✔ Clear your mind of other distractions — like when to do the shopping or who to ring up later.

✔ Be rested, and well fed!

✔ At the seminar, don't try to impress, just be 'normal'.

✔ And, of course, listen closely and carefully to everyone else.

Okay, half a dozen tips. But if you only followed two, for some reason, which would you say they should be?

Honing your listening skills

In a lecture or formal talk, listening is difficult. How do you avoid dozing off? Does taking notes count as active listening if you aren't really following the thread? Well, maybe. The thing

Learning with the Help of Other People

A Russian psychologist called Lev Vygotsky has had considerable influence on what is sometimes called 'sociocultural theory', an approach that includes important insights into the dynamics of learning. Vygotsky says that social interaction and social context are essential for real learning. Think about the experiences of young children — even babies — to understand why. For them, a world full of other people, who interact with them, is essential for their cognitive development. All the higher functions of the mind have their origins in actual relationships between individuals, says Vygotsky.

The range of skills that anyone can develop with guidance or peer collaboration exceeds what can be attained alone.

The ability to learn through personal efforts coupled with demonstrations and immediate feedback is characteristic of human intelligence. Vygotsky even says that intelligence is better measured not by seeing what they can do on their own, as in standard tests, but by seeing what they can do when working with a skilled guide. Sounds strange? But think of learning a foreign language. How much can you learn by 'teach yourself' methods, as opposed to lessons from a native speaker, while living in the relevant country and surrounded by a rich linguistic background. The broader and richer the language experience offered, the more someone is likely to learn — the same is true for other subjects too.

about lectures is that very, very little of what's said goes into your memory: certainly less than 10 per cent and maybe more like 0 per cent! (And that's garbled. . . .)

Listening skills aren't only about listening to formal talks — they're about listening to other people in a context where you can (and should) participate. A seminar isn't a sparring match, a debate in which one team wins — maybe with the teacher as referee — it's a co-operative venture in which discovering weaknesses in your argument is something to be grateful for.

That's why listening skills come into their own during seminars, where (unlike most formal lectures) you're allowed to talk. In a successful seminar, everyone listens closely, responds thoughtfully, clarifies statements and justifies their thinking. In a formal lecture, you can't keep butting in with questions, but you can ask them just the same — privately, to yourself. You can jot down queries as they occur to you — and also answer them as a scribbled note, either positively, if the meeting later seems to meet the point and satisfy your doubt, or 'negatively', if you think you begin to see a weakness in the position being presented. Either way, you become more active in the otherwise rather passive lecture process.

The ultimate value of seminars is to wean people off that comforting habit of relying on authority figures any time something complex or unexpected comes up, and instead to try to work out their own strategies and answers, harnessing the power of group interaction. This is the best preparation for the complex and unanticipated problems that people — students, employees, all — face in real life. Step one to being able to transfer your skills to real life is to be an active listener!

Transferring skills to real-life problems

Much of education is about preparing for what comes next *after* education. It's about the extent to which what you learn can be applied — transferred later. Laszlo Bock, a high-up at

Google, has some interesting insights on the importance of transferable skills, saying:

> *One of the things we've seen from all our data crunching is that G.P.A.s [Grade Point Average] are worthless as a criteria for hiring, and test scores are worthless — no correlation at all except for brand-new college grads, where there's a slight correlation. Google famously used to ask everyone for a transcript and G.P.A.s and test scores, but we don't anymore, unless you're just a few years out of school. We found that they don't predict anything.*
>
> *—Laszlo Bock quoted in 'Head-Hunting, Big Data May Not Be Such a Big Deal', Adam Bryant, New York Times,*
> *19 June 2013*

Yes, he really does say 'a criteria, (instead of criterion) but you should forgive him because this is good news for people (you can't see, but my hand's in the air!) who hate having to work out which funny diagram doesn't belong in a group of funny diagrams, or pointless maths puzzles.

Here's Laszlo again:

> *On the hiring side, we found that brainteasers are a complete waste of time. How many golf balls can you fit into an airplane? How many gas stations in Manhattan? A complete waste of time. They don't predict anything.*
>
> *—Laszlo Bock quoted in 'Head-Hunting, Big Data May Not Be Such a Big Deal', Adam Bryant, New York Times,*
> *19 June 2013*

Google found that what did seem to matter was how people had dealt with open-ended issues in the past. Those who'd succeeded then, were the ones who did best in the future too:

> *. . . when you ask somebody to speak to their own experience, and you drill into that, you get two kinds of information. One is you get to see how they actually interacted in a real-world situation, and the valuable 'meta' information you get about the candidate is a sense of what they consider to be difficult.*
>
> *—Laszlo Bock quoted in 'Head-Hunting, Big Data May Not Be Such a Big Deal', Adam Bryant, New York Times,*
> *19 June 2013*

Transferable skills

A number of studies have been conducted into what employers look for in graduates. The results suggest that: the specific facts and skills explicitly taught in degree courses are relevant to only about 50% of vacancies, and in most cases graduate recruits require further training; the qualities most sought after are general intellectual and personal skills which receive relatively little attention in most degree courses.

The idea that there **are** *general* skills which can be acquired, and that learning them in one context is transferable to a different context runs contrary to much educational thinking of the recent past, which has instead tended to break everything down into different areas which are artificially separated one from the other.

The distinction between thinking and personal skills is far from sharp, since many things that are usually counted as the later, as personal skills, are necessary if the intellectual skills are to be used effectively. For example, you often have to be able to be patient and persevering to make sense of new information, you have to be open-minded and tolerant of different options before you can evaluate and analyse them accurately. Similarly, it doesn't really matter how brainy you are if you can't communicate your insights and knowledge — as an exercise in public speaking makes clear very quickly!

Students — everyone — need less drill and practice and more opportunities to discuss things in an open-ended way, as well as opportunities to practise and apply ideas on real problems.

Whenever you can, try to opt for projects at school, college or in the workplace, which involve problem solving, and if nothing on offer seems to do this, try to create within the project an element in which you can develop your Critical Thinking skills. It can only make your work on the project better! Every time you successfully tackle a project or resolve a problem, or (just as useful) learn from an unsuccessful attempt — record it in a special place, maybe your personal CritThink notebook. Get those highlighters out!

Noting a Few Notes

More is not always better! I hope that anyone planning to do some Critical Thinking would immediately see that taking literal notes during a lecture or maybe a class is a pretty silly idea. (For tips on taking notes when reading, which is a very different matter, see Chapter 9.)

The obvious thing is for the lecturer or teacher to prepare the key points in advance, maybe in note form, and hand them out. Simple! So how come in some colleges you often find hundreds of students sitting in a hall scratching out identical notes while a professor recycles for the umpteenth time the core curriculum?

One claim often made for this tradition is that note-taking helps people to memorise information, maybe because handwriting uses a different part of the brain to that involved in listening. But if you think about it, this is a pretty feeble justification.

 In fact, the real explanation has much more to do with a tension between two very different approaches to teaching and learning, which can be categorised by recalling the differences between two Ancient Greek philosophers:

 ✔ **Socrates:** Favoured an interactive, debating style, in which he engaged people in conversation.

 ✔ **Plato:** Advocated a lecture-based approach to learning.

Engaging in debate: The Socratic approach

Socrates's educational ideas drew upon the practice of the *sophists,* who were an early kind of thinking-skills experts offering advice to the aspirational classes for a small fee. Their main role was to show private citizens how to win arguments in the public assembly, where all the decisions of the day were decided by a kind of mass vote, whether as politicians or as lawyers.

 The *Socratic technique* was, naturally enough, to engage people in debate — a process he often categorises using military or sporting analogies. The idea is that people learn best how to win arguments by trying to win arguments with a master. When eventually they can hold their own, they've been trained. The Ancients saw reading and writing as secondary activities that weren't much use for honing these argumentative skills or for improving the reasoning that makes arguments persuasive.

Dialogue not monologue

In both education and in social life, the traditional pattern has been long on monologues and short on dialogues: teachers as I say, traditionally saw themselves as experts whose task is to deliver chunks of information to students, ideally wedging it firmly into their permanent memory stores too.

The strategies for doing this were always monologues — one person speaks, maybe reading out from notes or printed materials, while a group listens and makes notes. This is not an environment in which Critical Thinking flourishes, instead there should be dialogues and debates, and even where new content is being delivered (which of course is not something to be avoided) it should be done so between teachers-as-performers and students-as-critical-audiences.

For Socrates, the very idea of taking notes would be anathema, because it represents a passive kind of activity.

Listening to an expert: The Academic approach

The *Academic approach* is named after the first university founded by Plato. In the Academy the style of teaching was quite different from the Socratic approach. The primary means of instruction was the lecture, a one-sided affair in which professors verbally delivered elements of their expert knowledge to an entirely passive audience.

No surprise then, that whereas Socrates seems to have never written any books, both Plato and his pupil, Aristotle, left behind comprehensive libraries of their ideas and research.

When comparing Plato with Socrates, however, bear in mind this important qualification: many of Plato's books are written in dialogue form. They purport to be recordings of little debates (starring Socrates), so that even if readers are passive in the sense of reading someone else's thoughts, they're active in that the dialogue constantly swings from position to position and obliges them in turn to reflect constantly on their own views and positions.

So both Plato and Socrates actually agree on learning needing to be active, rather than passive, even if Plato is heavily into delivering expert opinions too. Plato's dialogues are actually a radical kind of note-taking in themselves — the short plays are Plato's way of recording facts and views about his favorite great philosophers, with his personal insights added in.

Comparing the consequences for the note-taking process

Plato lived nearly 2,500 years ago, but his ideas have had a huge incluence over the form education and learning has takenn in universities and colleges ever since (take a look at the nearby sidebar 'Socrates and Plato go to school').

As a result, in modern universities students sit quietly through lectures or read set texts (books or handouts) in order to reduce them to notes; later they write essays. As you can see, Plato's Academic approach has won an almost total victory over that of his master, Socrates.

Socrates and Plato go to school

For hundreds of years, in the medieval colleges learning was a mixture of Plato's kind of professorial lectures complemented by more Socratic meetings with junior teachers in which ideas were vigorously debated. The assumption in the lectures was (and continues to be) that disagreement is inappropriate. Until relatively recently, books were very expensive to produce, and so the lecture was a reasonable tool for the delivery of information.

Yet nowadays, when not only books but also electronic tools have revolutionised the sharing of facts and ideas, the lecture is anything but efficient in terms of its original purpose. It has become an anachronism, along with exams that require the regurgitation of previously memorised facts. But anachronisms — persons or things that seem to belong to the past and not fit in the present — have always found a home in educational institutions!

To see what I mean, distinguish between the two kinds of activity when taking notes: one records what the speaker is saying and the other expresses your own views and responses. Often, note-taking in an academic context consists only of the first kind! After all, keeping up with all the information being delivered is hard.

But in real-life situations where taking notes is a useful skill — perhaps during a meeting where new ideas are being generated or previously unappreciated differences of opinion (perspective) clarified — notes are definitely going to be a mix of fact and interpretation. Plus these days, unlike in the days of the Ancient Greeks, people have access to all the background facts — often very speedily too, via the Internet. For more locally specific information the lecturer really ought to copy and hand out the data. Either way, time spent, say, recording grape yields in Aquitaine, France, 1960–69, or titles of pop songs with numbers in them, is wasted time.

So what does the smart note-taker put down? Perhaps very little. If the subject was those grape crops in Aquitaine, maybe the point the lecturer is making is that the yields have changed as small family vineyards gave way to larger businesses. If so, that's the kind of insight to note. If you also can think of some possible objections to the theory — make a quick note of that idea too. Insights disappear fast unless jotted down!

Smart note-taking, as opposed to the desperate and sometimes obligatory scramble to get everything down before the page changes — when a teacher lacking Critical Thinking skills is in charge — is all about selection, and selection is all about making judgements. Guess what: in many contexts, the decision about what's worth noting, or the reformulation of what's said, is highly subjective and very political.

Democratising the Learning Environment

Bias often operates in business meetings and in organisational structures — and can easily result in good ideas being lost. Awareness of, and paying attention to, the risk of all kinds of cognitive biases or dodgy mental shortcuts in meetings where decisions get made, is a pretty valuable Critical Thinking skill.

Here are some strategies (for those in charge) to avoid turning the audience into passive zombies taking notes but not actually thinking or learning much.

✔ **Create the right atmosphere:** How many times do meetings reach bad decisions because participants are unable or too fearful to contribute? Fear stalks the classroom much as it does the boardroom. Where a hierarchy exists, people such as teachers or CEOs can make an important contribution by demonstrating their willingness to be found wrong and to change their views on matters. The level of a discussion is raised by the participants' courage to express their convictions, no matter how unusual they may be.

✔ **Ensure a mix of views:** In areas where controversy is part of the game, have two or three different sets of facts — different proposals, different expert witnesses. But this also means a mix of roles, of personality types (including some cautious people alongside some enthusiasts and definitely some outside-the-box thinkers — the people who tend to disagree with the majority). They may not be right but they ensure that the meeting hears a wider range of views. If you can't see anyone obviously like this, give someone the role and make it their job!

✔ **Prepare the key facts and background:** In a college context, this means homework! In a business context, it means due diligence, preparing briefing notes and background papers for all the participants to have and refer to. Most real-life decisions are based at some point on reference to factual data, and it makes sense to ensure that this material is as accurate, up-to-date and complete as possible.

✔ **Get everyone involved:** At the outset, ask everyone to write down their initial positions, or maybe use a white board to ask everyone for their 'balance sheets' of pros and cons. This process increases the likelihood that people actually consider changing their positions later!

Seminar Skills

Critical Thinking encourages the development of the whole range of skills, from the intellectual ones like logical reasoning at one end, to inter-personal ones like the ability to work co-operatively with others in team at the other.

There are *communication skills*, which are things like being clear and relevant in your contributions, and to the point and succinct too.

There are *comprehension skills*, which are things like the ability to see the core ideas in difficult and complex texts and in rambling and disjointed presentations too! Comprehension skills start with listening to what others say, and being open to different points of view.

There are *contextualization skills*, which concern your *depth and breadth of view. Can you see* beyond traditional subject boundaries, can you remain objective and can you

sometimes, when necessary, return to first principles? Can you see ahead to practical applications, and make new connections?

Linked to this is the skill of originality, which emphasizes independence of thought, flexibility of approach and inventiveness. Originality shows itself in the ability to come up with new and stimulating examples and counter-examples.

Then there are *the reflexivity skills*, which are the skills needed to reflect on your own thinking. How well are you communicating and expressing yourself? How are your ideas being received?

Finally, there is the skill of *co-opera-tiveness*. This is essentially the ability to work with others, whether as the boss of the minions, while making a full and positive contribution both to discussion and any activities involved.

Doodling to generate creativity

What did Einstein, Thomas Edison and Marie Curie have in common? Yes, they were all physicists, but the answer I'm looking for is that they were all inveterate doodlers!

Anyway, that's the claim of people like Sunni Brown, who has popularised the doodle in some bestselling books. In fact, she's a 'visual-thinking skills' expert, who runs workshops for businesses such as banks, retailers and television networks. What she says to the executives is that doodling:

✔ Boosts comprehension and recall

✔ Allows you to organise information in novel ways with increased clarity

✔ Doesn't require any skill at drawing.

(That's why those little *For Dummies* icons are more than text decorations.)

To be honest, doodling does require some drawing skills and that's why most people give it up (along with being told off repeatedly by teachers, of course). For most teachers, doodling is associated with not concentrating, and that's the mark of a duffer, not an innovator. But even teachers can't know everything.

Recent research into doodling suggests that when students shift their focus from interpreting other people's diagrams or charts to creating their own, they end up with a greatly enhanced understanding of whatever they're studying. The doodling students generate new inferences and refine their reasoning — without even noticing it!

And that's the key thing about doodling — it uses parts of the brain that you're not actually aware of. In fact, the word means 'scribble absentmindedly', which sounds bad until you appreciate how incredibly subtle the mind is. Language taps only a tiny proportion of the power of the human mind and, doodling can draw on some of the rest. That's why some of the researchers have advocated that doodling be recognised as a key element in education, up there in value with reading, writing and joining in group discussions!

Okay, so research has shown that doodling really helps you stay focused, grasp new concepts *and* retain information. Trouble is, you can't doodle. So here's a chance to get the habit. Don't be put off by thinking that doodling has to be anything special; it doesn't. It could be pictures, abstract patterns or decorated letters and word clouds. If you are arty, it might be images of objects, or landscapes, or people. If you like cartoons it might be cartoons. The point is to draw and what it is doesn't really matter.

So just for fun, grab a pen, use the margin of this book — and doodle about the value of doodling. I'll have a go too, and you can see my effort in the 'answers' at the end.

Answers to This Chapter

The great intro

Of course, there's no one answer to this, but here are some general points that may be of help to you in deciding how promising your idea really is.

Start with a personal story — yes, these can be powerful and grab attention. Sad but true, a 'horror story' about a bad presentation probably gets the most interest!

Joke — In fact, a horror story about a bad presentation is a kind of joke — but be careful with this approach. Maybe you will accidentally step on some toes with the professor in the corner of the room — or maybe you will make yourself sound conceited. Plus, as every stand-up knows, being half way through a joke that your audience finds unfunny is an uncomfortable place to be.

Ask a question — well, this is a pretty direct way to engage with an audience. You might say, for example, 'How many people here have ever given a really duff presentation?' Questions like this might at least grab attention! However, you need a good follow-up; this would be back to 'telling a story'. The kind of question to avoid is the boring one. It's incredible how often the same question comes up over and over again. So don't start by asking 'How many of you have had experience at giving a presentation?'

Doodling on doodling

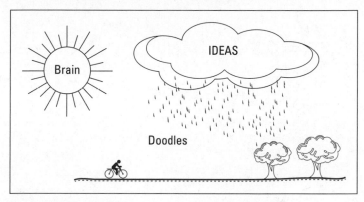

Figure 11-1: My doodle.

Okay, it's not great art. In fact, it's not art at all. But that's the point though — doodles aren't supposed to be. I let my hand do the thinking and it came up with this image that I can now see says that doodles are a way to make ideas come down out of the sky and maybe grow into useful things, like trees.

Part IV
Reason and Argument

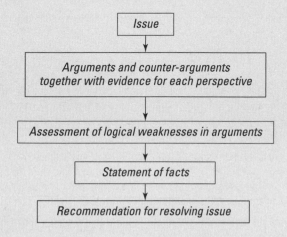

Issue

↓

Arguments and counter-arguments
together with evidence for each perspective

↓

Assessment of logical weaknesses in arguments

↓

Statement of facts

↓

Recommendation for resolving issue

In this part . . .

✔ Discover that logic is at the heart of Critical Thinking but also the less well-known fact that the kind of logic that Critical Thinkers do is firmly rooted in language skills and an appreciation of the general context of debate.

✔ Learn how to separate facts from values, because Critical Thinking requires a much broader range of skills than any introductory logic class ever will, and this part will put you on the right track to develop those skills.

✔ Get a solid grounding in informal logic and the all-important principle of logical implication.

✔ Bring yourself up to speed on Aristotle and those fallacies that everyone else is worrying about.

✔ Understand that most of the things you hear people saying, or even that you read, are not arguments in any sense. They're things like descriptions, exclamations, or instructions, with scarcely the whiff of a logical argument, but instead more powerful appeals to your hopes, your fears and your emotions.

Chapter 12

Unlocking the Logic of Real Arguments

In This Chapter

▶ Picking out the key elements in everyday arguments

▶ Examining reasoning in detail

▶ Thinking about your listeners or readers

Thinking is the hardest work there is, which is the probable reason so few engage in it.

—Henry Ford

*A*rguments lie at the heart of Critical Thinking ('oh no they don't!' you cry. 'Oh yes they do!' I reply. That's not an argument, by the way, just irritating contradiction!). Such arguments come in all sorts: hidden, irrational, polemical or whatever. But a difference exists between the 'real-life' informal arguments of everyday life — ones about real issues addressed to real people — as opposed to the neatly organised formal ones you often find presented in philosophy textbooks.

You encounter these 'real' arguments every day. On TV, politicians argue about policies, talent-show judges argue about 'talent' and two-dimensional characters argue in soap operas. In the pub, people argue about the relevant merits of their football teams (or even of different sports) and whose partner at home is 'just the worst'. Often these everyday exchanges aren't arguments in the philosophical or logical sense; they're more like disagreements and increasingly forceful statements of entrenched opinion.

In this chapter I examine some short but fairly typical real arguments both to see how they're constructed and so that you can practise your key Critical Thinking skills. In the process I take a look at aspects that people take for granted in everyday life, such as notions of cause and effect, and the different kinds of reasons — necessary and unnecessary, sufficient and insufficient — that people often confuse when trying to back up their conclusions.

Introducing Real-Life Arguments

In philosophy textbooks, the books on which most Critical Thinking guides are based, the arguments are usually tidy and precise (especially so-called *deductive* ones — the kind in which Sherlock Holmes specialises). The facts of the matter are clearly stated and the conclusion is neatly marked out with a line or the word 'therefore'. The focus of attention is definitely all on the logic — or lack of it.

But in real, everyday life, people don't argue like that. They rarely start by stating their factual assumptions but instead leave them to be guessed at, and they tend to leap instantly to the conclusion. Here's an example:

We must take urgent steps to reduce carbon emissions, or the world will overheat!

or

Children should not eat biscuits. They're bad for their teeth.

In addition, to confuse matters further, in everyday language people use the word *argument* to mean a bad-tempered quarrel or dispute, which is the last place to look for logic or structure.

Even so, you can still restate much of this type of emotional outburst philosophically. After all, most everyday disagreements start with a fact or claim, the argument then working backwards by offering reasons why the statement is true or false, depending on the point of view of the speaker.

In this section, I describe informal logic, the particular role of premises in arguments, and how images can also be used to back up claims. I also investigate the logical structure of arguments, revealing one common error that people — even professors — often make.

Coming as you are: Informal logic

Informal logic sounds intimidating, but needn't be at all:

✔ **Informal logic:** All about assessing and analysing real-life arguments and debates using everyday language. The work is really in the conversion of issues expressed in informal, everyday language into something more structured.

✔ **Formal logic:** In contrast, these arguments use symbols and letters to represent the argument. Once an argument has been reduced to symbolic notation, its structure should be easier to see and logicians can then manipulate it in the same sort of (very precise) way that mathematicians manipulate equations.

I know explanations can get more confusing when additional explanations are added into the explanation! Informal logic is really the topic, formal just crept in. . . .

Logic, science and everyday reasoning

People expect scientists to be good role models as regards crisp, clear thinking. But (as I discuss in Chapter 2) scientific thinking and logic are two quite different things.

Science is based on the principle of drawing general — universal — conclusions from a limited number of cases. It's a powerful method but, strictly speaking, illogical. Logicians

define this kind of reasoning, which they call *induction*, as *invalid* reasoning, and only see *deductive* reasoning — Sherlock Holmes's kind — as 'valid'.

The problem with deduction is that it doesn't provide any new information — it can't. So, in the real world, a lot of arguments are strictly speaking invalid.

The distinction isn't much more than that between formal and informal clothes: you dress formally for an interview and informally to cut the grass.

To illustrate, I need an everyday argument. Sure enough here comes one now!

You're a rotten husband!

You don't do the washing-up and you don't even do the gardening.

In philosophy, arguments are typically presented as a series of statements that are themselves true or false (these are generally called *premises*) coupled with a conclusion. Thus the Critical Thinker prefers to restate the above conversation with the following structure:

- ✔ **First premise:** Rotten husbands are men who don't do the washing-up and don't even do the gardening.

- ✔ **Second premise:** You don't do the washing-up and you don't do the gardening.

- ✔ **Conclusion:** You're a rotten husband!

As I explain in more detail in Chapter 13, if the argument is *valid* (constructed correctly) then as long as the premises are true, the conclusion must be true too.

This argument, by the way, *isn't* valid. (Hint: rotten husbands aren't the only people who don't do the washing-up and don't do the gardening.) But pointing out the error in the reasoning is hardly going to let anyone off doing their chores, which just underlines that getting the logical structure of an argument right isn't going to settle many real-life issues. But even so, it can help identify the real issues in a debate.

Try to keep the two notions of *truth* and *validity* separate, because only a valid argument is one in which you can be *sure* that if the starting assumptions are true then the conclusion is too. This is a pretty powerful reasoning tool, if you think about it! An invalid argument gives no such reassurance.

Circular reasoning

Here's an example of circular thinking by the German statistician Ernst Engel, who carried out (much praised) research into the relationship between spending patterns and income in the 19th century. Engel's law states that 'the poorer the individual, the family or a people, the greater must be the percentage of the income needed for the maintenance of physical sustenance, and of this a greater proportion must be allowed for food.'

Unfortunately, as Ian Hacking points out (in his book *The Taming of Chance*), treating this as a firm law is pushing things, because Engel had started off by taking the proportion of outgoings on food as the measure of material standard of living. That is, his 'law' simply says:

The more of your money you spend on food, the poorer you are.

The poorer you are, the more of your money you need to spend on food.

It's pretty circular! On the other hand, the reasoning seems to be 'valid'. Circular reasoning should be, because the conclusion is only restating the assumption!

In formal logic, arguments are either valid or invalid (that is, *sound* or *unsound*). They aren't true or false. Only the premises (and the conclusion), which are factual claims about the world, can be true or false. Informal, everyday arguments tend to mix up premises and conclusions, and often the distinction gets lost.

Spotting formal and informal arguments

Arguments expressed in the style of formal logic are essentially mathematical proofs with the aim being to demonstrate that a statement is true: if $x = 2$, does $x + 4 = 6$? But informal arguments aren't so different, because typically they're a series of statements offered as support for a conclusion. Words such as 'because', 'if' or 'since' and phrases such as 'if you really think that' and 'everyone knows that' often mark out the starting assumptions, while words such as 'then' and 'therefore' flag up a conclusion.

I say more about these sorts of textual clues and details in Chapter 10.

The problem with real arguments is that they come in every possible shape and size. Much of the reasoning isn't even spoken or written down! You have to guess, or decode, what's going on before you can judge whether the reasons support the conclusion, which is what arguing is all about.

Persuading with premises

Informal arguments that use everyday language should still set out an argument in good, persuasive steps, putting the assumptions (the *premises*) first and making sure that the real point is a *deduction* that follows on (or at least appears to!) later.

Here's a pretty good example of how to do it from logician and political activist Bertrand Russell. He's putting forward a deceptively simple argument concerning educational policy:

> *The evils of the world are due to moral defects quite as much as to lack of intelligence. But the human race has not hitherto discovered any method of eradicating moral defects. . . Intelligence. . . on the contrary, is easily improved by methods known to every competent educator. Therefore, until some method of teaching virtue has been discovered, progress will have to be sought by improvement of intelligence rather than of morals.*

> —Bertrand Russell, *Sceptical Essays* (1935)

Grab a pen and paper (or text it on your phone) and set out Russell's argument as three pithy, short sentences, split into two claimed statements of fact and a conclusion that's supposed to follow from them.

Prisoner Russell

The twentieth-century philosopher, Bertrand Russell, often argued against the views of the government of the day and its response was (surprise, surprise) not to fight him by pointing out logical errors in his political positions, but with the law courts and the police. He was imprisoned several times for 'catch-all' offences like 'anti-war activities' or 'breach of the peace', while campaigning on issues like nuclear disarmament and votes for women. Too often, in real arguments, logic is often the last thing that decides the issue.

Here's my attempt (but try forming your own before peeking):

- ✔ **First premise:** People's bad behaviour should be improved either by improving their morals or through education.

- ✔ **Second premise:** There's no known way to improve people's morals.

- ✔ **Conclusion:** *Therefore*, people's bad behaviour should be improved through education.

Using pictures in everyday arguments

Far better an approximate answer to the right question, which is often vague, than an exact answer to the wrong question, which can always be made precise.

—John Tukey

Real arguments don't depend just on words, of course. The most successful political broadcasts, for example, mix a voiceover with compelling images to persuade their audiences (a picture really is worth a thousand words); homeowners are supposed to be able to persuade potential buyers by having a pot of coffee brewing. In this section I discuss how these illogical elements persuade, showing that the process is often very subtle.

 With real arguments, the addition of visuals (whether pictures, diagrams or charts) can certainly make claims more persuasive, but whether visuals can make a logical difference (as opposed to reinforcing the emotional, rhetorical strength of an argument) is less clear:

- ✔ Some people are sceptical that images can do any work other than rhetorical.

- ✔ Others think that images can carry arguments independently.

- ✔ Still others believe that images can carry at least some parts of some arguments.

Many advertisements rely on pictures to support an argument. this fact. Imagine an advertisement for, say, Dummies Jeans, that says simply: 'Buy Dummies Jeans'. It wouldn't sell very many just for that. But coupled with a picture of some attractive, successful, fun-looking young people — it might well do. The reason is the implied connection between being attractive, successful, fun-looking and young — and the jeans: *if* you buy Dummies Jeans *then* you'll become like these people!

Or take the classic advertisement from the 1920s in Figure 12-1, which simply makes an assertion about the brand (of coffee) that's worth paying 'a little more' for. The evidence for the statement is in the pictures. The man is obviously drinking it with enjoyment, while the shadowy drinker just behind is obviously not getting the same 'satisfaction' from his cup o' Joe.

Have a go at expressing the coffee advert as a simple, logical argument. (Best is to jot something down before reading on).

Okay, this is how I 'deconstructed' the ad:

- ✔ **First premise:** Paying a little more for something is worth it if it brings you real satisfaction.

- ✔ **Second premise:** This kind of coffee brings you real satisfaction.

- ✔ **Conclusion:** *Therefore,* paying a little more for this kind of coffee is worthwhile.

That's the surface message, anyway. The subliminal (hidden) message is that the particular brand of coffee is superior to other brands. This message appears in the argument as one of the assumptions in the premises).

Checking a real argument's structure

Even though real arguments are phrased in ordinary language, they still have a structure that you can try to reveal by stripping away the unnecessary details and expressing the whole thing in its argumentative essence.

Figure 12-1: Such a little to pay! But where's the evidence?

Sometimes the use of everyday language itself causes problems with the argument's logic. One logical error is so common it has its own special name: the fallacy of affirming the consequent. You don't need to know the name, but you do need to be able to spot this mistake in reasoning, because it's probably one of the most common errors people — even famous philosophers — make.

The *fallacy of affirming the consequent* involves arguing that one event was caused by another merely because it occurred after that event. (It's also called making a *logic reversal*.) People who affirm the consequent imagine that the effect of a cause is also the cause of the cause. But no, *course* not!

Socrates debates the limited value of pictures

Most people think that pictures or TV clips are a rather poor way to argue — because they can be misleading, 'manipulative' and, of course, manipulated. Written materials, on the other hand, are often considered to be straightforward, 'serious' and 'honest'. But the Ancient Greek philosopher Socrates saw things much more radically. For him, written words play tricks and so *real* debates have to be live so that everything and anything can be immediately challenged and tested.

In one of Plato's dialogues (the little plays featuring Socrates and someone else buttonholed into having a debate) Socrates tries to persuade Phaedrus that not only pictures but also words themselves (when written down) are limited and inferior compared to real, verbal arguments.

'You know, Phaedrus that is the strange thing about writing, which makes it truly correspond to painting. The painter's products stand before us as though they were alive but if you question them, they maintain a most majestic silence. The same goes for written words; they seem to talk to you as if they were intelligent, but if you ask them anything about what they say, from a desire to be instructed, they go on telling you just the same thing forever'.

Analysing an example of a real argument

Here's a slightly dodgy real argument that illustrates the point from a recent book (*The God Argument*) by a university philosophy professor.

As presented in his book, religion is a nasty business, consisting of hanging homosexuals, beheading or stoning to death adulterous women, and subordinating 'women and children' in Bible Belt America. Because (says the author) religious belief, historically and today, leads to these awful things, people should always try to discourage religious belief.

This is a real argument in two senses: people really make it — as the professor does in his book (although not in so many words) — and it's expressed in everyday language.

Here's one way of looking at its structure, including the evidence offered:

- ✔ **First premise:** Religious belief leads people to do terrible things to other people, such as hanging them for being homosexual or stoning them to death.

- ✔ **Second premise:** Leading people to do terrible things to others, such as hanging them for being homosexual or stoning them to death, is bad.

- ✔ **Conclusion:** *Therefore,* religious belief is bad.

Premises don't have to be true and you don't need to prove them. They come with an implied 'if' before them, and the conclusion is only supposed to be true if the premises are.

On that basis the claims here look okay. To investigate whether the sweeping conclusion demands acceptance too — as the professor hopes — you can structure the argument a bit more formally, as follows:

- ✔ **First premise:** Religion leads to terrible things.

- ✔ **Second premise:** If something is terrible, it should be banned.

- ✔ **Conclusion:** *Therefore,* religion should be banned.

The structure looks to be something like this:

- ✔ If A then B.
- ✔ If B then C.
- ✔ *Therefore,* if A then C.

Expressed in this way, the argument certainly appears to be valid (in the sense I describe in the earlier section 'Coming as you are: Informal logic'). But in fact a bit of cheating is going on: it lies in the words of the original argument. Check out the first premise again, the one that says:

Religious belief leads people to do terrible things to other people, like hanging them for being homosexual, or stoning them to death.

The professor doesn't flatly say that religious belief always and invariably leads to each of its adherents doing terrible things but only that it *sometimes* leads to some people doing them. Clearly he can't state the former, because Mother Teresa, for example, didn't stone adulterers to death in India but helped sick children. So a more accurate way to represent the argument might be as follows:

- ✔ If A then sometimes B.
- ✔ If B then C.
- ✔ *Therefore,* if A then C.

However, this argument is certainly not valid. As long as some 'A' aren't 'B', any additional information, no matter how juicy, about 'B' is always going to be entirely irrelevant to them. On the other hand, maybe the professor isn't intending to argue this. Perhaps the essence is instead better summarised as follows:

- ✔ **First premise:** *If* religion is an evil influence on people *then* people's minds will be addled and lots of bad things result.
- ✔ **Second premise:** People's minds have been addled and lots of bad things have resulted.
- ✔ **Conclusion:** *Therefore,* religion is an evil influence on people.

Even if it is this version though, the conclusion is still rather wonky. (See the nearby sidebar 'Scientists arguing illogically' for more on this.) The problem now with this reasoning is that another explanation for the bad things may exist: maybe inbred sexism or aggressive pursuit of economic self-interest. But such issues are getting, I suppose, into the area of sociology. Explaining the world's problems isn't your task here — you're just looking at the structure of arguments. And in this case, it does seem that the logic of this real argument is rather wonky.

Discussing the usefulness of the fallacy

The fallacy of affirming the consequent is just one of a list of logical fallacies that Aristotle drew up thousands of years ago but are still going strong (see Chapter 14 for details). Indeed, it's such a common argumentative tactic that pointing it out can seem a cool trick to make you look much cleverer than your opponent. But in 'real life', is it really an error at all?

Scientists arguing illogically

You come across many famous historical examples of scientists committing the logical error of affirming the consequent. Take the grandest theory of them all, the Big Bang one, which supposedly explains the origin of the entire universe as resulting from a primeval atom, well, exploding. It includes within it an expectation that the universe should be filled with leftover radiation distributed evenly. The argument goes as follows:

✔ First premise: If the universe started with a Big Bang then there should be lots of stray background radiation left over for the radio telescopes to find.

✔ Second premise: Lots of stray background radiation is left over that the radio telescopes have found.

✔ Conclusion: *Therefore,* the universe started with a Big Bang.

Naturally, when radiation was discovered, the Big Bang theory was counted as confirmed. Only now, rather grudgingly, are some scientists reopening the case, because although lots of this background radiation is indeed scattered around the night sky, it doesn't seem to fit the more precise requirements of the theory, for example, instead of being evenly spread around, it is seems to be located in strange clumps.

Applying full logical rigour to the real world is difficult. Perhaps the moral is: don't throw out the useful science with the logical bathwater.

People who commit a logic reversal and affirm the consequent are implying that the effect of a cause is also the cause of the cause. To see why this is wrong, recall, from the logic vaults, the crown jewel of the logic, the valid argument called the *modus ponens* (from the Latin, for 'the way that affirms by affirming' — but, for all it matters, it is just a funny name), which has a special form which you can see in the following example.

Suppose you're talking about Paris. A correct argument proceeds like this:

✔ If it's December then it will be cold in the pavement cafés.

✔ It is December.

✔ *Therefore,* it will be cold in the pavement cafés.

The conclusion is true because the premises are taken to be true:

> ✔ If A then B
>
> ✔ A
>
> ✔ Therefore B

But look what happens if instead the argument is mangled to become 'B therefore A':

> ✔ If it's December then it will be cold in the pavement cafés.
>
> ✔ It is cold in the pavement cafés.
>
> ✔ *Therefore,* it must be December.

But no! It can be a cold day in January or in almost any month.

For logicians, this is definitely a silly mistake to make. But that's not quite the same thing as saying that it's wrong in everyday use and in real arguments, because the invalid argument is actually a way of offering evidence for a particular belief.

Delving Deeper into Real Arguments

In real, everyday, informal arguments, if people don't agree on the underlying facts (the starting points), no amount of persuasion ever allows one side to persuade the other of the rightness of their position. In this section I take a look at the classic 'if . . . then' formula, revealing some aspects that people can mix up: cause and effect, unnecessary and insufficient conditions, and independent and joint reasons.

Considering the formula 'if A then B'

In a sparky, recent book called *If A then B: How the World Discovered Logic,* two philosophy professors, Michael

Shenefelt and Heidi White, argue that reasoning, knowledge and rationality are first and foremost matters of logic: of applying that deceptively simple formula 'if A then B' to the world. What's more they argue that the history of the world is also the history of simple logical forms. For example, the simple arguments I discuss in this chapter — where statements are presented and then claimed to lead to a certain conclusion — emerged out of the Ancient Greek way of taking decisions. For the background history, see the nearby sidebar 'A history of arguing'.

The idea is that if everyone agrees to be logical and let rules decide arguments, people should eventually reach decisions that everyone can see the reasons for and by and large can accept.

A history of arguing

In Ancient Greece, political issues were decided at public meetings in which the 'facts' were represented and the citizens voted, after drawing their conclusions. In this sense, the Ancient Greeks invented not so much democracy (the rule of the people) but something much more useful: arguments.

Of course, arguments lead to conflict, such as the long battle between Catholics and Protestantism in Medieval Europe. Although some historians disagree, Michael Shenefelt and Heidi White think that the conflict was about 'whose version of Christianity was theologically correct', and that this social debate made people 'especially concerned with problems of logic'. Later, by encouraging people to refer to the Bible themselves, Martin Luther, for the Protestant side, encouraged people to examine 'the premises' (through personal reflection and individual reasoning) instead of just accepting the conclusions of others (notably the Church authorities).

As Shenefelt and White see it, logic didn't help to sort out the war because the two sides started with different and opposed premises, 'and so a great collision between Catholicism and Protestantism became inevitable'.

Assuming a causal link

Causal links in nature are central to the way people make sense of the world — and just as in logic, they're often not thinking directly about the mechanisms, about *why* A leads to B. For example, consider these arguments or claims:

- ✔ Don't eat wild mushrooms — they're poisonous.

- ✔ If you study hard, you'll get a better grade in the exam.

They are very different kinds of statements. One seems more 'causal' than the other — yet in another way they're both similar because they're both statements of the kind 'all A are B':

- ✔ All wild mushrooms are poisonous.

- ✔ All people who study hard get good grades.

The philosopher David Hume is credited with a great insight into everyday arguments. He says that the deeply held belief of causal links — for example, that not watering plants causes them to wither or that throwing rocks at windows causes them to break — isn't logical but merely psychological. His rather abstract point about 'cause and effect' has many practical implications for Critical Thinking, because he's challenging the root of logic itself.

David Hume says that the idea that one thing causes another is a human construction, based on past observations and experience. This is his argument

And what stronger instance can be produced of the surprising ignorance and weakness of the understanding than the present. For surely, if there be any relation among objects which it imports to us to know perfectly, it is that of cause and effect. On this are founded all our reasonings concerning matter of fact or existence . . . Our thoughts and enquiries are, therefore, every moment, employed about this relation: yet so imperfect are the ideas which we form concerning it, that it is impossible to give any just definition . . .

In other words, a key idea that human beings use to make sense of the world around us, that what we have observed one day, in one set of circumstances, can be learnt from and assumed to apply another day in similar circumstances, is based itself just on faith! Why should the same cause always have the same effect? His idea is so radical that it makes nearly all arguments fall to pieces straight away! Hume admits himself that he can see no answers to his problem, but suggests shrugging and carrying on anyway. In a sense that is what we have to do. But Critical Thinkers can benefit from the warning by always doubly sceptical and asking questions when someone asserts that a certain outcome will always follow, given a certain action.

Discussing unnecessary and insufficient conditions

Here's another way in which drilling down into logical reasoning and revealing an their formal structures can help in even informal arguments: specifically, the difference between necessary and unnecessary conditions.

Everyone's familiar with the concept of something being necessary. For example, in order to keep fish in an aquarium alive, it is necessary to make sure that it's full of water. If you let the water evaporate out, the fish perish.

 In the all-important 'if . . . then' statements of reasoning, the second bit that follows the word 'then' (technically known as the *consequent*) gives a *necessary condition* for the first part (which philosophers call the *antecedent*):

If Phyllis the goldfish is to be happy and healthy [the antecedent] then the water in the aquarium must be kept topped up [the consequent].

So important are necessary conditions that in ordinary language people have many ways to express them. For example:

  ✔ Water is necessary for fish to live.

  ✔ Fish must have water to live.

  ✔ Without water, fish die.

  ✔ No fish can survive long outside water.

A condition X is said to be *necessary* for another condition Y, if (and only if) the *falsity* (the non-achievement) of Y guarantees (or brings about) the falsity of X.

But keeping the water level topped up isn't a *sufficient* condition for keeping Phyllis the fish happy and for having a successful aquarium. For example, you need to make sure that the water is clean, that oxygenating weeds are present and that the water is the right temperature. So the water level is a necessary but insufficient condition. So far so useless! But this insight does lead you towards being able to make a new suggestion:

If Phyllis the goldfish is to be happy and healthy then I must place a plastic castle for her to swim around at the bottom of the aquarium.

Certainly this is a very nice thought and I'm not against it at all, but is it absolutely necessary to provide plastic castles for goldfish? Not at all. You could provide some interestingly shaped rocks instead or maybe more weeds.

So clearly this is an *unnecessary* condition, because Phyllis can be healthy even without the castle. But is the plastic castle also an *insufficient* condition? Yes it is, because if you fail to feed her, or let the water level drop, or lots of other things, the plastic castle isn't enough to keep Phyllis healthy and happy.

Condition A is said to be *sufficient* for a condition B, if (and only if) the implementation of A guarantees the truth (the bringing about) of B.

Before reading on, pause for a moment and make a list of necessary conditions for Phyllis the goldfish to be happy and healthy.

Okay? Here's a couple that you probably didn't think of: you mustn't have any cats that can gobble up Phyllis or any nasty anchor worm eggs introduced into the aquarium, say on the pond weed!

Don't kick yourself if you missed those two. Instead, award yourself one mark if you listed ten points and three marks if you wrote less. Because a Critical Thinker soon realises that it isn't too useful to spend too long on that list because it is potentially an infinite task.

The moral is that, in real arguments, specifying either *necessary* or *sufficient* conditions is often impractical. Instead, a huge amount of shared assumptions are needed.

Investigating independent and joint reasons

One quite subtle distinction in critical thinking is between independent and joint reasons.

Many arguments work quite happily on just one reason. You can see these arguments as assertions:

Killing animals for meat is wrong. Therefore, everyone should become vegetarians.

The argument 'works' because the word 'should' contains a judgement about what's right and what's wrong — and the first part of the argument says that killing animals is wrong. The hidden structure is probably as follows:

✔ Killing animals is wrong.

✔ People shouldn't do things that are wrong.

✔ *Therefore*, people shouldn't kill animals.

✔ (next step)

✔ People who aren't vegetarians are involved in the killing of animals.

✔ Killing animals is wrong.

✔ *Therefore,* everyone should become vegetarian.

In contrast, a *joint reasoning* argument is one in which you need at least two reasons in order to draw the conclusion. In other words, you can't draw the conclusion from any one of the reasons on its own: Take a look at this one, with four reasons offered to support the eventual conclusion, for example.

✔ Two thirds of the world's surface is covered in water.

✔ If people stop eating fish then pressure on the fragile ecosystems on land will be increased.

✔ Increased pressure on the fragile ecosystems on land is bad for the environment.

✔ Vegetarianism requires people not to eat fish.

✔ *Therefore,* vegetarianism is bad for the environment.

There! In this section, you've used logic to prove two opposite sides of the argument! (Vegetarianism is morally right, and vegetarianism is morally wrong.) That's a pretty handy Critical Thinking skill.

Being aware of hidden assumptions

Looking at arguments from the point of view of those making them helps you to spot hidden assumptions that they're making, assumptions that you may want to discuss openly and perhaps challenge.

Similarly, turning a critical eye on your own beliefs and values allows you to identify premises or beliefs that may not be accepted at face value by the people listening to or reading about your views.

Elements that influence your views (often without you really realising it) include the following:

✔ Race, nationality and culture.

✔ Language and your education.

✔ Family status (do you have children who depend on you? Are you reliant on others?).

✔ Economic or social class.

✔ Whether you're religious or non-religious.

✔ Views of your peer group (for example, teenagers are notoriously sensitive to and influenced by whatever their friends are doing!).

If you can identify the hidden assumptions in other people's positions or the problematic aspects of your own, you're better able to do two useful things:

✔ Anticipate the kind of counter-arguments that may be put.

✔ Make a kind of 'pre-emptive manoeuvre', by rethinking and if necessary strengthening your own assumptions, especially ones you hadn't really been properly aware of.

Chapter 13

Behaving Like a Rational Animal

It is important to remember that the informal fallacies are just 'rules of thumb'. If violating the informal fallacies is necessary in order to describe social systems, then a decision is required. Should traditions concerning the form of arguments limit the scope of science? Or, should the subject matter of science be guided by curiosity and the desire to construct explanations of phenomena?

> —Stuart Umpleby ('The Financial Crisis: How Social Scientists Need to Change Their Thinking', 2010, www.gwu.edu/~umpleby/recent.html)

*P*rofessor Stuart Umpleby is a social scientist rather than a philosopher (otherwise he'd never use a fallacious argument). He's sounding a cautionary note about the too literal, too narrow use of logical rules, a view that I clarify in this chapter.

This chapter is about how to use logic to strengthen your own arguments and help you spot weaknesses (or indeed strengths) in other people's. I emphasise that logic is a tool that suits only certain applications and isn't a universal shortcut to proving points and finding the truth. If you don't believe me and think that logic can settle everything, check out this chapter's discussion on Aristotle's three Laws of Thought.

I also include an opportunity for you to hone your skills via a deceptively important little argument that highlights the role of link terms in producing a good, sound argument — and the danger of ambiguous language for producing a bad one.

Setting out Laws for Thinking Logically

The Ancient Greeks provide many of the foundations for both logic and good, rigourous thinking in general.

The first philosophers strove to eliminate ideas that seemed vague, contradictory, or ambiguous, and the best way to accomplish this, they thought, was to work out the rules of thinking that would reliably lead to clear and distinct ideas. In other words, to discover and then follow the laws of thought themselves. This chapter explains what those laws are, but it's also important to remember (and much less often actually done) that in spite of how dominant these ideas have been over the centuries in both science and philosophy, they have not been without their critics, and for every point in their favour there are equally powerful arguments against them. That's what a Critical Thinker should expect, of course! The real issue seems to be not so much whether the principles are true or not, but where and when are they applicable? The laws of thought have an important role to play in Critical Thinking, but they are not the whole story by any means.

But, having said that, Aristotle's ancient book on common logical errors, and also on *sound* ways of theorising, is a great way to start thinking more precisely and methodically. His Big Idea is that an argument is *valid* when the conclusion follows logically from its starting assumptions (the premises) — and he's not too bothered if a conclusion can still be complete nonsense if there's a problem with those assumptions. If you start with true, relevant and non-contradictory assumptions *and* structure the argument correctly then you have a copper-bottomed guarantee that the conclusion is true. This is what is meant by a *sound* argument in this context.

Asking Aristotle about reason

For the Ancient philosophers, like I guess most people today too, a good argument was one that brought people to agree with the speaker, and it really didn't matter quite how that was achieved. It might be by careful use of rhetorical devices, such as making three points in sequence, or through ridiculing the opponent. (For more on this, see Chapter 15.) Or it might be by recalling the legends told about the Gods of Mount Olympus. Probably the most influential philosopher of them all, Plato, used the whole range of persuasive techniques in his philosophical writings, which included a fairly detailed blueprint for running a small country — his famous playlet called *The Republic*. Ironically, I think it could have been a jealous reaction to Plato's literary and rhetorical skills that prompted his pupil, Aristotle, to look instead at the nuts and bolts of arguments, and to try to tease out the elements of the most powerful ones. Whatever Aristotle's real motives, this was really innovative work — and it changed the way people thought and argued forever.

Neither Aristotle nor the other Greek philosophers made any distinction between scientific and philosophical investigations: for them everything was 'philosophy'. So what was a bad argument in politics was a bad argument in science too — and vice versa. But as I will explain in this chapter, different elements of an inquiry actually need different kinds of approach. Experimental science, for example, often uses inductive reasoning, drawing general conclusions from limited evidence — a procedure which is by definition invalid. This is what the experimental method is all about. But scientists are often also philosophising — presenting premises and claiming certain conclusions follow — so these parts of their work require 'logic-checking' just as much as anyone else's.

A typical academic book or essay is a mix of science and philosophy, of facts discovered through research and arguments newly developed by the author and will certainly include sections that need to be logically rigorous!

Logic is all Greek to me!

Aristotle (384–322 BCE) is generally considered the 'father of logic', even though the Chinese got there before him and many other ancient philosophers had talked in detail about the issues. Aristotle didn't even come up with a lot of the stuff you can see attributed to him. But he wrote the original 'book on logic' and so he gets the credit (rather like under-16s today think that Simon Cowell invented the talent show).

Aristotle worked on every subject under the sun with alarming zeal, particularly interested in observing nature, but nothing more so than in sorting out all the different kinds of reasoning that people use. The way that Aristotle approached any question had a great influence on how other people did so for centuries after — for better or (as it more often was) for worse. One of his influential ideas, which still affects the way that most of people think, is his view that every organism has its own particular function, or place, in nature, and the particular role of humans is to *reason*. 'Thinking' is what people are better at than any other member of the animal kingdom.

He came up with three mental rules that he called the *Laws of Thought*. Philosophers tend to understand these Laws as part of an attempt to put everyday language on a logical footing, which, like many contemporary philosophers, Aristotle regarded as the key to human progress.

 Don't make the mistake of thinking that Aristotle's Laws of Thought are just Ancient History: they remain a pretty big deal. Some 2,000 years later, George Boole, whose logic is vital for today's software and computers, acknowledged Aristotle's influence and pioneering role.

Here are Aristotle's Laws of Thought:

- ✔ **Law of identity:** Whatever is, is.
- ✔ **Law of non-contradiction:** Nothing can both be and not be.
- ✔ **Law of excluded middle:** Everything must either be or not be.

Doesn't sound too difficult, does it? Read on!

Posing problems for logic

Perhaps you're wondering what these three laws mean in practice and whether they stand up to Critical Thinking.

Well, for a start, avoiding contradiction isn't as easy as it sounds. Many of the fallacies in arguments come from asserting two contradictory things. Plus, many of the ambiguities and confusions that create unbridgeable differences of opinion can be traced back to a failure to apply the law of the excluded middle.

Plato, who, remember, was Aristotle's mentor, was well aware of the Laws of Thought, but he was more interested in where they seemed to *not* apply. You see, in certain cases, they lead to absurd conclusions.

For example, in one of Plato's little plays, someone argues that Socrates must be the father of a dog, because the dog has a father and Socrates admits that he's a father. The law of non-contradiction (nothing can both be and not be) says that one can't both be a father and not be a father at the same time, and so logic seems to require that Socrates must be the father of the dog.

Of course, Socrates is obviously *not* the father of the dog, but the problem is seeing where the thinking has gone wrong. In other words, where and how to apply the laws raises as many questions as those the laws are supposed to settle.

Don't be so in awe of Aristotle that you rush to agree on all his thoughts (Critical Thinkers should never rush to agree . . .). Aristotle has his fair share of foolish views, such as the influential but false doctrine that bodies fall to Earth at speeds relative to their mass, or the dreadful (but popular with men) claim that women don't and can't reason but are a kind of domestic animal. Yes, he really said that, even as (or perhaps it was because?) his boss, Plato, was writing the opposite and counting women as great philosophers too.

Is logic a 'boy thing'?

Many people think that logic is something that suits males better than females. In popular language, the term 'female logic' is derogatory. This view, like so many 'everyone knows that' opinions, is wrong.

The research evidence is quite clear that on almost all the thinking skills, word skills, analogy making, intuitive thinking, method and organisation, very little difference exists in the ways that men and women think. And if any difference does exist, education (by which I mean things like reading this book) has the potential to eradicate it completely.

But some evidence *does* show a gender gap in formal logic and maths. Formal logic — the kind expressed using symbols rather than in words — is a kind of maths, not a part of philosophy although it has crept in there, claiming, for example, to be a good way to look at arguments. Tests that ask students to rotate shapes and so on also seem to favour boys at the expense of girls. It seems that these tests involve abstract logical manipulations that at some level call on the same mental architecture, use the same processing elements of the brain.

Four points are worth making about the issue:

✔ Expectations have a very clear influence on outcomes. An interesting 1999 experiment (led by Steven Spencer, a Canadian psychologist) gave the same logical reasoning test to two groups of students. One group was told that the test was to measure how great the logic gap was between boys and girls. The other test was presented without any implication of a gender gap. The girls performed significantly better in the test when no 'seeds of doubt' were planted in their minds beforehand! This is what social scientists call the problem of *stereotype threat*.

✔ Any differences in certain skills are emphatically not the true Critical Thinking skills at all, but arguably certain ones involving logical manipulations of abstract information.

✔ The boy—girl differences are cancelled out by the differences between people who are left-handed and people who are right-handed. Left-handed boys are worse at the 'traditionally male' logic and spatial awareness tests than right-handed boys, but left-handed girls are better at them!

✔ You'd think it pretty odd if teachers taught left-handed and right-handed children in separate classes — handing out tea sets to play with to one and electronic circuits to program for the other, but something like this can happen later in life when logic is taught.

The bottom line is that it's not clear that males have any advantage in informal logic, which is what Critical Thinking is about. And even if a gender gap does exist in some related thinking skills, the differences are small. Data on average performance of large groups tells you very little about an individual's abilities, and so no one should suppose anything about the thinking style of individuals solely on the basis of their gender.

Seeing How People Use Logic

In this section I look at some of the key logical structures that people use — for better or worse.

Identifying convincing arguments

What makes an argument convincing? The evidence advanced for a position being correct isn't enough; you also need some reason to accept that the conclusion follows from the evidence.

Accepting that true premises don't make for true conclusions

In logic, *true* premises (all the assumptions an argument starts out by simply asserting are true) don't ensure that a *conclusion* is true. They only do so if the reasoning used, the argument, is *valid,* which in this context means structured correctly — respecting things like the 'Laws of Thought' (described in the section above).

The easiest way to 'prove your point' is to structure it as a hypothetical — an 'if one thing then another thing', followed by a demonstration that the 'first thing' really is the case. This kind of argument is called *affirming the antecedent* (the antecedent is the thing that comes before).

Philosophers often express arguments in symbols, whereas Critical Thinkers use ordinary in English. But noting that the validity of arguments is most easily tested using symbols helps you to remember two important things:

  ✔ Making your argument valid means logic-checking its structure.

> ✔ Starting off with false premises (assumptions) doesn't
> actually make the argument invalid — but it does make it
> unsound and unpersuasive!

Here's this affirming-the-antecedent argument in
symbolic form:

If P, then Q

P
_____

Therefore, Q

And here's an example:

If there is evidence of design in the universe *then* there must
be a Designer

There is evidence of design in the universe
_____

Therefore, there must be a Designer

Goodness, does that settle the huge old debate simply
through logic? Not really. You can still disagree over whether
the premises are true. What's meant exactly by 'a designer'
(or indeed one with a capital 'D')? Unless the starting assumptions are true the structure of the argument can be as excellent as you like, but you still can't be sure of the conclusion.

Another way of making this point is to say that a valid argument
is *truth preserving,* in the sense that if you put true premises in a
true conclusion comes out the other end. But not the other way
around, mind you! If the premises are false, you can't assume
that the conclusion is false too. A politician can still be right,
after all, despite having all her facts and arguments wrong.

Aristotle came up with 256 variations of arguments that have
two assumptions followed by one conclusion, of which he
thought 19 were truth preserving; the rest were fallacies and
hence ones to avoid — mostly obviously so. Actually, people
think nowadays that at least 4 more of his 19 'safe forms' are
dodgy — showing just how difficult being fully logical and
rigorous is. But that doesn't mean you shouldn't try.

Denying the consequent

A great valid form of argument is *denying the consequent* (*modus tollens* in Latin). As the name rather gives away, instead of proving that the 'if bit' is true, you prove that the 'then bit' ('the consequent') is false. For example, if being a real king *requires* having a crown, then not having a crown implies not being the king.

In logic-speak, assuming that a real (and an unbreakable) connection exists between the antecedent and the consequent (the 'if' and the 'then'), and the consequent is false, then the antecedent must be false also. Denying the consequent (the thing after) thus involves the denial of the antecedent (the thing before) as well.

Here's an example, both in symbols and plain English:

If P, then Q

Not Q
_____

Therefore, not P

If I eat lots of sweets made of sugar, then my teeth will fall out

My teeth have not fallen out
_____

Therefore, I haven't eaten lots of sweets made with sugar

Denying the consequent is a great argument form to use — simple and effective. Even if, as the example hints, it proves no more than what the first premise asserts. In other words, if any possible circumstance (such as someone cleans her teeth very thoroughly each night) makes the first claim untrue, then the fact that the argument form is valid doesn't save it from being unsound (see my explanation of this important concept in the section above **Setting out Laws for Thinking Logically**), because this practical qualification of the first premise makes it effectively untrue. Remember, untrue premises lead nowhere!

Falling over fallacies

Here I examine a bit more how to 'logic-check' the structure of your arguments, which means checking how the parts of the argument fit together — or don't.

In logic, a *fallacy* is an invalid argument, one in which a flaw in the way it is constructed meanst that it's possible for all the premises to be true and yet the conclusion to be false. As such, you clearly want to avoid fallacious reasoning — it leads you astray as well as your readers or listeners. People also often use the term colloquially to include arguments they consider 'false', because they disagree with one or other of the premises. The two ways of using the word should not be confused.

Not just any old type of mistake in reasoning counts as a logical fallacy. To be a fallacy, a type of reasoning must be potentially deceptive (in other words, look plausible): it must be likely to fool at least some of the people some of the time.

The statement 'it's a fallacy that paying people welfare benefits encourages laziness' is probably a critique of the following informal and politically incorrect argument:

If people can get money without working then they'll become lazy

Unemployment benefit is a form of getting money without having to work for it

Unemployment benefit encourages laziness

Is the argument valid? Skip to the Answers section at the end of this chapter for my comments.

The rest of this section covers the idea of fallacies. To see why that's all you need to know, check out the nearby sidebar 'Focusing on fallacies that matter'.

Choosing your words carefully

Ambiguity is the enemy of a solid argument. One commonly spotted ambiguity is *amphiboly* (from the Greek verb to 'throw around'). This fallacy results from the way a sentence is constructed (instead of from the ambiguity of words or phrases, called *equivocation*). Amphiboly occurs when a bad argument trades upon grammatical ambiguity.

Here's a suitably Classical example: the emperor Croesus is said to have consulted the Oracle at Delphi to see whether the omens were good for his planned attack on Persia. The reply seemed to auger well: 'If Croesus goes to war, a great empire will be humbled.' Thus encouraged, Croesus went to war, had

Focusing on fallacies that matter

An incredible number of fallacies exist. People have written long books on them — starting with 'affirming the consequent' (see Chapter 12) and finishing with 'unaccepted enthymemes' and the 'undistributed middle'! Imbetween are fallacies with exotic names such as 'poisoning the well' and Latin tags such as *Post hoc ergo propter hoc* (it's the same thing as 'affirming the consequent'), not to forget *quaternio*

terminorum (also known as the 'fallacy of equivocation'). Such terms are imposing — they can make you feel like doing a course in logic or more likely slinking away with your tail between your legs to the nearest bar.

Don't be put off or intimidated. Only a few fallacies count, and the jargon terms used to categorise variants aren't worth learning or even understanding.

a terrible time and promptly lost. A mighty empire was indeed humbled — but it was his one.

Watching out for circular reasoning

You can all too easily accidentally produce a *circular argument*. This is a type of reasoning in which the conclusion is supported by the premises, which are themselves relying on the truth of the conclusion, thus creating a circle in reasoning in which no useful information is shared. (See the box in Chapter 12 for more on this.)

Choosing the appropriate kind of reasoning

Don't start to see fallacies everywhere — because science — and real life generally — is all about *inductive reasoning* — drawing general conclusions from a limited amount of evidence. The trouble with doing this is that the next bit of evidence along could destroy the theory — as (for example) recently nearly happened to the entire Western banking system when it turned out that certain kinds of investments were not actually safe 'as long as they were all bundled together', as the dominant economic theory at the time predicted. In real life we use inductive reasoning all the time, even though it is by definition invalid, and it caries with it the risk of being proved wrong by future events.

The alternative approach which promises conclusions that are rock-solid and eternal is called *deductive reasoning*. It is exemplified by logic and geometry with their ability to demonstrate that, for example, that $3 + 4 = 7$, or that the angles of a triangle add up to 180 degrees, or that 'Socrates, being a man, is mortal'. Claims like these tend to stay true. The trouble with this kind of reasoning is that, in practice, it tells you nothing you did not already think already. It can't; that's why it's 'valid'. Thanks, Aristotle!

Central to the distinction between inductive and deductive reasoning is that you can't get any new information out of deductive arguments — all that you can do is rearrange them. So, when people accuse someone of producing an 'invalid' argument, they usually mean something different: that someone is misstating a deductive argument.

Spotting a fallacy

Suppose that you're having an argument with someone about whether or not starfish have fins. You know that starfish are beautiful marine animals that can be a variety of colours, shapes and sizes, and all have five 'legs', which make them resemble a star. But for the sake of this argument, you don't know whether they have fins or not. Can logic help you to settle the question?

Major premise: All **fish** have fins

Minor premise: All starfish are **fish**

Conclusion: All starfish have fins

Doctor, we have our answer! Or do we? Does this prove that starfish have fins? Check out the answers at the end of the chapter for a full discussion of this surprisingly important riddle.

Putting Steel in Your Arguments with Logic

In this section I give some general tips on how to make your arguments more effective.

Logic always has a rather frightening aspect: perhaps you think that things in it are 'black and white' and you'll look ridiculous if you make a mistake. That's often how teachers present it in philosophy classes, too. But Critical Thinking is concerned with real life and logic is a valuable tool and a friend.

When you're trying to assess the truth of someone elses's argument, or indeed trying to construct one yourself , think of logic as a guide-rope that helps you to navigate the treacherous paths through the mountains of political and scientific controversy. So, crampons and grappling hooks at the ready!

Taking a clear line

The first thing to consider when constructing an argument is whether you're contradicting yourself. Of course, any areas of social or scientific debate often include opposing arguments and conflicting evidence, and good writers are aware of this fact and able to include the controversy in their accounts. However, for readers, conflicting messages and inconsistencies are confusing.

Here are some tips on how you square this circle in your own writing:

- ✔ Make clear early on the general line you're going to take.

- ✔ Use signal words to flag up that what follows is an alternative point of view, contrary to the main message. For example, 'On the other hand', or 'Alernatively . . .'.

- ✔ Explain how any contradictory perspectives and views that your research may have revealed can be resolved, perhaps by introducing a third perspective. Or at the very least, make clear to the reader the presence of an unresolved contradiction and that it's not just the reader who can't solve it.

Choosing your words carefully

Many arguments are really just confusions about terminology. In fact, Socrates insisted that all human disagreements come down to this problem, but then he was executed by his fellow citizens after a vote, which implies he misjudged their characters. He was somewhat naïve about how and why different economic interests can lead people to have a *reason* to see things a certain way.

You need to word your arguments precisely, if they're to have any chance of being logical. Imprecise wording is a recipe for inconsistency, the error that brings an argument tumbling down later. See the exercise in the earlier section 'Spotting a fallacy' for how even everyday words can mislead.

A sound logical argument depends on terms having one fixed and precise meaning. But in ordinary language (as opposed to artificial languages such as symbolic logic, or mathematics) no terms have a fixed meaning. They're all to varying degrees a little bit nuanced, a little bit context-dependent and a little bit ambiguous.

Here's an easy question: do the angles of a triangle add up to 180 degrees? Not when the triangle is drawn on the surface of a sphere, they don't. So even maths and logic are context-dependent, and logic can't get going until the precise meaning of the terms has been agreed.

To this extent, all claims made using ordinary language depend on a degree of subjectivity, and on, at the very least, a consensus about meanings and usage.

Employing consistency and method

In a good, logical argument, the points made support the eventual conclusion. Another pitfall you want to avoid here is providing reasons that don't support the conclusion — perhaps because they're basically irrelevant or because they imply the reverse of the desired conclusion. This happens easily if you don't really know at the outset why you think that such-and-such, but are 'cobbling together' reasons and evidence to support your opinion anyway.

Getting the reasons in the right place is important. Often, people link reasons to each other that don't directly support the overall conclusion, but instead lead to an intermediate conclusion. A logical structure requires a line of reasoning in which first things come first and related arguments are dealt with together (see Figure 13-1).

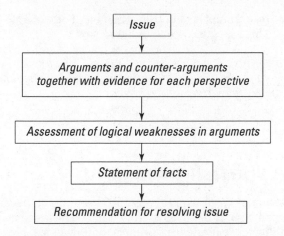

Issue

Arguments and counter-arguments
together with evidence for each perspective

Assessment of logical weaknesses in arguments

Statement of facts

Recommendation for resolving issue

Figure 13-1: Structure of a persuasive paper.

You can find out more about this aspect in more detail in Chapter 12.

Answers to Chapter 13's Exercises

Here are my answers to the two exercises.

The 'Does welfare encourage slacking?' argument

I say that this argument is valid. But I'm not a fascist, and you don't have to accept premises are true. Let me explain. Here, the argument hinges on 'if people can get money without working then they will become lazy', which looks plausible, when understood as '*sometimes*, if people can get money without working then they will become lazy'. But it seems less so when understood as 'in all cases' and even less so when the amount of money is included. Plenty of scope for disagreement exists about the assumptions in this argument. For example, suppose that the first premise is expanded to say:

> *Invariably, if people can get just enough money to survive from the State without having to work for it, then they will all become lazy.*

Looks less plausible, doesn't it? But it's not a change to the logic, only to the content.

The starfish argument

The argument as it is presented proves nothing, because the word 'fish' is being used in two different ways: in a strict scientific sense in the first premise and in a looser, every-day sense in the second premise. The end result is that the conclusion is unreliable. For the record, in this case, not just unreliable but flat wrong.

The fallacy is given the fancy name *quaternio terminorum!* In plain English, it's the *fallacy of four terms.* The logic depends on there being just three terms, with what logicians call *the middle term* being the vital link between the others. (It's called the middle term because of its link role, rather than because it appears in the middle of the sentence.) When you have four terms, you have no link, and the whole argument becomes random assertions.

Here's a valid argument, to remind you of how the middle term (in bold) acts as the vital link:

Major premise: All **fish** have fins

Minor premise: All salmon are **fish**

Conclusion: All salmon have fins

In plain English, the argument is that salmon have fins because they're a kind of fish and all fish have fins.

An invalid argument doesn't tell you that the conclusion is false (that would be useful in a way!). But although starfish live underwater they aren't 'fish' in the scientific sense that the term is used in the first premise. (Whereas fish propel themselves with their tails, starfish have tiny feet to help them move along.)

Chapter 14

Using Words to Persuade: The Art of Rhetoric

• •

In This Chapter

▶ Discovering the nature of rhetoric

▶ Using rhetoric to wow when giving a presentation

▶ Boosting a failing argument with rhetorical tricks

▶ Analysing a series of rhetorical statements

• •

*R*hetoric is the study of how to persuade with words. It's an ancient topic, as ancient as anything academics talk about. Perhaps the dominant theme of this book, in line with most Critical Thinking advice one way or another, is how to impose structure on ideas, turn claims and counter-claims into arguments, while allowing other kinds of thinking only a supporting role to the central role that logic plays.

But real life isn't like that. Most of the things you hear people say, or even read, aren't arguments in any sense: they're more like descriptions, exclamations or instructions. When people try to persuade you, the chances are that they don't come up with much by way of a rational argument, but instead try to appeal to your hopes, fears and emotions. They may even tell a few jokes.

You can call these tactics *rhetorical flourishes* if you like, but they're all an important part of persuading people. Therefore, they deserve to be part of any book on arguments and certainly part of any examination of Critical Thinking.

In this chapter I look at some of the ways you can use rhetoric to persuade — whether your efforts are already going well or not, and in informal and more formal situations (such as work presentations). I even include a section on how jokes can get your audience thinking.

 Although logic tries to force people to agree with you, to convince an audience in any meaningful way you will usually do much better by trying to *win* them over. Invariably, the person who triumphs in the debate comes across as co-operative rather than confrontational — and that's something that Critical Thinkers can certainly take onboard.

Introducing Rhetoric: When an Argument Isn't an Argument

Arguments, in the sense I use it in most of this book, are a series of statements for or against something, all set within a logical framework that makes them persuasive. But throw away that framework now, and what you have left is rhetoric.

 Rhetoric is still a series of statements designed to persuade — but with the logic taken out. And it works — no doubt about that. This section identifies some of the elements rhetoric uses in place of remorseless logic.

Choosing the overall approach

When the Ancient Greeks first studied rhetoric, they identified three basic distinct approaches — three different ways to win an argument:

- ✔ **Logos:** Facts and figures make the speaker look knowledgeable and impress the audience. Critical Thinkers do this automatically, of course. Join the facts up using logical arguments and you convince people who are following carefully and are open minded.

    In other words — *logos* doesn't win most people over! So the good speaker adds in some of the other two approaches too.

- ✔ **Pathos:** Reaction in the listeners or readers. Politicians of course dwell on sad tales people have asked them to help with. But even the most clinical social scientists or academics can't resist dressing up their essays with a little tirade (angry speech) at a social injustice, or stop themselves dwelling a little longer and in a little more detail than necessary for the point they're making on examples of misfortunes or tragedies. All this is pathos.

But beware you don't overdo it and end up with *bathos,* which is an abrupt transition in style, for example, from a lofty scholarly account to a highly subjective personal view, producing a ludicrous effect.

✓ **Ethos:** Involves convincing your audience that you're trustworthy and expert. You speak (or write) with quiet authority. Achieving this goal is of course the tricky bit — the skill is linked to having *charisma,* a certain magical, even 'godlike', quality. One practical tip is to be honest, accurate and modest.

Making a great speech

A Spanish-born lawyer, called Quintillian, set out what he saw as the key elements of rhetoric in the first century CE. Although Marcus Fabius Quintilianus (to give him his impressive full name) focused on public speaking, his points also apply to all sorts of attempts to put forward a particular point of view.

Here are his five ingredients for a great speech:

✓ **Invention:** The key stage of thinking of something to say! Invention is concerned with the 'how' and the 'what' of the issue. It covers questions such as how to come up with a strategy to argue a point, a task that's often equivalent to thinking of some good reasons to support a conclusion.

✓ **Arrangement:** How you're going to set the speech out, in the sense of how to order and arrange the ideas and any arguments being included. Should you say a bit about yourself first? Or keep the conclusion secret to the end?

✓ **Style:** Involves decisions such as would it be effective to pause here, and maybe insert a joke? And how about a little personal anecdote in the middle? Politicians often like to end their speeches with an appeal to action, wrapped in an emotional glow: 'Yes, we can!'

✔ **Memory:** This is something where I fall down: I can never remember my points. Fortunately (unlike in Quintillian's day) keeping a sheaf of notes handy is usually acceptable. But these are little use if you haven't got the important points you need written down clearly on them. There's nothing worse than having to flounder through your notes with a crowd of people waiting on your next word! So make sure your notes have a clear structure that makes them easy to dip into if necessary.

✔ **Delivery:** The original Greek word for this is *hypokrisis,* which roughly translates as 'acting'. Acting skills are what make all the difference between a good presentation and a lousy one. You have to empathise, 'to bond' with your audience, create a sense of personal dialogue with everyone present. Plus, of course, your speaking needs to come across 'loud and clear' and also sound melodious and varied, a combination that's rather harder to achieve.

Write a two minute speech — a simple 'presentation' — and (via the wonders perhaps of modern cameras or phones, record yourself giving it. Short of a topic? Why not just make it your own short version of the 'Art of Rhetoric'?

Are rhetorical skills a bad thing to have?

The most famous rhetoricians were the Sophists of Ancient Greece. These were the original 'wise men' (the name in Greek, signifies wisdom). They included many great and respected philosophers such as Protagoras, famous (and controversial) for having said that 'man was the measure of all things', a view which makes truth itself up for grabs, and indeed many a rabble-raising speaker has also believed it justified their positions. The Sophists made pots of money by offering advice to Greek citizens, particularly those seeking public office, or those accused of crimes and having to defend themselves in court.

The Sophists drew a line between two kinds of knowledge: the kind that describes the natural world and the kind that relates to the more complex case of human beings. Despite owing the Sophists for many of his inspirations, Plato regularly attacked them for, in a sense, 'selling arguments' as part of their rhetorical skills, and putting a price tag on the pursuit of knowledge. Soon, their reputation sunk to such a low point that Plato's student, Aristotle, mocked them as people who take money for appearing wise without actually being so. Cruel! But elegantly expressed, as only to be expected from someone who himself wrote a book on rhetoric.

In the last century, however, the philosopher of science Karl Popper called for the ancient rhetoricians to be given a little more credit for their work. Popper even says that what Plato and other later philosophers *really* had against the Sophists was their principle of treating everyone as equals and their willingness to take on the elites, including the philosophical ones.

Clever old Quintillian's five elements of rhetoric are so good that people continue to use them today. The first one, invention, is the part that overlaps most with the usual ideas of Critical Thinking. But in rhetoric, you don't just draw upon arguments. You may want to offer authorities to back your view — maybe even to present yourself as such — or perhaps overwhelm with facts and figures (see the approaches of ethos and logos, respectively, in the preceding section).

A vital part of speaking and writing effectively is to tailor what you're doing to the particular audience, a skill I cover in more detail in Chapter 10. For example, don't deliver a complicated, fact-heavy account to people who just need an overview, or give a weepy, emotional account to a sceptical audience. And don't tell dirty jokes to a Select Committee at the House of Commons looking at teaching thinking skills!

Winning When You're Right

Rhetoric provides some great strategies for making your points more persuasive, say, as part of a spoken presentation or debate. These tactics work whether you're right or wrong, but I assume you want actually to be right and so I concentrate on that for the moment.

To discover some shadier approaches to bolster a weak argument though, check out the later section 'Debating Successfully When You're Wrong'.

Favouring a simple but effective structure

The simplest way to structure your speech is the same way that you structure an essay, in order to aid comprehension:

1. **Outline the points you're going to make with a short introduction.**

2. **Give the meat of the argument, following the out-lined structure.**

3. **Summarise the argument.**

As the lawyers' dictum has it:

Tell them what you're going to tell them. Then tell them. And then tell them what you told them.

When you identify in advance your points, you let the audience know what to expect and encourage them to mentally prepare for what's coming up. Explaining in advance helps the audience to file information and ideas away, and to see connections better. Summing everything up at the end, reprising the key points you've made, isn't going to bore anyone. Instead it reassures those who got the point the first time and gives a second chance to those who didn't.

Speeches in particular, and arguments in general, are much more persuasive when they're clear — which requires a structure. A structure is most useful when it is explicit and audience can see it. (*For Dummies* books do this all the time, with their hierarchy of headings and the mini-intros at key points telling the reader what's coming up.)

Repetition is a bit of a no-no in academic books and articles, but in speeches, and journalism, it's a key tool. In such contexts, don't be embarrassed to repeat points. Novice speakers are often shy of doing so, feeling that the audience may spot and frown upon it ('borrring!'), but great speakers love to repeat things. Think of some of Winston Churchill's epic speeches, such as: 'We shall fight on the beaches, we shall fight on the landing grounds, we shall fight in the fields and in the streets, we shall fight in the hills; we shall never surrender'!

Repetition is valuable in creating a pattern, reinforcing the structure of a presentation and providing a powerful aid to comprehension.

Remembering the difference between denotation and connotation

In real life conversations and exchanges, words rarely mean one thing. And often the thing that the speaker intends to communicate is hidden behind another, more diplomatic, form of language. It is useful to both be able to tell what the deeper meaning of words is, and to be able to communicate extra levels of meaning in your own words.

Many words can denote roughly the same thing, but have very different connotations:

- **Denotation:** Using something as a sign for something else. For example, the jargon buster icon denotes that the text near it explains the use of an obscure or specialised term. In other words, when you mean what you say, literally, or, at the very least, *figuratively* (that is, metaphorically).

  For example, if you say that a new pop song *literally* blew your head off, you better stop talking and seek medical advice.

- **Connotation:** When you mean something else that may be initially hidden. The connotative meaning of a word may be based on implication, or shared emotional association with a word.

  Take the world 'greasy', for example: a completely innocent, lovely word. Many things, such as the moving parts of engines, should be greasy. But if you describe a meal in a restaurant, or worse still, your boss, as greasy, it contains negative associations. That's connotation.

Here's another example of language being used to make a point subtly. The words say one thing on the surface, and quite another in practice. A message that might be impolitic to give bluntly is being sneaked in by sleight-of-hand.

A lecturer is asked to write a reference for a student who has applied to be an administrator in a large organisation. The lecturer writes that the student is 'a very original thinker who often comes up with unusual ideas'. It sounds like a nice thing to say — the denotation is positive — but given the context the connotation is negative, and indeed may set off alarm bells! Not a team player! Possible fruit cake!

Conducting your argument with jokes

Jokes are a great way to 'break the ice' and get an audience on your side.

But what if you're speaking or writing? A sheaf of favourite Snoopy cartoons won't do. Ideally, if you're a natural wit, you can ad-lib and make the joke relevant. But otherwise try to have a few prepared jokes up your sleeve!

Here's a joke that I think illustrates an otherwise abstract idea about how humour often involves an unexpected shift in perspective.

A man, who lives in a flat in a hot town centre, goes on holiday, leaving his neighbour to water his prize Bonsai Tree and look after his dog. A few days later the neighbour sends him an email to say his beloved Bonsai Tree has died.

The news spoils the man's holiday and he writes back rather crossly to say that at the very least his neighbour might have led up to it more gradually, for example by saying in a preliminary email that the tree was looking a bit thirsty and he was worried about it. The neighbour apologies. The next day he emails to say that his dog seems rather thirsty.

Get it? As well as being pleasurable, humour is a valuable way of getting people to think: it seems to 'loosen up' the thought processes.

In many contexts, jokes are going to be considered not very respectable. Even when funny, they can be seen as inappropriate, bad form and frowned upon. So by all means include a joke in your presentations and public speaking, But show a little, ah, discretion.

Speaking in triples

This method for achieving rhetorical effect is simple: whenever possible speak in triples. Trios, triplets and triads abound in Western culture. Just consider the memorable triads in the nearby sidebar 'Famous triples'.

What is it about triples that makes them so effective? Three creates a pattern, and offers a structure. Each triple is also a beginning, a middle and an end. And even where there's no grand sense to the triple, it sounds right. Go for it! Just do it!

Some of the most famous speeches ever delivered feature triples prominently. Julius Caesar proclaimed: *Veni, vidi, vici* (I came, I saw, I conquered). Abraham Lincoln's Gettysburg Address played on the power of three by saying: 'We here highly resolve that these dead shall not have died in vain, that this nation, under God, shall have a new birth of freedom, and that government of the people, by the people, for the people, shall not perish from the earth'.

In more recent years, that natural orator Barack Obama (a self-proclaimed fan of Lincoln), played on the power of three as he campaigned with: 'Yes we can'. His Inaugural Speech included memorable lines such as: 'We must pick ourselves up, dust ourselves off and remake America', and unmemorable ones too, such as: 'Homes have been lost; jobs shed; businesses shuttered'. That's style for you!

Famous triples

Something works about the number three and rousing speeches. Consider these famous triples. From Christian theology come:

✔ Father, Son and Holy Spirit.

✔ Heaven, hell and purgatory.

✔ Three Wise Men with their three wise gifts: gold, frankincense and myrrh.

From the world of politics come the three branches of government:

✔ Executive, Judiciary and Legislature

(continued)

(continued)

And of course populist appeals to the deepest aspirations include:

✔ Life, liberty and the pursuit of happiness (in the US).

✔ *Liberté, Égalité et Fraternité* (in France).

✔ *Ein Volk, ein Reich, ein Führer!* ('one people, one empire, one leader' in Nazi Germany). Nowadays the German motto is completely different except that it's still a triple: 'Unity, justice and freedom'.)

Tell people what they want to hear

In his barnstormingly success-ful book, *How to Win Friends and Influence People* (1936), Dale Carnegie makes a very useful point for public speaking: don't talk about yourself and what you want and need, but talk about your audience and what they want and need. Address their concerns — not yours.

To be an effective communicator, pin up this little reminder: 'People aren't interested in me. They're interested in themselves — morning, noon and after dinner.' Only then can you start to find a way to make what you want something they may want too, but vice versa: communications should always be a two-way street.

To be a good speaker, you have to also be a good listener. To be inter-esting, you have to be interested. To be admired and appreciated, you have to make other people feel appreciated too.

Debating Successfully When You're Wrong

In this section, I look at a few slightly dodgy tactics that, of course, you'd never stoop to, but which you may find useful to know about anyway, because other people certainly use them! These great debating tricks can make even a weak hand into a winning presentation.

Making a virtue of not knowing

Audiences are much more sympathetic to people who admit not knowing than they are to someone who reveals through a mistake that they're ignorant. After all, most of the audience doesn't know either and no one likes a smart alec. So if you don't know, shout it out loud! This is a legitimate tactic in arguments.

But a more sophisticated kind of 'admission of ignorance' is a little bit less honest. Funnily enough, when it suits them, subject experts often back up their positions by saying that no one knows certain things about an issue. The tactic has a grand Latin name: the *argumentum ad ignorantiam*.

For example, physicists, astronomers and cosmologists regularly announce firmly that no one knows (and no one can know) anything about the state of the universe before the Big Bang — the primordial explosion that most scientists think brought the universe into existence. But when facts are based on a claim about ignorance — for instance, that the age of the universe is that which can be calculated from the Big Bang onwards (because no one can know anything about the universe before) — strictly speaking, such claims are fallacious.

Don't let the grand rhetorical flourishes that often accompany this tactic blind you to errors in reasoning.

Employing convoluted jargon

The rhetorical strategy here is to use big, complicated words so that you seem to be an expert. Academics and specialists of all kinds invariably think that the more obscure their terms, the more expert they are. This style also looks rather impressive. Indeed, people have written books using the method — even in the area of Critical Thinking where in principle the method should be shunned.

The good news is that this strategy isn't so difficult. Anyone capable of regurgitating a dictionary or thesaurus can learn the technique. And it never hurts to quote some phrases from long-dead foreign languages, too. Check out the nearby sidebar 'You says what now?' for an example.

You says what now?

The 20th-century French philosopher, Giles Deleuze, is often accused of using words in a meaningless, jargonised way. Professor Eric Alliez of the University of Kingston in Surrey, will have none of that. He says that if you know enough about the background, when you read Deleuze's words, it all makes good sense. Well, have a look and see for yourself:

> What is neither individual nor personal are, on the contrary, emissions of singularities insofar as they occur on an unconscious surface and possess a mobile, immanent principle of auto-unification through a nomadic distribution, radically distinct from fixed and sedentary distributions as conditions of the syntheses of consciousness.

> Singularities are the true transcendental events.... Only when the world, teaming with anonymous and nomadic, impersonal and pre-individual singularities, opens up, do we tread at last on the field of the transcendental....

—Giles Deleuze (The Logic of Sense, 1969)

I've got a bit of the background, and I still say that this passage is impossible to follow! The method is a strange one in which obscure terms are strung together as if by a mad computer.

All professions (and not just professors) have their special, expert language. But they have to translate it if they want to talk to everyone else.

Throwing in a koan

A *koan* (pronounced Co-ann or perhaps Cohen even) is a paradoxical statement designed to force people to 'think outside the box'. The original *koans* were used to train Zen Buddhist monks so that they no longer depended on conventional reasoning to understand the world, but instead understood it through sudden, intuitive enlightenment.

A famous example is to ask someone to imagine the sound of two hands clapping and then to ask them to imagine the sound of one hand clapping. Another example from literature and philosophy is Jean Paul Sartre's description of a waiter. Sartre explains grandly that the waiter is a being who is not what he is and is what he is not, a contradictory claim which is, in its own way, a koan.

This method of asking people to think about things that literally don't make sense is characteristic not only of many academic philosophers, but also of many other people in public life (I'm thinking of those political types again). These people advance a position, qualify it and then finally suggest a contrary position that negates the original assumptions. They then tell the audience their answer is present somewhere in this contradictory mix of assumptions, if only the audience were clever enough to follow them.

Conducting your arguments via questions

'What for?' you may say, immediately using the strategy. 'Why not?' I would reply, doing likewise, and maybe add 'Doesn't everyone?' and 'How many of the great thinkers can you name who didn't do that?'

The built-in advantage for the questioner is that asking a question is almost always easier than answering it. (But beware the 'yes/no' variety, which can leave the questioner looking long-winded.)

Take a complicated and long-running debate like that about evolution, for example. The issues are things like whether or not human beings really are the random product of billions of years of random mutations or whether some kind of supernatural element needs to be imagined (such as God). Someone sceptical of scientific explanations can easily ask: 'If you think the theory of evolution explains the world, then can you at least give the basic outline to explain how people evolved from hydrogen atoms?' The questioner barely needs to know the first thing about what he's asking. Great!

What's more, even if the speaker brilliantly deals with that question, the sceptic can simply nod appreciatively and bide his time for another complicated query. The speaker does the work and the questioner gets the credit. (Smart students know this trick, of course.) Or the person can turn the question into a list of things to be explained, just to be on the safe side.

Complex questions (to use the technical term) where a series of things that ought to be kept separate are strung together can be useful too, but the more complicated they get the more they run the risk of annoying the listeners.

In the evolutionary debate example, a complex question might be: 'How did birds develop wings, and in what ways is it similar, or different to, the mechanism that explains how birds evolved from dinosaurs?' The fact that the issues joined together in the question may be logically quite different isn't the questioner's problem: he or she can smile sweetly and leave the expert to sort out the mess.

Above all, never underestimate the power of the 'loaded' question, such as the celebrated 'When did you stop beating your wife?' By implying that the questioner is simply unable to imagine a universe in which the other person isn't beating his wife, the question has a more profound influence than the answer. Politicians who struggle to be logical or reasonable, often excel at this kind of question, offering them as sound bites to the media: 'Is the government going to stand up for our fishing industry — or carry on kow-towing to European Union bureaucrats?'

Watch out though: the arguing-through-questions technique is a bit of a boomerang, just as likely to generate confusion as to shed light. After all, people can all too easily confuse themselves even without people firing questions at them.

If you're making a presentation or giving a talk and some annoying person in the audience comes up with a killer fact that seems to put you in the wrong, don't be too keen to find some obscure counterexample or suchlike to save face. Think instead about revising your position. At least any Critical Thinkers in the audience will respect your openness.

Getting personal: Ad hominem

Ad hominem argument tactics are criticisms directed at the person making the argument, rather than at the argument itself. The method was very popular in the ancient world, where it was considered perfectly reasonable, indeed quite scholarly. It was particularly favoured for philosophical debates! But today *ad hominem* attacks are usually seen as the resort of scoundrels and count as fallacies.

In fact, nasty though such tactics sound, they're sometimes sensible and useful. Lawyers can legitimately use them to undermine evidence. For example, the evidence of an expert medical witness may be undermined if the lawyer can show, say, that the expert has previously made many misdiagnoses in his career. Alternatively, a scientist who claims to have made a dramatic new discovery may usefully be challenged over her record if she made similar grand claims in the past and was found to have been mistaken.

Another little piece of Latin jargon exists that means roughly the same thing: *tu quoque*. The form of the argument, familiar from everyday disagreements, is as follows:

> You tell me not to leave my dirty cups around the house!
>
> You leave dirty cups around all the time!
>
> (Therefore, your view is dismissed.)

The argument carries legal weight too. At the Nuremberg Trials, held at the end of the Second World War, German officers accused of violating the laws of war by using American uniforms to infiltrate Allied lines successfully used the *tu quoque* argument to defend themselves. They introduced evidence that the Allies themselves had on at least one occasion worn German uniforms.

In 2012, Prince Harry was embarrassed after he was photographed at a 'private party' wearing a German uniform Alas, despite having had one of the most expensive private educations money can buy, he didn't seem to know to use the *tu quoque* argument — and respond 'but the best British heroes have worn Nazi uniforms too!' — to defend himself.

I've had a hard day!

Human nature means that people tend to think more generously of themselves than other people. When you're looking at your own actions, lots of reasons can explain why you didn't do something as planned.

For example, when you forget an assignment was due, it was because there were exceptional circumstances. The coffee ran out and when you went to borrow some you got talking. Or maybe you had a really bad headache, or perhaps the car broke down again. But when someone else forgets, they're disorganised and lazy. When people feel 'let down'

(continued)

(continued)

by someone else, they rush to find a negative pretty quick, when other people 'mess up', it's always tempting to blame them and see personal faults. And maybe they have some. But best to resist this kind of reasoning, which has a special name: 'attribution error'.

Discerning a Message

This section contains an exercise in Critical Reading that also illustrates the point in this chapter about the different rhetorical techniques used to win an argument.

You can find out more about Critical Reading in Chapter 9, but the key point here is not to settle for just the 'top level' read, which is more or less a paraphrase of what the author or text states anyway, but to go the crucial step further and work out 'what's going on' under the surface.

Let me give an example to explain what I mean by that. Imagine someone in charge of a nuclear power plant. That person's job isn't just to read the dials (for example, showing temperature, pressure and so on), but to understand the context and what the dials display. Maybe the reactor is in danger of overheating and exploding? Only this deeper understanding gives guidance as to what should be done next.

Estimates suggest that 80 per cent of people who smoke started before they were 20 years old, and half of this number before they were 16. With these 'young smokers' primarily in mind, tobacco companies were first obliged to print health warnings on cigarette packets in 1971. The first warnings simply ran:

WARNING by H.M. Government, SMOKING CAN DAMAGE YOUR HEALTH.

Notice the weasel word 'can'. Twenty years later, the warning was 'strengthened' to say:

TOBACCO SERIOUSLY DAMAGES HEALTH

Not just upping the stakes to 'seriously', but also removing he element of doubt. In 2003, new EU regulations stipulated that the warnings cover at least 30 per cent of the surface of the pack and that a variety of more specific warnings should be used, such as:

SMOKING KILLS

SMOKING CLOGS THE ARTERIES AND CAUSES HEART ATTACKS AND STROKES

SMOKING CAUSES FATAL LUNG CANCER

SMOKING WHEN PREGNANT HARMS YOUR BABY

SMOKE CONTAINS BENZENE, NITROSAMINES, FORMALDEHYDE AND HYDROGEN CYANIDE

Right, that's the background. So what, with your Critical Thinking hat on, do you think is the message now being delivered to the public by the governments?

Answers to Chapter 14's Exercise

Here are my thoughts on the smoking warnings exercise.

Literally and 'logically', of course, the message is that smoking is very dangerous and maybe should be avoided. That's the message if *logos* (facts and figures) decides the target readership's reactions. But some psychologists, such as the contemporary Swiss-American Clotaire Rapaille, say that the message being delivered, particularly to the young people (including children), who were the governments' main targets for their campaign, was that smoking was part of a forbidden, adult, risky world. In short, the message that smoking's desirable and cool! Paradoxically, the more dire the warnings, the more many young people felt that smoking was something subversive and hence desirable. It's that difference between denotation and connotation again. You maybe won't disagree with smoking being dangerous, but most of us know that the effect of being told something is strictly forbidden is to make doing it seem more attractive!

Perhaps realising this, or maybe just because the figures for youth smoking showed the warnings were less effective than anticipated, in 2003 the EU decided to add not more arguments but ghastly pictures of supposedly smoking-related diseases to packets. This approach was a shift away from the use of *logos* and logic to the use of *pathos* and its appeals to fear and the emotions.

Chapter 15

Presenting Evidence and Justifying Opinions

● ●

In This Chapter

▶ Spotting everyday unreliable evidence

▶ Questioning scientists

▶ Struggling with statistics

● ●

> *Physicists have shown that all matter consists of a few basic particles ruled by a few basic forces. Scientists have also stitched their knowledge into an impressive, if not terribly detailed, narrative of how we came to be . . . I believe that this map of reality that scientists have constructed, and this narrative of creation, from the big bang through the present, is essentially true. It will thus be as viable 100 or even 1,000 years from now as it is today. I also believe that, given how far science has already come, and given the limits constraining further research, science will be hard-pressed to make any truly profound additions to the knowledge it has already generated. Further research may yield no more great revelations or revolutions but only incremental returns.*
>
> *—John Horgan (The End of Science: Facing the Limits of Knowledge in the Twilight of the Scientific Age, 1996, Addison-Wesley)*

Sounds pretty authoritative? Since John Hogan, sometime editor of *Scientific American,* wrote these words, astronomers have decided that about 90 per cent of the universe consists of previously unappreciated 'dark matter', not the stuff John Horgan was thinking of at all. Plus, even familiar 'facts' such as the number of planets in the Solar System have been put up for debate.

Astronomy's a good example of a 'hard' science where many people think that 'facts are facts' and opinions are at their best 'facts in waiting'. But in plenty of cases, the facts turn out to be a matter of opinion and the consensus view changes over time.

In this chapter I have a thorough look at the difference between facts and opinions, in everyday life as well as the realm of 'scientific knowledge', to try to separate those that deserve your respect from those that don't. I also cover the confusions that can result from numbers and statistics and give you a chance to test your own Critical Thinking skills with a look at the debate on whether smoke alarms save lives.

Challenging Received Wisdom about the World

I don't want to startle you (well maybe a little!) but an awful lot of what people tell you they know for certain is wrong. This section will give you some new perspectives on how facts and opinions become blurred and impact on the decisions you take in your everyday life, such as what to do if you have a cold, who you vote for or what you choose to eat.

Lesson One in Critical Thinking is that you need to always be aware that what you think on any issue may be wrong. For most people, that bit's easy. That's why students often look things up in encyclopedias instead — as do scholarly authors and journalists.

Lesson Two is harder learnt: what you read others saying may be wrong too. A lot of people never seem to quite get to grips with this idea.

Even prestigious academic journals regularly publish papers that are factually challenged. Some of the views ought to be suspect, because they're facilitated by large research grants, or based on studies conducted by activist campaigners. Remember that claim that the Himalayas would melt in 30 years? That went past the highest and most distinguished panel of scientific experts ever — the International Panel on Climate Change. Yet the original research was the work of a couple of green campaigners and amounted to little more than speculation.

Investigating facts and opinions in everyday life

Definitely, at some point or other, in order to be a Critical Thinker, you have to decide what is a 'fact' and what is a subjective opinion. The need to do this touches every area of life, far more than you probably realise. (See the nearby sidebar 'Defending society against science' for some warnings.)

Defending society against science

Paul Feyerabend, a radical philosopher of science, is best known for his anarchic rejection of the existence of universal methodological rules. For example, he sees astrology as just as good a way to investigate many things in the world as mainstream science. Sounds crazy? Well maybe. But what he means is that he would treat his findings based on astrological lore sceptically, just as people should treat findings based on, say, the latest scientific experiments or surveys.

Here's a taste of his views:

> Science is just one of the many ideologies that propel society and it should be treated as such . . . there must be a formal separation between state and science just as there is now a formal separation between state and church. Science

may influence society but only to the extent to which any political or other pressure group is permitted to influence society. . . . Science is not a closed book that is understood only after years of training. It is an intellectual discipline that can be examined and criticized by anyone who is interested and that looks difficult and profound only because of a systematic campaign of obfuscation carried out by many scientists.

—Paul Feyerabend ('How To Defend Society Against Science', Acta Sociologica, 22(2), 204, 1979)

That last point is a good one for Critical Thinkers to remember, because they can understandably feel nervous of challenging mainstream scientific claims.

Part of living in a modern technological age is that nobody understands the world around them — how it works, who runs it and why — and so they rely on other people to understand it for them. That's why when you research a topic, you head straight for a book, and why that book relies on the views of other books and other people, in a long chain of research and opinions. Read enough such things and you become an expert — but only in a tiny area. Very few areas are left to 'ordinary folk' to have an opinion.

In all areas of life — not just in the artificial, protected world of student essays — people need Critical Thinking skills. In this section I give you some examples to illustrate why. In other words, I construct an argument using hypothetical examples as evidence.

Treating a troubled child

Take child psychology, my first example as to why you should be sceptical of what may at first appear to be a settled consensus. Because even if all the experts agree on something today, that doesn't mean they will tomorrow (and maybe they already don't if you look a bit further).

If you're a parent and you have children who just don't seem to want to behave in school or at home, an expert opinion from a psychoanalyst is often part of the solution. In the US particularly, these experts frequently diagnose medical disorders such as attention deficit disorder (usually abbreviated to ADD or sometimes ADHD) and recommend drugs such as Ritalin or Adderall to alter the behaviour of children and young people. Some of the children are as young as age 3!

The drugs, despite being stimulants, are considered to have desirable effects in terms of curbing 'hyperactivity' and helping the individual to focus, work and learn. Experts have prescribed them for *millions* of children, as well as school and college students too. With so many experts agreeing, presumably the drugs work, and at the very least the disorder is real enough. But where's the line between fact and opinion here?

Sceptical voices certainly exist, but more remarkably, in 2014, the most consulted professional reference work for psychiatry itself decided that the 'disorder' didn't really exist. One of the most respected experts in the area, Dr Bruce Perry, told the London newspaper *The Observer* that the label of ADHD covered such a broad set of symptoms that it would cover perfectly normal people. You can't cure people of being normal!

Choosing who to trust

My second everyday example is that big issue of 'who to trust'. Which programs or columnists to rely on to find out about what's really going on around the world? Where to turn for medical advice? And, of course, which journalist to read for good advice on who to vote for. Rather than decide for yourself or maybe chat to some friends, wouldn't it be better to take some of the insightful analysis from highly respected (and highly paid) newspaper columnists or TV and radio pundits?

Actually, research shows that pundits have less influence than we (or indeed they) think. The reason is that people choose the pundit (or the newspaper) that says the kind of things they think anyway. We all do this, don't be ashamed! But nonetheless deciding to read certain newspaper columns or watch certain TV programs means you start to soak up a flood of information that, well, you can't check, but you assume is true anyway.

Advice offered by a newspaper columnist, or in an editorial for that matter, that the way to prosperity lies in building lots more houses and sending Polish plumbers home, will be presented as sound reasoning — but may really be windy rhetoric and hot air, maybe fuelled by errors or gaps in the writer's research and topped by popular prejudices. Even if the articles are better than that, readable summaries of complex issues — even then, they're just not things to rely on for accuracy or as evidence.

Fixing a sickly car

My final example involves another everyday problem — who do you believe when your car breaks down? Yourself, the neighbour or the garage mechanic?

This example illustrates how being much more knowledgeable (as someone who works everyday with cars certainly is) does not necessarily equate with being right.

I admit I'd take my car straight to the garage — no tinkering under the hood with a pair of nylon tights (not to wear, that is, but to replace the fan belt) or poking a long piece of wire into engine orifices to spot any build-up of carbon.

But although I rely on garage mechanics to mend my car, I certainly don't believe automatically what they say. I've had too many completely contradictory opinions on the same car to imagine that whatever mechanics do know, it's somehow infallible and beyond sceptical challenge. As many a consumer TV programme has shown, a car secretly prepared to have no faults or (more excitingly) to have one dangerous one, can be taken around as many garages as you like and have as many different expert diagnoses (and expensive repairs) as you choose to pay for. Only very occasionally, it seems, does the diagnosis and repair correspond to the fault. Put another way, it pays to be a bit sceptical next time someone says your 'big end' needs replacing.

However, if people sometimes suspect that scruffy dungaree-wearing mechanics aren't as expert as they seem, the experts

Trust me — I have a PhD

The top economists were insisting that they'd solved the problem of 'boom and bust' a few years ago – and then the whole US banking system collapsed, dragging the rest of the Western world into recession. Robert Lucas, the winner of the 1995 Nobel Prize for economics, even declared in 2003 that the problem of economic depressions had been finally eliminated, and then in 2008 came the bursting of the bubble.

What about doctors? Not long ago they travelled in wooden wagons painted with outrageous claims, dispensing coloured water in fancy bottles to cure various ills. Evidently, these were not real doctors but crooks and charlatans! But brightly painted wagons impressed people back then. Nowadays, doctors must train for many years and read lots of books and 'government advisories' to achieve the same effect.

And huge transnational companies with gleaming steel and glass-fronted laboratories today make modern-day coloured water. What do I mean by that? Only that for all the advances in medical science, which have certainly produced some remarkable improvements in human health, research also shows that many treatments and many prescriptions continue to be not only inappropriate – but actually dangerous! In recent years, some heavily prescribed drugs, such as Sibutramine, Rezulin (troglitazone) and Vioxx (rofecoxib) — three high-profile examples of drugs approved by the drugs watchdog in the USA — were later withdrawn from the market for posing unacceptable risks to patients.

in suits still get automatic respect. Expertise is all about appearances. Check out the nearby sidebar 'Trust me — I have a PhD' for more examples.

'Eat my (fatty) shorts!': What is a healthy diet?

This section describes some food controversies to illustrate how medical experts sometimes present opinions as facts.

Don't be confused by its constant claims to the contrary: medicine is just as much a creature of 'fashion' as any teen-ager buying into the latest fad. Take one myth you probably assume is a fact: fat in food is dangerous for you. A consensus built up around this idea during the 1970s (along with that conviction that enormous flares on trouser legs were cool). This consensus — the food one! — still exists, even though it never had any scientific basis, by which I mean hard facts and careful research. (You can read more about this in Chapter 2.) The key point however is this: the evidence for fatty goods causing heart disease involved cherry-picking the research. Countries where there seemed to be the expected 'fatty diets = high levels of heart disease' were included in the final survey, and countries where the evidence pointed the other way were excluded.

This research preference for 'positive' outcomes, often also findings which fit the researcher's (or company's) require-ments, is the elephant in the room for 'evidence-based — medicine'.

Take, for example, a US study of drugs prescribed as anti-depressants published in the New England Journal of Medicine in 2008. Television ads promote their benefits. One in four middle-aged American women are apparently on these! But do the drugs help? Of 74 trials ever submitted to the Food and Drug Adminstration for evaluation, about half had posi-tive outcomes — but only 40 papers ever saw the light of day by being published, of which 37 were positive. Of the 36 nega-tive outcomes, only 3 were published. So, do anti-depressants work? The evidence in reality was roughly 50:50 — or 'maybe'. The evidence as published was a resounding 92 per cent positive — 'yes'!

When a view becomes so widespread that everyone you come across thinks it must be true, you have a 'consensus'. But unfortunately, it still doesn't make the view true. Notice that no one is lying about the drugs — but the evidence has been skewed and distorted.

Digging into Scientific Thinking

It's easy to assume that with so many things being discovered every day, and the internet apparently providing one-click answers to everything you can think of to ask, that there must be a simple, and hence 'knowable' answers to everything. This section is about how, in fact, many questions have no answer. Paradoxes and contradictions sit at the heart of maths and physics — every bit as much as they do in other areas of life where you might more expect to find them — areas such as politics or even human relationships. Sounds weird? Read on! In the process you will pick up some big ideas for the evaluation of even little debates. One such idea, invaluable for Critical Thinkers, is to recognise that arguments that neglect the complexity of issues often mislead, and generalisations need to be openly admitted — and abandoned where necessary.

Changing facts in a changing world

The idea that facts are facts and fixed forever is one of the things that makes them so useful and seem so very different from opinions (which people change all the time). That's certainly one of the assumptions in the famous claim (well, within philosophy anyway) of the French mathematician Pierre Simon Laplace back in the 18th century that knowledge of facts bestows almost God-like powers. He wrote:

> We may regard the present state of the universe as the effect of its past and the cause of its future. An intellect which at a certain moment would know all forces that set nature in motion, and all positions of all items of which nature is composed, if this intellect were also vast enough to submit these data to analysis, it would embrace in a single formula the movements of the greatest bodies of the universe and

*those of the tiniest atom; for such an intellect nothing would
be uncertain and the future just like the past would be
present before its eyes.*

*—Pierre Simon Laplace (A Philosophical Essay on
Probabilities, 1951, translated into English by Truscott,
FW and Emory, FL, Dover Publications)*

If Laplace were alive today, Google's immense collection of
facts would appear to be getting near to his dream! Or would
it? Problems exist with the idea that facts are facts and that
you can dream one day of collecting so many of them that you
can start to predict everything else from the ones that you
have already.

Most of the time, most people think this way, but good and
practical reasons compel Critical Thinkers to be a lot more
careful.

Take the work of Edward Lorenz, a mathematician and a
meteorologist. In the 1960s, as weather modelling was starting, he quite by chance found that if he adjusted the numbers
entered into his weather models by even a tiny fraction, the
weather predicted could change from another sunny day in
Nevada to a devastating cyclone in Texas.

Or take the length of the lunar month. You've got a calendar
on your wall that seems pretty reliable, but (as Hindu priests
realised thousands of years ago) the exact time between two
full moons as seen from Earth is actually *impossible* to ever
calculate — because of what scientists call 'feedback effects'.
The moon is affected by both the Earth and the Sun, and in
turn affects the movements of the Earth are a very different
matter.

Clearly, many things in the world aren't predictable in practice or in theory. In fact a lot of things that affect the world
aren't just hard to express precisely — they're impossible,
from weather patterns to lunar months. And chaos reigns
from stock movement fluctuations to the rise and fall of
populations or the spreading of diseases.

In terms of weather, as Edward Lorenz memorably put it, the
mere flap of a butterfly's wing in one country can 'cause' a
hurricane a week later somewhere else, as a cascade of tiny
effects change outcomes at higher and higher levels.

Here's a quote to muse on:

> *The truth is that science was never really about predicting.*
> *Geologists do not really have to predict earthquakes;*
> *they have to understand the process of earthquakes.*
> *Meteorologists don't have to predict when lightning will*
> *strike. Biologists do not have to predict future species. What*
> *is important in science and what makes science significant*
> *is explanation and understanding.*

—*Noson Yanofsky (The Outer Limits of Reason: What Science,*
Mathematics, and Logic Cannot Tell Us, 2013, MIT Press)

Critical Thinking is all about explanation and understanding —
and even the best explanation involves both facts and opinions.

Teaching facts or indoctrinating?

Sceptical philosopher Paul Feyerabend wrote that facts, especially 'scientific facts', are taught at a very early age and in the
same manner as religious 'facts' were taught to children for
many, many years. Nowadays, people frown at children being
fed 'dogma' by priests in religious schools, yet the truths of
science and maths are held in such high respect that in many
subject areas no attempt is made to awaken the critical abilities of children or students. Indeed, Feyerabend, a university
teacher himself, says that in his experience at universities the
situation is even worse, because what he calls the indoctrina-
tion is carried out in a much more systematic manner.

You probably think that scientists are quite above indoctrina-
tion — forcing their views on others — and that such things
are objective, neutral and, well 'scientific'. Aren't their theories, according to the influential account of Karl Popper, only
accepted after they're thoroughly tested?

Certainly, Popper says scientists must test their theories
properly, under the most difficult circumstances. For if
we're uncritical, he says, then

> *. . . we shall always find what we want: we shall look for,*
> *and find, confirmations, and we shall look away from, and*
> *not see, whatever might be dangerous to our pet theories.*

—*Karl Popper (Poverty of Historicism)*

Popper described himself as a *critical rationalist,* meaning that he was critical of philosophers who looked for certainty through logic. He argued that no 'theory-free', infallible observations exist, but instead that all observation is theory-laden, and involves seeing the world through the distorting glass (and filter) of a pre-existing conceptual scheme. To cut a long story short, all measurements and observations are a matter of *opinion.*

Popper categorically rejects the inferring of general laws from particular cases, the process which is the basis of scientific method. Such inferences, he says, should play no role in scientific investigation, because securing the 'verification' of a universal statement is logically impossible. You can't prove that all rocks are heavier than water, for example, because someone may discover a new one that isn't (pumice stone floats on water) or even that the properties of water itself changes.

All scientific theories are like this, making universal claims for their truth unverifiable.

Despite what you were probably told at school, science rests on inspiration, and not on facts: that's why the fact that no number of positive confirmations at the level of experimental testing can ever confirm a scientific theory. It doesn't matter how much evidence you can produce to support a theory — the next case along can still destroy it. The sun may not rise tomorrow and the next time you open the fridge a gorilla may leap out. It seems unlikely, but something being unlikely has no power over whether or not something happens.

Tackling the assertibility question

How do you separate out cranky views that aren't supported by evidence from reasonable theories that maybe worth serious consideration? This problem is sometimes called *the assertibility question* (AQ), because you're asking what evidence allows you to assert that the claim is true.

Here's a useful checklist for scientific theories from a recent book called *Nine Crazy Ideas in Science* (Princeton UP 2002). Professor Robert Ehrlich advises everyone to test theories considered controversial by 'mainstream' scientists, as he puts it, on a 'Cuckoo scale'. He offers various questions to ask about theories such as 'radiation exposure is good for you', or 'distributing more guns reduces crime', which I sum up as follows:

- ✔ How well does the idea fit with common sense? Is the idea nutty?

- ✔ Who proposed the idea, and does the person have a built-in bias towards it being true?

- ✔ Do proposers use statistics in an honest way? Do they back it up with references to other work that supports the approach?

- ✔ Does the idea explain too much — or too little — to be useful?

- ✔ How open are the proponents of the idea about their methods and data?

- ✔ How many *free parameters* exist (see the nearby sidebar 'Parameters: The elephant in the theory' for an explanation of the term)?

Ehrlich thinks that these questions will root out dodgy theories, and most likely they would, along with all other new ideas. But Ehrlich has his own dangerous assumptions. He seem to assume that orthodox opinion is to be preferred to new ideas, and thereby shows a surprising blindness to the true history of science. Yesterday's cuckoo theory is today's orthodoxy and today's orthodoxy is tomorrow's cuckoo theory.

Resisting the pressure to conform

Informal thinking is social — what you think is influenced by what other people think. The idea that *the way* people think (and not just the 'things' they think about) is influenced by social factors seems strange at first hand, but it's a well-established fact.

A much-cited experiment by the American social psychologist, Solomon Asch, back in the 1950s, found that people are quite prepared to change their minds on even quite straightforward factual matters in order to 'go along with the crowd' or in many cases, the experts.

Parameters: The elephant in the theory

A *parameter* is kind of artificially decided setting that constrains and affects a theory or situation. A practical example: if you have central heating in your house, two parameters that may be set are the times when the system comes on, and the maximum and minimum temperatures.

The presence of parameters and their settings is important when you're examining and evaluating theories and situations. John von Neumann, the famous mathematician once joked that with four parameters he could fit an elephant into any theory, and with five he could even make the elephant wiggle his trunk!

The point is that if parameters are set arbitrarily, although they may well help to make the theory work, they can also make the theory meaningless. Too often, parameters are artificially set to 'make the theory fit the facts' or otherwise serve a particular, preconceived purpose, rather than because the parameters reflect anything in the real world.

Dr Asch showed a group of volunteers a card with a line on it, and then a card with three lines drawn on it, and asked them to determine which of the lines matched the first card (see Figure 15-1). Unknown to one of the group, all the other participants weren't, in fact, volunteers, but stooges. These people had been previously instructed to assert things that were obviously not the case, for instance, by choosing a line that was obviously shorter than the one sought, or that was a bit longer. Revealingly, when enough of their companions told them to do so, around one third of people were prepared to 'change their minds' and (disregarding all the evidence) bend pliantly to peer pressure.

Cheating when choosing lines is one thing, but changing your answer to fit in with everyone else on complicated issues you don't really understand is well, sort of understandable. You can't really blame people for doing so, especially when to do otherwise would mean exploring scientific issues they're unused to processing.

On the other hand, most things aren't as complicated as particular experts like to make out. Experts such as Albert Einstein, and the founding father of modern atomic theory, Ernest Rutherford, were highly concerned to ensure, at least in principle, that anyone could understand their theories.

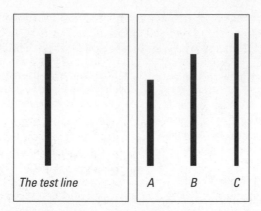

Figure 15-1: The lines test: Which line do you think is the match? Sure?

Common sense is a powerful way to interpret the world, but unfortunately it's constantly being bamboozled by scientific sales chatter, and in some cases, deceit (the wheels of commerce and life itself are amply greased on both). People have to create hierarchies of expertise for their own purposes and to satisfy their own needs. The relationship of experts and people seeking guidance needs to be symbiotic and serve the wishes of both parties.

Following the evidence, not the crowd

In many areas of life, people are in the position of having to make irrevocable decisions on the strength of others' advice.

China has a popular new antiques TV show called *Collection World* in which amateur collectors meet professional experts. The amateurs get their most prized Qing dynasty vases, or delicately carved wooden chests, authenticated (authoritatively dated and valued by the experts). The twist is, however, that if the experts say the work is a modern reproduction (a fake) the owner must immediately take a sledgehammer to their pride and joy, and smash it to pieces!

But the 'expert panel' is in reality constructed of people who had no knowledge of antiquities: just people who happened to be handy — researchers or technicians. How many ancient vases and works of art have been smashed for the amusement of TV audiences, no one will ever know. That's showbiz! If watching it makes you want to cry out — 'Stop! That's a work of art, you cynical frauds!' — then the programme is twice as much fun. After all, even the best experts make mistakes, don't they. . . . Tune in next week!

The real question is, of course, not so much whether to reject all claims of expertise, but how to tell which claims are right. In that sense, although people don't know a great deal about a great many things, and experts know a lot about small areas of life, the masses should never be asked to suspend their own judgement, to accept passively the views of experts.

Black swans and the unknown facts

Economists are people paid very large sums of money by governments to predict important things such as how much the national economy will grow in the next year. The Organisation for Economic Co-operation and Development (OECD), charged with promoting the 'economic and social well-being of people around the world', for example, collected the assessments of the top economic experts in 2007 and came up with an average growth rate of 2.5 per cent for its 34 members. It didn't foresee that the US house price loans bubble was about to burst. The eventual growth rate for all the member countries the next year was 0.2 per cent. The next year, slightly chastened, the economists predicted growth of around 1 per cent, but instead economies worldwide plunged 3.5 per cent as banks and stock markets collapsed all round the world.

Drawing painful lessons today from this, the OECD and the IMF (International Monetary Fund) now specifically consider 'alternative scenarios', when trying to forecast future economic events. They try to anticipate *black swan* events – events that are essentially unanticipated because nothing like them has been encountered before. The general lesson that you may already know from everyday life is that *something* unlikely is almost certain to happen! It's just hard to know what, or when.

The other lesson these powerful international organisations have drawn is also worth noting – they aim in their discussions and meetings to encourage a range of views and not to prejudice minority ones in favour of a too-early, even if very comfortable, consensus.

Take big questions like: When does life begin? When does life end? What should people do in between those two points? These are scientific questions, yes, but they are also ethical, human issues. An interaction is necessary — a kind of democratic interaction — between those who say they know, and those of us who rely on them to be our guides.

Rules of the scientific journal: Garbage-in, garbage-out

One of the most downloaded papers in recent years on scientific method is 'Why Most Published Research Findings Are False', by John Ioannidis, a Greek-American professor of Hygiene and Epidemiology. He writes that across the whole range of supposedly precise, objective sciences a research claim is more likely to be false than true. Moreover, he adds that in many scientific areas of investigation today, research findings are more often simply accurate reflections of the latest fashionable view (and bias) in the area.

A number of reasons exist for this situation, which all can be shown quite objectively, by considering the context of modern scientific research. Much hinges on the correct use of statistics, and scientists are no better at this than anyone else. In particular, the smaller the studies conducted and the smaller the effect sizes in a scientific field, the less likely the research findings are to be true. The later section 'Counting on the Fact that People Don't Understand Numbers: Statistical Thinking' illustrates how statistics can mislead.

At the same time, the greater the number and the lesser the selection of tested relationships in a scientific field, and the greater the financial and other interests and prejudices in a scientific field, the less likely the research findings are to be true. A similar story relates to how trendy the research is, with increased numbers of competing scientific teams resulting in an increased likelihood of the published research being, well, false.

Finally, Professor Ioannidis warns, the greater the flexibility in designs, definitions, outcomes and analytical modes in a scientific field, the more dodgy the research findings. This is simply because flexibility increases the potential for transforming what would be 'negative' results into 'positive' results. All this explains why you often read in the paper or see on the TV news about some major new discovery making scientists very excited — followed some months later by a teeny-weeny story about the findings being 'not quite all they seemed at first to be'.

Selecting evidence

When you're writing a piece, assume your readers are Critical Thinkers! Explain your reasoning, and offer them plenty of evidence. In a court of law, evidence is what usually settles the case: the suspect's fingerprint on the knife, the witness report of the argument followed by the shout. Evidence is factual. But plenty of innocent people have gone to prison because evidence was misinterpreted, or maybe misrepresented. The same sorts of problems dog evidence in all academic areas too.

In theory, evidence gives an objective foundation to arguments, and makes your writing more than a mere collection of personal opinions. Evidence takes the form of: facts and figures; case studies and historical examples; personal accounts and interviews — or maybe images and films.

The evidence, or data, used in your research are known as sources and are split into two broad categories called *primary* and *secondary*.

Primary sources provide direct or firsthand evidence. Usually they're contemporary accounts. Examples include:

✔ Personal correspondence and diaries

✔ Speeches

✔ Newsreel footage of events

✔ Photographs and posters

✔ Census or demographic records

✔ Physical examples, such as plant and animal specimens, or archaeological finds

Secondary sources, on the other hand, are produced some time after an event happened: they contain information that has been interpreted, summarised, analysed or processed in some way. Textbooks, encyclopedias, commentaries in newspapers, are all examples of secondary sources.

But the difference isn't quite black and white. Take, for example, this book. Is it a primary or a secondary source? The answer is both. If you quote it as your source for the controversy over fatty foods (see the earlier section '"Eat my (fatty) shorts!"': What is a healthy diet?' of this chapter) it's definitely a secondary source. The primary source would be a journal article accusing Dr Keys of skewing his findings. But this book would be the primary source if you want to argue that some Critical Thinking books are encouraging students to be suspicious of experts in certain circumstances.

Proving it!

Proofs that produce good reasons have been studied since the time of Aristotle (I discuss his three types of proof — *logos, pathos* and *ethos* in Chapter 14). More recently, academics have added one other form of proof: *mythos* — proof based on the traditions, identity and values of a group. Mythos is what drives things such as the emphasis in the climate change debate that 'all the experts agree . . .'.

All reasons for claims must answer the assertibility question (AQ) (see the earlier section 'Tackling the assertibility question'): 'How do you know that such-and-such a claim is true?' You're asking what evidence allows someone to assert that the claim is true. You ask it when you're presented with a claim and the proponent should respond with a reason to believe the claim is true.

Claims are rarely as objective as they seem. In some cases, no evidence is produced — because none is needed. Instead, the effort is put into showing that the conclusion follows from the certain stated assumptions.

You can look at arguments from three standpoints:

- ✔ **As neutral observer:** Looking at an argument put by someone else.

- ✔ **As participant:** Trying to judge your own argument.

- ✔ **As referee:** Looking at arguments being debated and perhaps evaluated by others, say, in a text.

If it's your argument, you need to provide sufficient evidence to support it. Sufficient is something of a value judgement though — do you really need to prove that say, water flows downhill, in order to argue that the collapse of a dam will threaten the village just underneath it?

If you're evaluating someone else's argument, you also need to judge whether the person has provided sufficient evidence. Ask yourself, what reason is the author giving to support the conclusion and why should I believe her?

In both cases you need to judge whether evidence offered is true *and* relevant. In my collapsing dam example, discussing the political situation in the country isn't relevant unless you can provide there are direct links between that and the issue at hand. There may well be! For example, the government may be in the habit of ignoring earthquake risks in order to increase the amount of electricity generated. In this case, politics is part of the apparently objective task of evaluating an argument.

The other part of evaluating argument is checking that the structure of the argument is valid. This is much less of a matter of judgement, and much more a matter of applying a rulebook. A valid, sound and logical argument has to be free of fallacies (as I discuss in Chapter 13).

Critical Thinking is about bringing things upfront that may otherwise remain in the back of your head. Another advantage of putting them upfront is to make sure that they're going on and have not been overlooked or forgotten!

Here are some tips for evaluating arguments:

- ✔ Get the feel of the shape of the argument — is it a chain of reasoning or a piecing together of a jigsaw of evidence? Assign weights to reasons and note any weak points in the logic of the argument.

- ✔ Reverse the conclusion to see how this perspective changes your view of the argument and evidence presented. It should be in direct conflict: if not, the reasons aren't persuasive after all.

- ✔ Sort the reasons into similar kinds. Look for purely logical reasons to support the form of the argument, but also examine the quality of the evidence and the methodology behind any statistics.

- ✔ Treat methodological assumptions with especial care. In many, many practical areas, the methodology chosen determines the results that emerge — yet the validity of the methods themselves isn't challenged. Make sure to look for bias in the starting points that decide the methodology.

- ✔ Use mind maps (see Chapter 7) and doodles.

If it's your own argument, you need to be particularly careful to avoid bias, which is easier said than done. Of course you're always right! Use strategies to force yourself to evaluate your own arguments. Ask yourself — what would it mean if you were wrong? How come other people disagree — what are they seeing differently? See the nearby box 'Hats off to Edward' for some ideas.

Hats off to Edward

Edward de Bono, the writer and philosopher who made the term lateral thinking famous, has a novel suggestion for evaluating arguments. He says people should imagine putting on one of six different coloured hats — and then evaluate the material in a particular way for each hat. Here's my summary of his six hats:

White hat: How you're probably used to being told to think, treating texts as factual information and looking at it coolly and objectively.

Red hat: Look at the text allowing full rein to your intuitions, your emotions — even your prejudices!

Yellow hat: Look for things that you like about the text.

Black hat: Look for faults, errors and weaknesses. Find fault. Ask yourself — what has the author forgotten to look at — maybe even deliberately left out?

Green hat: The hippy hat. Think about how the ideas in the text could be freely adapted, taken in new directions. What might have happened if the author had followed a different approach? Speculate.

Blue hat: Get the big picture. Put the argument into a wider context. Ask yourself — has the case been made for the methodology used? What assumptions have been made?

Counting on the Fact that People Don't Understand Numbers: Statistical Thinking

If a man stands with his left foot on a hot stove and his right foot in a refrigerator, the statistician would say that, on the average, he's comfortable.

—Walter Heller (quoted in Harry Hopkins, The Numbers Game: the Bland Totalitarianism, 1973, Brown & Co)

Strangely, many people find statistical flukes perturbing and extraordinary: for example, a run of 40 'tails' when tossing a coin or a set of perfect hands dealt out in Bridge (all spades to one, all hearts to another and so on).

I say 'strangely' because such events and such arrangements are no less likely than any other: the significance is only in people's minds and yet they think it extraordinary. (In a sense, any sequence is unique, but only some of them seem to form a pattern.) Plus, people do put an absurd amount of faith in 'rare events' never happening. As George Carlin, the US social critic, puts it: 'Think about how stupid the average person is; now realise half of them are dumber than that.'

George mocks those of us whose eyes glaze over a bit when statistics are introduced. But well, facts and stats are hard to separate so everyone really has to learn strategies for dealing with numerical claims. The first step though is to become aware of the issue. So now try assessing this real-life issue.

Test your skills on the following argument on smoke alarm advice:

The fire service estimates that you are twice as likely to die in a house fire that has no smoke alarm than a house that does. The figure is based on US research that shows that between 1975 and 2000 the use of smoke alarms rose from less than 10 per cent to at least 95 per cent, and that over the same period the number of home fire deaths was cut in half.

In the average year in the UK, the fire service is called out to over 600,000 fires. These result in over 800 deaths and

> *over 17,000 injuries. Many of the fires are in houses with no smoke alarm fitted. If people had an early warning and were able to get out in time many lives could be saved and injuries prevented. Smoke alarms give this kind of early warning. Conclusion: Smoke alarms save lives.*

Assuming of course that the argument does contain a flaw, which of the following objections best describes that flaw:

✔ **1: A factual objection:** Actually, only about 50,000 of the 600,000 emergency call outs to fires are household ones in the home, and so the great bulk of lives and injuries can't possibly be saved no matter how many alarms are fitted in homes.

✔ **2: An objection on the principles:** Millions of people never experience a household fire. Why should they be told that they have to fit a smoke alarm because of the tiny minority who do?

✔ **3: A logical objection:** Correlation isn't causation. The drop in lives lost in domestic fires could be for other reasons than that of more smoke alarms being fitted.

✔ **4: A 'causal' objection:** This argument assumes that having a smoke alarm means that an early warning will sound, but no one may be around when the alarm goes off! Even if someone is, the alarm may make next to no difference as to how quickly the person spots the fire and it certainly doesn't mean that the fire service gets to the house in time.

✔ **5: Another logical objection:** The argument is a non-sequitur, because it assumes that having a smoke alarm gives early warning of fires, whereas, in fact, the alarm may be broken. A broken alarm may lull residents into a false sense of security by their presence and thus make them more likely ignore early signs of fires and sensible procedures in general.

✔ **6: A practical objection:** The argument overlooks the possibility that fires may not be anywhere near the room with the alarm.

✔ **7: Another practical objection:** The argument ignores the fact of different kinds of smoke and that only some kinds (burning toast, for example) set fire alarms off.

Answers to Chapter 15's Exercise

The real objection and weakness to the argument is Objection 3 — correlation isn't causation — and it's a very common error!

The argument doesn't allow for the fact that during the 20th century a steady trend downwards already existed in deaths from fires. In the decades before smoke alarms started to be installed the trend downward was actually steeper! In the 1920s and 1930s, homes used open fires for heating rooms and water, as well as candles or gas for light. By 1950 electricity had taken over these functions in most houses, and solid fuel or gas boilers were providing hot water in posher homes. These changes clearly reduced the likelihood of domestic fires, and thus saved lives.

Here's my view of the other objections:

✔ **Objections 1, 4, 6 and 7:** All miss the point — a reduction is claimed for deaths in fires in homes thanks to smoke alarms — despite many of them not working, different kinds of smoke and so on.

✔ **Objection 2:** Although I agree with the principle of not forcing people to have the alarms, this wasn't the argument, which is about whether or not alarms save lives.

✔ **Objection 5:** More of a counter-argument than a *non-sequitur*. It seems to say that if smoke alarms save some lives by giving early warning, they may cost some lives by lulling people into a false sense of security. As I say above, some evidence for this makes it my 'second best answer'.

Part V

The Part of Tens

 For Dummies can help you get started with lots of subjects. Go to www.dummies.com to learn more and do more with *For Dummies*.

In this part . . .

✓ Discover my ten favourite logical fallacies, to give a rather grand title to what are really just dodgy argument techniques.

✓ Take a whistle-stop tour of arguments in history. You may learn a few tips here, but mainly it's a snapshot view of the role ideas expressed in words have played in history — and will doubtless continue to do so in the future.

✓ Develop your view about why some things seem interesting and about how people tend to join the dots even when really the dots are pretty random.

Chapter 16

Ten Logical Pitfalls and How to Avoid Them

- -

In This Chapter

▶ Picking up tips for real-life debates

▶ Looking at how newspapers and politicians spin arguments

- -

*A*rguments are all about providing reasons to support a position. Reasons are often, in practice, limited to producing so-called authorities who're claimed to hold the same view (perhaps important people, important books or of course God). Or perhaps they're claimed as links to future events, for good or bad: for example, countries should put a hefty tax on lightbulbs and petrol or else the seas will rise and drown coastal cities.

Such arguments are very weak, but not necessarily invalid. Why do I say they're weak? Because in the first case they require others to accept your judgement of who's an authority, and in the second case they 'beg the question' of exactly what is the causal link. (Remember, in logic, premises are assumed to be true, however implausible. The thing that makes an argument invalid is an internal contradiction.)

Here, however, I provide ten common argumentative tactics that I strongly suggest you avoid!

Claiming to Follow Logically: Non Sequiturs and Genetic Fallacies

Non sequiturs and genetic fallacies involve statements that are offered in a way that suggests they follow logically one from the other, when in fact no such link exists.

The term *non sequitur* comes from the Latin, simply meaning 'that which does not follow'. It's spelt with a 'u' at the end and not the expected 'e', and so watch out if trying to impress! A good example is that of someone arguing against wedding rings on the grounds that they must be bad because they have their origins in something bad — the historical fact of the unequal submission of women to men. The argument is fallacious, because the use of wedding rings today carries no such associations – at least not 'logically'.

This example is actually a special kind of *non sequiter,* oops, *sequitur,* called the *genetic fallacy.* This occurs where people draw assumptions about something by tracing its origins back, hence 'genetic', even though no necessary link can be made between the present situation and the claimed original one.

Making Assumptions: Begging the Question

Begging the question is the dodgy argumentative tactic of assuming the very point at issue. In effect, the conclusion is one of the premises in an argument supposedly intended to prove it. Therefore, it's a form of circular argumentation.

But, in logic, a valid argument has to have all the true information needed in the premises to work too. So in a sense, in order to be logically valid you have to beg the question! Nevertheless, in Critical Thinking argumentation, don't do it. The reasoning of your argument should extend the information contained in the premises a little bit further.

Restricting the Options to Two: 'Black and White' Thinking

In black and white thinking, or *the false dichotomy* to give it its slightly grand title, the arguer gives only two options when other alternatives are possible. For example, 'If you want better hospitals for everyone, then you have to be prepared to raise taxes. If you don't want to raise taxes, you can't have better hospitals for everyone.' Logical nonsense! Plenty of other options are possible between these two extremes. (Maybe money could be swapped from building roads . . . or new missiles.) Someone using this type of argument is probably deliberately trying to obscure other available approaches.

You may also spot another failure of logic in this example (like buses, fallacies often come in twos and threes) — mistaking correlation for causation (see the later section 'Mistaking a Connection for a Cause: Correlation Confusion'). Better hospitals and higher taxes aren't necessarily linked: healthcare can improve without increased funding and increased funding for hospitals doesn't necessarily improve it either.

Being Unclear: Equivocation and Ambiguity

Equivocation and ambiguity involve using a word or phrase that has two or more meanings as though it has just one. You can hardly avoid encountering various types of ambiguity, including:

- **Lexical:** Refers to individual words.
- **Referential:** Occurs when the context is unclear.
- **Syntactical:** Results from grammatical confusions.

Politicians rely heavily on this kind of bad argument. Actually, here's an example of referential ambiguity from recent political life in the United States. President Clinton was accused of not having 'taken out' Osama bin Laden (the man who later organised the crashing of the hijacked planes into the Twin Towers in New York).

Clinton insisted that, on the contrary, he'd approved every request that the CIA and the military made of him involving the use of force against Osama bin Laden. But he didn't disclose that he'd also instructed the CIA and military, in writing in several Memoranda of Notification, that he wanted bin Laden captured and treated humanely, but not killed, unless it was in the process of capture.

So yes, he agreed with all the requests, but he also instructed them not to use lethal force unnecessarily. Another, rather better-known, Clinton example concerned one of his lady friends — Gennifer Flowers — who alleged she had had a 12-year affair with him. He said her story was untrue and that she was 'a woman I never slept with'. The story was 'untrue' however only in the sense that it was not exactly 12 years and he never literally fell asleep with her.

Mistaking a Connection for a Cause: Correlation Confusion

Correlation confusion is also summed up as the adage: 'correlation is not causation'. Anyway, this common fallacy consists of assuming that because two things often go together a link must exist. For example, children are eating more biscuits and cars are getting bigger. But did the one cause the other? The link is spurious — children who eat a lot of biscuits may need larger clothes, but not larger cars. Don't jump to an unsound conclusion.

As I discuss in more detail in Chapter 12, one particular form of this fallacy, usually known as *affirming the consequent,* is a surprisingly common error. The logical structure of the argument is of the form:

If P then Q.

Q

Therefore P.

(In other words, the dodgy argument is saying that since 'Q' really is the case, then 'P' must have caused it.) Another example, 'If there's a serious drought, the leaves will fall off the trees. The leaves *are* falling off the trees, therefore there's a serious drought.' You can seen that such reasoning is dodgy when you remember that leaves can fall off trees for plenty of other reasons — like because it's autumn!

Resorting to Double Standards: Special Pleading

Special pleading (or 'stacking the deck') involves employing values or standards against an opponent's position while not applying them to your own position, and without being able to show a relevant difference to justify the double standard.

For example, a motorist may complain about other people driving too fast while claiming that his or her own ignoring of the speed limits is justified by superior driving skills. You can see the problem when you realise that almost all motorists have a firm belief in their excellent driving skills!

The notion is related to the *principle of relevant differences*, according to which, say, two people can be treated differently if and only if a relevant difference exists between them. For example, an elderly lady can ask the strapping young footballer to let her have the seat beside the door of the bus by arguing that she's frail and he isn't.

Thinking Wishfully

Wishful thinking is about assuming conclusions just because you want them to be so. Despite the obvious problems of relying on reasoning that involves this fallacy, people do so surprisingly often — surprising, that is, when looked at coolly and rationally. A likely explanation is that the subconscious mind finds the tactic a very good way to make its points, turning its desires into assumptions of truth.

People who use wishful thinking often supplement it with emotional states such as aggression or pleading, seeking to batter others into accepting their assertions. Appeals to 'majority opinion' to back up a factual claim is a particular kind of wishful thinking, for example when children tell their parents that 'everyone else' is wearing Nike trainers to school.

Detecting the Whiff of Red Herrings

Red herrings are irrelevant topics or arguments that people bring into a discussion with the effect of allowing the real issue to go unexamined. Apparently, smoked herrings (which are red) were sometimes used to confuse dogs chasing after foxes.

When the BBC ran programmes looking into the reason behind the UK government's unpopular and controversial decision to go to war in Iraq in 2003, the then Prime Minster's press spokesman, Alastair Campbell, was accused of trailing red herrings after he managed to change the focus of the debate into one about the BBC's coverage of the issue. He claimed the coverage showed a disgraceful bias. Many public debates seem to consist of a series of red herrings being dragged round — and often the only outcome is a bit of a stink!

Attacking a Point that Doesn't Exist: Straw-Man Arguments

Straw men are similar in many ways to the red herrings of the preceding section — at least when you're talking about arguments, which I am. They're both kinds of arguments that introduce and attribute a weak or absurd position to an opponent, before swiftly proceeding to demolish it.

Here's one classic example of the straw-man tactic. President Nixon had to respond to criticism that he seemed to have been caught red-handed misappropriating campaign funds for his personal use. Instead of attempting to deny or defend his actions, he started talking about whether or not people thought he should have let his children keep a black and white cocker spaniel dog, which a supporter had sent in a crate all the way from Texas: 'And, you know, the kids, like all kids, loved the dog, and I just want to say this right now, that, regardless of what they say about it, we are going to keep it.'

Nixon is no longer talking about what his opponents asked, but instead about a much weaker charge for which he could expect to win public support and understanding. Indeed, he was elected a little later, by a landslide. Smart fellow, but illogical.

Particularly in terms of writing, the straw-man fallacy often involves misrepresentation of someone else's argument, perhaps by distorting the context, perhaps by crudely paraphrasing the opponent. This kind of tactic is closely connected with the fallacy of *ignoratio elenchi*, or more simply, the fallacy of offering irrelevant conclusions.

Redefining Words: Playing at Humpty Dumpty

This error is named in honour of Lewis Carroll's egg-shaped character who sits on a wall (but at least he's not sitting on the proverbial 'fence'). Humpty insists 'When I use a word . . . it means just what I choose it to mean — neither more nor less.'

Here's a real-life example that involved me as part of the Global Warming debate. I noticed that the London *Guardian* (like other newspapers) kept telling its readers that carbon dioxide was the main greenhouse gas. The implication being that it was essential to get control of it in order to influence the so-called greenhouse effect (which keeps the Earth from icing over, but is now suspected of making it too hot).

Being a stickler for accuracy, I wrote to the *Guardian,* citing about ten articles where the newspaper had said this, along with some sources to show that it was unambiguously accepted in the scientific community that the major greenhouse gas is in fact water vapour. (Water vapour in the atmosphere is responsible for about 80 per cent of the greenhouse effect.) The paper, very responsibly, investigated, found that I was right, but then replied that they'd continue to say that carbon dioxide was the main greenhouse gas it was using the words 'the main greenhouse gas' in a special way which everyone understood and had got used to.

The moral is, of course, that the decision on usage was political.

Chapter 17

Ten Arguments that Changed the World

● ●

In This Chapter

▶ Seeing how the experts argue

▶ Unscrewing the secret formula for influencing people

● ●

*W*ho says arguments don't change anything? Here are some famous arguments that have been seriously influential. These views certainly changed the way human society developed and evolved. Yet, curiously, all the arguments are a bit dodgy. They're not logically sound — and often not very cunning. (If you think arguments have to be logical to be useful, turn to Chapter 4 to see why life's more complicated than that.) The good news is that you don't have to be super-logical or mega-cunning to construct a great argument.

These arguments are great not because they're brilliant and complex, but because they offer simple answers to difficult questions. In fact, you can easily pick holes in many of these arguments, but afterwards enough is left standing to still be thought-provoking.

Naturally, many of the great arguments belong to philosophy, but don't be put off by that. Plato, Marx and the like produced arguments by the bucket-load, yet these philosophers are of a quite different kind from those in academia today. In fact, I'd say that they'd be more likely to write *For Dummies* books than be professors, because of their love of communication!

But this book is about Critical Thinking, and so don't take my word for it. Instead have a look for yourself at this argumentative top ten.

Suggesting That Only a Small Elite Is Clever Enough To Be In Charge

Who made this claim? Plato does, in *The Republic*, written over 2,000 years ago!

The big issue: Plato says that altruism, the virtuous desire to serve other people, is the motivation of all really clever people and so it will be for those he'd choose to form the ruling elite. These are the people that he calls *the Guardians*. (No relation to *Guardian* newspaper readers, or even columnists, of course!)

As for everyone else, Plato thinks that most people couldn't recognise a good thing even if they had it plonked right in front of their noses, and certainly shouldn't be allowed much say over how to run something as complicated as a society. Instead, his prescription for the masses is a diet of propaganda to give them a false, but satisfying, view of their lives.

The flaw: Don't focus on whether this approach is ethical or not. The practical problem isn't so much with the argument but with the starting assumptions — the premises: in other words. The theory is good, the facts cause problems. Although ruling elites can start out finding that the rewards of helping other people are the most satisfying thing, somehow they always end up succumbing to the gravitational pull of greed and self-interest.

As for keeping the masses happy through a diet of crowd-pleasing lies, history shows that people simply can't be kept munching contentedly — they're never quite satisfied and need conflict. Democracy is a way of providing the masses with a safe way to protest and fight each other.

This first argument is still relevant to the way that many modern countries run their affairs. Russia, for example, has a tightly defined ruling elite, who exercise formal and total control of the mass media and education.

Crossing the Line: An Argument for Breaking the Law

Uh oh! That sounds dodgy . . . not suitable for a *For Dummies* book. What's worse, the guy who came up with the argument was spending eight days in a US jail at the time for doing just that. But I press on because his argument is justly famous.

The big issue: Basically the argument is a response to the critics' challenge: 'How can you advocate breaking some laws while urging people to obey others?'

The explanation and the justification for picking and choosing which laws to obey, rests on three, linked claims:

✔ **Two types of laws exist:** *Just* laws and *unjust* laws. That's the least controversial part of the argument.

✔ **People have no obligation to obey unjust laws:** Somewhat trickier, I think you'd agree.

✔ **'From God's perspective, an unjust law is no law at all':** This quote offers some extra support to the controversial second step with an 'appeal to authority'. In this case, the authority is a religious and philosophical one, because Saint Augustine wrote these words long ago.

The flaw: Arguments from authority are always dodgy, except where the authority clearly has the right to set the recommended policy. If, for example, a child is told off for drawing funny faces on the blackboard, she can properly call as support the authority of the school teacher who 'said it would be okay to draw funny faces on the blackboard': the teacher has the appropriate responsibility for loosening the rules. But even Saint Augustine doesn't have the authority to cancel a great swathe of human laws.

The other problem is, of course, that people may have many views about what's just or unjust, and so the advantages of living in a law-governed society soon disappear if this principle was applied generally. This is why people often say that you should obey even an unjust law, but you can use your democratic rights (letters to the newspaper, petitions to your Member of Parliament) to argue for change.

But what may affect your opinion on this issue, however, is that the prisoner in jail for eight days was Martin Luther King, the famous civil rights advocate in the United States in the 1960s. The laws he was challenging were segregationist ones that split things such as buses and schools up into separate ones for white children and black children only.

History offers plenty of instances where essential political reform comes only through the willingness of people to break laws that they feel are unjust. But, although a brilliant speaker, Martin Luther King never produced a logical proof for his views — instead he relied on powerful, rhetorical appeals.

Staying on the Right Side of the Law: An Argument for Always Obeying the Law

In a 17th-century book called *The Leviathan,* the influential English thinker Thomas Hobbes argued that governments can do anything they like to their citizens, because the alternative is anarchy and this would be worse. The book's publication was said to enrage God so much that he arranged the Great Fire of London as a punishment.

The big issue: Hobbes says that people are basically driven by simple desires — notably for power, fame and wealth. Not everyone can be top of the heap, though, and so conflict is inevitable. The only way out of this problem is to make someone *Numero Uno,* Top Dog — and hand that person absolute power.

Hobbes sees the Sovereign (which could be a parliament as well as a monarch) as being all-powerful, but the argument today is more about the rights of citizens versus their governments. Think about the recent US government strategy of kidnapping people off the street and flying them to secret prisons in far-off countries to be tortured. Sounds like bad government, yes? But Hobbes argues that this kind of thing is better than allowing people so many rights that the governments can no longer control things.

In fact, Hobbes says the public must accept anything the rulers say, with the one important exception that they're allowed to resist being killed! He thinks that even allowing the courts to watch over the government is a mistake, because it's a step along a path that leads to anarchy, chaos and the famous nasty, brutish end.

The flaw: Hobbes presents the issue as an 'all or nothing' deal — no middle ground allowed. Yet governments can adapt, survive and even flourish in the face of demands, pressures and challenges. So Hobbes's argument seems to rely on the logical fallacy of black and white thinking, offering a 'false dichotomy' or choice (flip to Chapter 16 for more on false dichotomies — or don't, it's your choice!).

Arguing that Human Misery is Due to a Greedy Elite Exploiting Everyone Else

Karl Marx and Friedrich Engels made this argument in their political tract, the *Communist Manifesto,* which appeared in the middle of the 19th century. At this time, a cruel contrast existed between a few rich factory owners and aristocratic farmers and lots of desperately poor workers.

The big issue: Given their definition of the problem, the conclusion they drew is straightforward: abolish class distinctions and make everyone equal.

The flaw: This argument is kind of the opposite of Plato's vision (see the earlier section 'Suggesting That Only a Small Elite Is Clever Enough To Be In Charge'): getting rid of the ruling elite and giving the masses power. In practice, though, Marxism creates an administrative elite to look after things on behalf of the masses. Unfortunately, as many countries found, even supposedly socialist elites have a habit of being greedy and exploiting everyone else. So, the original divide is back.

Proving That, 'Logically', God Exists

How would you prove that God exists? For some people, a good method is to arrange some miracles, say by getting a lot of people together, instructing 'step forward all the sick or lame folks' and getting God to cure them.

These events are *arguments by demonstration,* with each miracle providing a little bit more evidence for believers. Unfortunately, sceptics insist that every cure that doesn't happen must also be taken into account, and so they remain unconvinced. To persuade sceptics and wannabe believers alike, you'd do better to find a sharp-edged logical proof. Saint Anselm, a medieval monk and logician based in Canterbury, England, came up with this argument, probably the most influential 'pro-God' one of them all.

The big issue: He starts by providing a tight definition of God, such as God is the greatest, most perfect and wonderful thing in the universe. Right? Not because religious folk say he is, but by definition. Then Anselm asks whether it's better to exist in reality or only in people's imaginations. Or put another way, which is better — having a lovely house or having an imaginary lovely house? Obviously, being real is better than being imaginary, and that goes for gods too. Conclusion: because God is the Greatest, he has to exist.

The flaw: Beware arguments that start by offering definitions: often the conclusion is built into the definition. Having said that, to be logically sound, the conclusion *has to be* contained in the starting assumptions. So, let that flaw go?

But a contemporary of Saint Anselm pointed out that people could use this 'proof' to demonstrate the existence of anything, as long as it's defined as the best example of its kind. For example, imagine the most perfect holiday restaurant possible. It's open 24/7, full of celebrities (no rowdies) and serves only veggie food. Well, that's my definition. Will the meals be free? Yes — because that's better still. Does it exist? Perhaps, but surely not because of the logic of my definition.

Proving That, 'in Practice', God Doesn't Exist

Lots of people don't think that a God — or gods — exist, but how do you persuade others? Probably the most influential 'there is no God' argument is the one called 'The Problem of Evil'.

The big issue: 'The Problem of Evil' is a simple but persuasive argument. It says that if an all-powerful, all-knowing God exists who wants the world to be the best possible place, full of happy people and good things (something like you see imagined in TV adverts for wash-powders), God wouldn't allow at least some of the very nasty things that evidently go on all the time.

The flaw: I'm afraid one doesn't exist! This argument seems pretty watertight.

God is required by definition to be all-powerful, all knowing and set on making the universe a good place. However, if evil and suffering exist, then God is either not all-powerful and all-knowing or not totally committed to making the universe a good place. But evil and suffering do exist, and so it follows that this kind of God doesn't.

Actually, many gods in the past have been quite violent and even prone to acts of astonishing cruelty! But these days we don't think those gods ever really existed. Nonetheless, the compassion that is the key characteristic of the Christian god does seem to require that either God is not omnipotent or not quite as loving as the churches tell us. Houston, we have a contradiction!

Perhaps the best response that believers can come up with is to say that God allows things that seem bad to humans to occur in order to achieve greater things. For example, people have to die to make room for new people. But arguments like this put God firmly under the rule of natural laws, which seems odd. Omnipotent-lite.

Defending Human Rights

Do you think that people have certain basic human rights? Well, fine, so do I. But what are they and how would you prove it?

The big issue: In practice, arguments for the 'reality' of certain human rights hinge on legal precedents. This makes sense, because the idea of a 'right' is essentially legal. The US Bill of Rights is one text people often think of when they consider the issues of human rights. It's the name for the first ten amendments to the United States Constitution that attempt to limit the central government's power and guarantee some personal freedoms, such as that unfortunate one about the 'right to carry arms'.

The flaw: Legal rights are all very well, but they only survive because people think that the law is protecting something more fundamental. The law has to fit with public perceptions of what's right and wrong.

Alas, people's views differ so widely that what is a 'human right' in one place can be completely illegal in another, and *vice versa.* Eating your grandparents seems pretty bad to most people today (rather chewy, for a start!), but some historical societies considered it the responsible thing to do. In some countries today, homosexuality is against the law and gays are barred from jobs and can even be executed. In the UK and lots of other places, by contrast, homosexuals are protected from workplace discrimination and can marry and adopt children.

Arguments about ethics are some of the most tricky around. Have a look at the next section to see one nice way, however, to make a simple point.

Making Everything Relative

One of the great sages of Ancient China, Chuang Tzu, produced this great argument for the relativity of 'right' and 'wrong'. 'Chusi' (for short, and pronounced 'Choosey') stressed the unity of all things, and the dynamic interplay of opposites. 'Good' and 'bad', he pointed out, are like everything else, interrelated and interchangeable. What's 'good' for the rabbit is 'bad' for the farmer.

The big issue: Here's how Chusi attempts to show the relativity of moral judgements. Assume as some sages say, that *killing is wrong:* therefore, is it wrong to kill a hare when it's the only way to save yourself from starving? Surely not. Perhaps, though, this only makes killing animals okay. How about people? Suppose first that, yes, killing another human being is always wrong. But what then about a robber intent on killing an innocent family? Surely it's then not wrong to kill him, especially if this is the only way to stop him?

Chusi's point is that all moral knowledge depends in this way on context and situations: it's relative.

The flaw: You can argue that the Chusi makes his own categorical and not-at-all-relative assertions about right and wrong in the process of proving his point. For example, he implies that if the only way to save the innocent family is to kill the robber you can kill the robber. This looks like a pretty categorical and 'universal' moral judgement.

Getting All Relative with Einstein

This argument is one of the most famous 'thought experiments', and maybe doesn't immediately look like an argument. Indeed, people often mischaracterise thought experiments as colourful examples — metaphors or analogies — rather than arguments. But true thought experiments come down to arguments. This one, very influential in its time, illustrates the need to rethink what people (or at least physicists) mean when they say that an event happened at such-and-such time.

The big issue: First suggested by Albert Einstein more than 100 years ago, the experiment concerns the effects of time in the context of travel at near the speed of light. Einstein originally used the example of two clocks — one motionless, one in transit. He stated that, due to the laws of physics, clocks being transported near the speed of light would move more slowly than clocks that remained stationary.

What's true for clocks is true for people too. So now suppose that one twin goes flying off to the nearest star which is four and half light years away (and back again), while the other waists patiently on Earth? It seems that if the twin on the spaceship travels near the speed of light, lets say at 86% of it, while the remaining twin potters around on the Earth, the astronaut twin would have aged ten years, but the earthbound twin would have aged dramatically more — 20 years!

The flaw. Yes, there is a flaw. In fact, a paradox. Because from the point of view of the spaceship, the earthbound twin is the one who could be considered to be in motion — in relation to the sibling — and therefore should be the one aging more slowly! (If you're not happy with that idea — suppose that both twins are astronauts and the experiment starts off with them in two twin spaceships before separating.) Einstein and other scientists have attempted to resolve this problem, but none of the solutions they have come up with are completely satisfactory.

Posing Paradoxes to Prove Your Point

Some of the most influential arguments are in the form of riddles:

- **Zeno's paradoxes of time and motion:** An example is the race between the hare and the tortoise, which leaves the hare unable to ever catch up with the tortoise. Zeno's teasers show up illogicalities in how even the most logical people think.

- **Galileo's paradoxical thought experiments:** See Chapter 5 for more on one of these that ushered in a whole new way of understanding nature.

- **Einstein's deceptively simple stories of paradoxical events:** Perhaps the best-known paradoxes of all, involving things like the time and the speed of light (such as his argument in the preceding section).

But here's a simpler argument that nonetheless is supposed to prove something about the universe: time travel will never be possible. Or, at least, not time travel backwards.

The 30-second argument: Suppose Dr When invents a time machine in 2020. Can he promptly step into it and travel back to the 1920s to shoot the young Hitler, as a way of avoiding much misery for everyone? What matters isn't how likely this ability is but whether the argument is logically impossible.

The flaw: One logical problem is that if Dr When did manage to change history, then how, when he invented his time machine in 2020, would he have known what a menace the young Hitler would be, and that he needed to go back to the 1920s to save the world?

This paradox tends to convince me that time travel like this will never be possible. But if you really want not to be convinced by this argument, you have a perfectly reasonable way out. You can continue to insist on time travel and reject the paradox instead.

Aristotle is supposed long ago to have advised that the best approach to all arguments is to treat them like timepieces. If the time on your watch is near to what you expect, then you should assume that the watch is telling you the right time. However, if it's wildly different, you can assume that it has stopped or is faulty. This policy, like the best arguments, relies not on a logical point but on common sense. But hey . . . you can disagree with me on that!

Index

About the Author

Martin Cohen is a well-established author specialising in popular books in philosophy, social science and politics. He is best known for his two introductions to philosophy, *101 Philosophy Problems* and *101 Ethical Dilemmas*. The books are used precisely to stimulate CT skills — in the case of the *101 Ethical Dilemmas* the book is seen as part of decision-making skills too. They are both texts directly relevant to this book, as they encourage and show their readers how to argue and how to dig down to the structure of issues.

He also published a popular overview of *Political Philosophy*, a radical survey of the world structured as a travel guide, *No Holiday: 80 Places You Don't Want to Visit,* and an 'anti-history' of great philosophers, called *Philosophical Tales*. Martin has also co-founded a wiki-site, www.philosophical-investigations.org, and has contributed to top-ranked internet sites such as the economics blog at *The Guardian*, and environmental ones at the *Daily Telegraph* to mention just a few of the more prominent ones.

His most recent projects include the UK edition of *Philosophy for Dummies* and *Mind Games: 31 days to rediscover your Brain,* which was a featured book on the national arts program of France Culture, where its emphasis on the social context of individual thought was appreciated.

There are only a few UK academics in philosophy who actively promote these kinds of transferable CT skills (most of them are narrow specialists), but Martin is one of them, researcher for a UK national report into how to use philosophy to turn students of all brands and types into Critical Thinkers ready for a wide range of jobs.

Dedication

'To Wod, without whom this book, and much else, would not have been possible'

Author's Acknowledgments

I'd like to thank the team at Wiley for all their support. Taking any book through production is always a challenging process and I really appreciate their help. I'd also like to offer a special thank you to Dr Zenon Stavrinides for his painstaking and informative technical review.

Publisher's Acknowledgments

Acquisitions Editor: Drew Kennerley/
Miles Kendall

Project Editor: Simon Bell

Developer: Andy Finch

Copy Editor: Kate O'Leary

Proofreader: James Harrison

Technical Reviewer:
Dr Zenon Stavrinides

Project Coordinator: Kumar Chellappan

Cover Image: © iStock.com/VLADGRIN

Apple & Mac

iPad For Dummies, 6th Edition
978-1-118-72306-7

iPhone For Dummies, 7th Edition
978-1-118-69083-3

Macs All-in-One For Dummies,
4th Edition
978-1-118-82210-4

OS X Mavericks For Dummies
978-1-118-69188-5

Blogging & Social Media

Facebook For Dummies,
5th Edition
978-1-118-63312-0

Social Media Engagement
For Dummies
978-1-118-53019-1

WordPress For Dummies,
6th Edition
978-1-118-79161-5

Business

Stock Investing For Dummies,
4th Edition
978-1-118-37678-2

Investing For Dummies,
6th Edition
978-0-470-90545-6

Personal Finance For Dummies,
7th Edition
978-1-118-11785-9

QuickBooks 2014 For Dummies
978-1-118-72005-9

Small Business Marketing Kit
For Dummies, 3rd Edition
978-1-118-31183-7

Careers

Job Interviews For Dummies,
4th Edition
978-1-118-11290-8

Job Searching with Social Media
For Dummies, 2nd Edition
978-1-118-67856-5

Personal Branding For Dummies
978-1-118-11792-7

Resumes For Dummies,
6th Edition
978-0-470-87361-8

Starting an Etsy Business
For Dummies, 2nd Edition
978-1-118-59024-9

Diet & Nutrition

Belly Fat Diet For Dummies
978-1-118-34585-6

Mediterranean Diet For Dummies
978-1-118-71525-3

Nutrition For Dummies,
5th Edition
978-0-470-93231-5

Digital Photography

Digital SLR Photography
All-in-One For Dummies,
2nd Edition
978-1-118-59082-9

Digital SLR Video & Filmmaking
For Dummies
978-1-118-36598-4

Photoshop Elements 12
For Dummies
978-1-118-72714-0

Gardening

Herb Gardening For Dummies,
2nd Edition
978-0-470-61778-6

Gardening with Free-Range
Chickens For Dummies
978-1-118-54754-0

Health

Boosting Your Immunity
For Dummies
978-1-118-40200-9

Diabetes For Dummies,
4th Edition
978-1-118-29447-5

Living Paleo For Dummies
978-1-118-29405-5

Big Data

Big Data For Dummies
978-1-118-50422-2

Data Visualization For Dummies
978-1-118-50289-1

Hadoop For Dummies
978-1-118-60755-8

Language & Foreign Language

500 Spanish Verbs For Dummies
978-1-118-02382-2

English Grammar For Dummies,
2nd Edition
978-0-470-54664-2

French All-in-One For Dummies
978-1-118-22815-9

German Essentials For Dummies
978-1-118-18422-6

Italian For Dummies, 2nd Edition
978-1-118-00465-4

 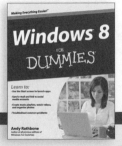  

Available in print and e-book formats.

Available wherever books are sold.

For more information or to order direct visit www.dummies.com

Math & Science

Algebra I For Dummies,
2nd Edition
978-0-470-55964-2

Anatomy and Physiology
For Dummies, 2nd Edition
978-0-470-92326-9

Astronomy For Dummies,
3rd Edition
978-1-118-37697-3

Biology For Dummies,
2nd Edition
978-0-470-59875-7

Chemistry For Dummies,
2nd Edition
978-1-118-00730-3

1001 Algebra II Practice
Problems For Dummies
978-1-118-44662-1

Microsoft Office

Excel 2013 For Dummies
978-1-118-51012-4

Office 2013 All-in-One
For Dummies
978-1-118-51636-2

PowerPoint 2013 For Dummies
978-1-118-50253-2

Word 2013 For Dummies
978-1-118-49123-2

Music

Blues Harmonica For Dummies
978-1-118-25269-7

Guitar For Dummies, 3rd Edition
978-1-118-11554-1

iPod & iTunes For Dummies,
10th Edition
978-1-118-50864-0

Programming

Beginning Programming with C
For Dummies
978-1-118-73763-7

Excel VBA Programming
For Dummies, 3rd Edition
978-1-118-49037-2

Java For Dummies, 6th Edition
978-1-118-40780-6

Religion & Inspiration

The Bible For Dummies
978-0-7645-5296-0

Buddhism For Dummies,
2nd Edition
978-1-118-02379-2

Catholicism For Dummies,
2nd Edition
978-1-118-07778-8

Self-Help & Relationships

Beating Sugar Addiction
For Dummies
978-1-118-54645-1

Meditation For Dummies,
3rd Edition
978-1-118-29144-3

Seniors

Laptops For Seniors
For Dummies, 3rd Edition
978-1-118-71105-7

Computers For Seniors
For Dummies, 3rd Edition
978-1-118-11553-4

iPad For Seniors For Dummies,
6th Edition
978-1-118-72826-0

Social Security For Dummies
978-1-118-20573-0

Smartphones & Tablets

Android Phones For Dummies,
2nd Edition
978-1-118-72030-1

Nexus Tablets For Dummies
978-1-118-77243-0

Samsung Galaxy S 4
For Dummies
978-1-118-64222-1

Samsung Galaxy Tabs
For Dummies
978-1-118-77294-2

Test Prep

ACT For Dummies, 5th Edition
978-1-118-01259-8

ASVAB For Dummies, 3rd Edition
978-0-470-63760-9

GRE For Dummies, 7th Edition
978-0-470-88921-3

Officer Candidate Tests
For Dummies
978-0-470-59876-4

Physician's Assistant Exam
For Dummies
978-1-118-11556-5

Series 7 Exam For Dummies
978-0-470-09932-2

Windows 8

Windows 8.1 All-in-One
For Dummies
978-1-118-82087-2

Windows 8.1 For Dummies
978-1-118-82121-3

Windows 8.1 For Dummies, Book
+ DVD Bundle
978-1-118-82107-7

Available in print and e-book formats.

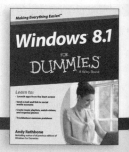

Available wherever books are sold.

For more information or to order direct visit www.dummies.com

Take Dummies with you everywhere you go!

Whether you are excited about e-books, want more from the web, must have your mobile apps, or are swept up in social media, Dummies makes everything easier.

Leverage the Power

For Dummies is the global leader in the reference category and one of the most trusted and highly regarded brands in the world. No longer just focused on books, customers now have access to the For Dummies content they need in the format they want. Let us help you develop a solution that will fit your brand and help you connect with your customers.

Advertising & Sponsorships

Connect with an engaged audience on a powerful multimedia site, and position your message alongside expert how-to content.

Targeted ads • Video • Email marketing • Microsites • Sweepstakes sponsorship

LOVE IS LETTING
GO OF FEAR

Other books by Gerald G. Jampolsky, MD
Teach Only Love: The Twelve Principles of Attitudinal Healing
Good-Bye to Guilt: Releasing Fear Through Forgiveness
Out of Darkness into Light: A Journey of Inner Healing
Shortcuts to God: Finding Peace Through Practical Spirituality
Forgiveness: The Greatest Healer of All
The "Oh Shit" Factor: Waste Management for Our Minds

Books co-authored with Diane Cirincione, PhD
A Mini Course for Life
Finding Our Way Home
*Change Your Mind, Change Your Life: Concepts
    in Attitudinal Healing*
Love Is the Answer: Creating Positive Relationships
Wake Up Calls
Simple Thoughts That Can Change Your Life
*Me First and the Gimme Gimmes: A Story of Love and
    Forgiveness, Choices and Changes*

Books edited with children
There Is a Rainbow Behind Every Dark Cloud
Another Look at the Rainbow
Advice to Doctors and Other Big People from Kids
Children as Teachers of Peace

LOVE
IS LETTING
GO OF FEAR

Third Edition

GERALD G. JAMPOLSKY, MD

FOREWORD BY CARLOS SANTANA

ILLUSTRATED BY JACK KEELER

CELESTIAL ARTS
Berkeley

Library of Congress Cataloging-in-Publication Data
Jampolsky, Gerald G., 1925-
    Love is letting go of fear / Gerald G. Jampolsky ; foreword by Carlos
Santana ; illustrated by Jack Keeler. — 3rd ed.
        p. cm.
    1. Love. 2. Fear. I. Title.
    BF575.L8J33 2010
    158—dc22

                                                        2010029480

ISBN 978-1-58761-118-6

Third edition

Printed in the United States

Design by Colleen Cain

10 9

To the children of the universe
Who by the essence
of their being, Love,
Bring light into a darkened world.

This book is dedicated to Helen and Bill, who have been both teachers and friends. It was because of their joint willingness that *A Course in Miracles* came into being, a work that provides the foundation for this book.

—G.G.J.

CONTENTS

ACKNOWLEDGMENTS

I would like to express my deep and loving gratitude to Dr. William Thetford for his continued support and encouragement, and the many hours he contributed to modifying and adding content to this book.

In addition, I wish to give my warm, heartfelt thanks to Jules Finegold, Hugh Prather, Mary Abney, and Diane Cirincione, PhD.

The twelve lesson titles in this book are quotations from *A Course in Miracles.**

* *A Course in Miracles*, published by the Foundation for Inner Peace, P.O. Box 598, Mill Valley, CA 94942-0598.

PREFACE 2011

When I was fifty-four years old, I embarked on a miraculous journey that began with the publication of my first book, *Love Is Letting Go of Fear*. In fact, in many respects, it was a miracle the book was ever written at all. Dyslexic since childhood, I entered the University of California at Berkeley in 1943 knowing that a "dumbbell" English course was in my future. I struggled through it and received a D, and on the final day of class my professor said to me, "Jampolsky, I don't know what you're going to do in life, but for God's sake, don't ever try to write a book."

I was fifty years old before I decided to no longer give my power away to other people's judgments about my limitations and do what I had been told was impossible—and write a book. I am still in awe that this little book has sold millions of copies and been translated into dozens of languages. Miraculous? Absolutely! What's more, at age eighty-five, the journey and the miracles continue for me.

Since 1979, the book has grown wings of love that have taken it to just the right people at precisely the right time in their lives. It seems as though the angels have been hovering from above, guiding it to those in need of its simple message. Over the years, I have been fortunate enough to hear from readers who have opened their hearts and changed their lives. Their stories are, to me, miraculous, and I would like to share a few with you that have come my way.

The first edition of *Love Is Letting Go of Fear* had been out for several months and was selling steadily, but modestly, when I received a telegram from a person I had never met. His name was Orson Bean, a talented actor and television personality. The telegram simply said, "Watch Johnny Carson tonight." Although I rarely stay up late, I did that night. At one point during the interview, Mr. Bean pulled a copy of the book from his pocket saying that it had changed his life. From the next day onward, *Love Is Letting Go of Fear* began its climb up the bestseller list.

Since then, whenever people ask me who my public relations person is, I always answer, "God."

A number of years ago at an event hosted by the Center for Attitudinal Healing, I was approached by a woman who shared the following story. Many years earlier, my son Lee and her son had been close friends in high school. Lee threw a party one night at my office when I was out of town. There was music and alcohol, and the party got a little wild. At one point, her son became a little unsteady on his feet and crashed into some bookshelves, whereupon a book toppled from the shelf and hit him in the head. The book was *Love Is Letting Go of Fear*. He was attracted to the illustrations and decided to take it home.

When his mother found the book in his room a month or so later, she decided to read it. At that time she was going through some major life challenges, and she said the book changed her life and she wanted to thank me for writing it all these years later.

A book will come to a person when he or she is ready for its message, and often it will come in an amazing way. The truth also comes to people—ready or not—in some pretty amazing ways. I decided to phone my son Lee just to remind him that the truth will always come out eventually, even if it's years and years after the fact!

It has also been gratifying to learn that *Love*'s influence has traveled the globe.

When teaching in Iran several years ago, we were surprised and delighted to learn that *Love Is Letting Go of Fear* and five of our other books had been translated and published in Farsi and were circulating throughout the country. Although these were clearly bootlegged editions, we decided not to make an issue of that fact. It is more important to us that *Love*'s message reaches those who need it.

Following a lecture at the University of Tehran, an Iranian professor shared his personal story with us. He and his wife had had a most difficult marriage, marred by constant arguing. At wit's end, he was seriously considering divorce. Although he loved his wife deeply, he yearned for a more peaceful existence and simply couldn't envision a calm relationship with her. One day while browsing in a bookstore, he came across a pirated copy of *Love Is Letting Go of Fear*. As he spoke to us, he spread his arms wide and, smiling, said that simply reading the book was the first step toward saving his marriage.

Diane and I made many trips to Russia when it was still the former Soviet Union. During one of our visits to Moscow, as was typical at that time, we were assigned a translator and a guide from the Soviet Tourist Bureau. What we didn't know then was that they actually were KGB agents!

We brought with us a number of Russian language editions of both *Love Is Letting Go of Fear* and *A Mini Course for Life*. Each day our translator asked us for a few copies, which we gladly turned over to her. As the days passed, she asked for more and more copies. Our supply was starting to run low, so we finally asked her where all the books were going. She explained they were being used to teach English to other translators (agents) because the concepts were so new and interesting to them.

Needless to say, we were delighted that the study of English was being supplemented by the study of practical spiritual principles that emphasized love and forgiveness.

Love Is Letting Go of Fear has found its way into the hands of people of all ages and from all walks of life.

Following a talk in Florida recently, a ten-year-old girl spoke with us. Her parents' decision to divorce had been deeply upsetting and very confusing. Looking for someone to blame, she wasn't sure which parent to be angry with so she decided to be angry with them both. One afternoon at a friend's house, she saw a copy of *Love Is Letting Go of Fear* and borrowed it. The book's message brought her peace of mind even though her parents continued to threaten each other with divorce.

Eventually, she gave the book to her parents to read in the hope it would help them heal their relationship. She then introduced her mother and father who were standing nearby, still married, and who enthusiastically validated their daughter's story.

An inmate in Arizona wrote me an angry letter claiming that *Love Is Letting Go of Fear* was the worst book he had ever read. He went on to say that if I were in solitary confinement and had been beaten by guards, I would never be able to forgive. He ended his letter with the accusation that I must be some flaky shrink from California who couldn't possibly know what real life was all about. I responded, not with self-righteous indignation, but with an open-minded, nondefensive letter. And so began a lively and mutually rewarding correspondence.

While on a lecture tour in Arizona, I arranged to visit him in prison. During our meeting he told me that after rereading the book, he realized it wasn't prison that kept him in bondage, it was the fear he carried in his own mind that was keeping him incarcerated. Some time later, following his release, he began the process of forgiving the significant people in his life. This enabled him to launch a vocation of working with people who had been incarcerated and who were facing death from terminal illness.

After a recent lecture on Maui, a woman came up to us in tears. She explained that in 1980 her husband had had an affair. Her anger had been like molten lava, and she had bought a gun with the intention of shooting him—a plan that would have irrevocably changed her life. The same day, a friend gave her a copy of *Love Is Letting Go of Fear*. Despite her pain, she read the book and abandoned her dangerous impulse—and altered the course of her life in a positive direction.

A man attending a workshop conducted by the Center for Attitudinal Healing shared the following story. As an adult, he made the upsetting discovery that his father had been a member of the Nazi party and served in the SS during World War II. Reading *Love Is Letting Go of Fear* had helped him take the necessary steps to get past the shame and anguish and forgive his father for being an active participant during such a cruel period of history. As a result, he decided to make a radical change and gave up his business for a very different kind of vocation. Of all things, he became a clown, explaining that the best way he could think of to heal the world was by making his life's work about bringing other people joy and laughter.

He described his costume to me, including a huge pair of extra-long shoes. When I asked him why the extra-long shoes, his immediate reply was, "So my father can walk along with me in my shoes as we heal the world together."

❧❦❧

In 2009 alone, this book and its mighty wings landed in Mongolia, Cameroon, Nigeria, Mali, Romania, and so many other places. A woman in Mongolia went through the experience of her deeply loved brother committing suicide. It was a devastating experience that left her deeply depressed. She wrote that after reading *Love Is Letting Go of Fear* she found the tools to heal herself, and her life changed. Since then, she has started the Center for Attitudinal Healing—Mongolia and wants to devote her life to helping others as a way to continue to heal herself.

A man in Cameroon, Central Africa, wrote that he had developed three businesses and was quite successful. He had a wife and two children. He became addicted to drugs, and his wife and children left him and his businesses collapsed. In his words, he became a derelict. One Sunday while taking a walk on an out of the way country road, he came across an old man selling used books from a small cart. He saw the title *Love Is Letting Go of Fear,* and with the very last few coins he had, he purchased the book. It became like a bible to him, and he proceeded to read it more than a dozen times. He stopped using drugs, and his wife and children returned to him. He went on to start a health clinic for her and a new business for himself. He said he was so transformed by the concepts and experience of the book that he has started Attitudinal Healing Support Groups and is now in the process of starting a Center for Attitudinal Healing in Cameroon.

The former ambassador to Mexico from Nigeria visited the Cecura in Mexico City, the first Center for Attitudinal Healing in Mexico (to date, more than twenty Mexican cities have centers or groups). There she located this book and found it began to nourish her spiritually. As an elder stateswoman in her country known for her work in anticorruption, she became convinced that the concepts in the Principles of Attitudinal Healing were a viable way for an "attitudinal shift" in her country. She went on television and spoke about this, generating a huge response nationwide and encouragement to go further. She has since incorporated the Center for Attitudinal Healing—Nigeria, and the work continues to grow.

Love Is Letting Go of Fear was written not only for you, but also for me. I still do my best to apply its practical principles to my own life. I find them even more timely, valid, and helpful today than I did thirty-two years ago. The lessons in *Love Is Letting Go of Fear* are grounded on the very same principles from which Attitudinal Healing has evolved.

It was in 1975 that I helped found the first Center for Attitudinal Healing located in Marin County, California. In 1981, Diane Cirincione, PhD, came into my life, and we later married. Diane has been both an angelic partner and a teacher of love, peace, patience, gentleness, and forgiveness. After thirty years, the principles in *Love Is Letting Go of Fear* are still indispensable to us as a couple and as individuals. We continue to nurture a relationship of equality and unconditional love. Attitudinal Healing has become our life work together and has given us the opportunity to meet and speak with people in more than fifty countries throughout the world.

Attitudinal Healing is based on the principle that it is not other people or situations that ultimately cause us to be upset. Rather, it is our own thoughts and attitudes about those things that are responsible for our distress, and the actions we take as a result of those thoughts and attitudes that can hurt us. Healing results when we concentrate on changing our own attitudes rather than trying to change the attitude of others. Thus, the goal of Attitudinal Healing is self-healing in the face of each life challenge, regardless of the source. Attitudinal Healing is not a religion or religious. It is a practical spirituality that supports and is compatible with all faiths and belief systems. People from many cultures, faiths, and denominations, as well as those who follow no faith at all, are welcome to use the principles of Attitudinal Healing.

The first Center for Attitudinal Healing, founded in Marin County, Northern California, began with support services for children with catastrophic illness and their families. All direct services are free of charge. Over the decades, the Centers have grown and developed support groups for children and adults facing illness, loss, and grief, as well as school programs focused on violence prevention through peer support and award-winning home and hospital visitation programs. Support groups for men and women continue, as do groups for bereavement and spousal and caregiver support during challenges, crisis, and change. Workshops for businesses that wish to apply the Principles of Attitudinal Healing in the professional environment are also being offered.

At the core of these principles is forgiveness. Forgiveness does not mean condoning or agreeing with a horrendous act. It is a decision to no longer attack one's self. Forgiveness is, quite simply, the decision not to suffer. To forgive is to make the decision to be happy, to let go of judgments, to stop hurting others and ourselves, and to stop recycling anger and fear. Forgiveness is the bridge to compassion, to inner peace, and to a peaceful world. It is my hope that forgiveness becomes as important, as involuntary to us, as breathing.

To my utter amazement Attitudinal Healing is now worldwide, in hundreds of locations consisting of centers and support groups in thirty countries on five continents. *Love Is Letting Go of Fear* has served, and still serves, as the cornerstone of our work.

It is our hope that this little book will continue to find its readers, one at a time, when the time is just right. It is our prayer that as we heal our own minds of fear and negativity, the world we see will be healed along with us.

Jerry Jampolsky
Sausalito, California
January 1, 2011

AUTHOR'S NOTE

We teach what we want to learn, and I want to learn to experience inner peace.

In 1975, the outside world saw me as a successful psychiatrist who appeared to have everything he wanted. But my inner world was chaotic, empty, unhappy, and hypocritical. My twenty-year marriage had recently ended in a painful divorce. I had become a heavy drinker and had developed chronic, disabling back pain as a means of handling guilt.

It was at this time that I came across some writings entitled *A Course in Miracles*. The *Course* could be described as a form of spiritual psychotherapy that is self-taught. I was perhaps more surprised than anyone when I became involved in a thought system that uses words like *God* and *Love*. I had thought that I would be the last person interested in such writings. I had been extremely judgmental toward people who pursued a spiritual pathway; I saw them as fearful, and I believed they were not using their intellect properly.

When I first began studying the *Course*, I had an experience that was surprising but also very comforting. I heard an inner voice, or possibly it would be more accurate to say an impression of a voice, which said to me, "Physician, heal thyself; this is your way home."

I found the *Course* essential in my struggle for personal transformation. It helped me recognize that I really did have a choice of experiencing peace or conflict, and that this choice is always between accepting truth or illusion. The underlying truth for all of us is that the essence of our being is Love.

The *Course* states that there are only two emotions: love and fear. The first is our natural inheritance, and the other our mind manufactures. The *Course* suggests that we can learn to let go of fear by practicing forgiveness and seeing everyone, including ourselves, as blameless and guiltless. By applying the concepts of the *Course* to both my professional and personal life, I began to experience periods of peace that I had never dreamed possible.

I would like to add that I still get depressed and at times feel guilty, irritable, and angry. These moods now last for only brief periods, whereas they used to last for what seemed eternity. I used to feel that I was a victim of the world I saw. When things would go wrong, I would blame the world or those in it for my misery and feel justified in my anger. Today, I know I am *not* a victim of the world I see, and therefore tend to take responsibility for whatever I perceive and for the emotions I experience.

We are all teachers of each other. I have written this book because I believe that in teaching what I want to learn, inner peace, I can become more consistent in achieving it for myself. This approach is not for people who want gurus, since it views everyone equally as both a teacher and a student.

As each of us moves toward the single goal of achieving peace of mind for ourselves, we can also experience the joining of our minds that follows the removal of the blocks to our awareness of Love's presence.

Together, therefore, let us demonstrate in our own lives this statement from *A Course in Miracles*:

Teach only Love for that is what you are.

Jerry Jampolsky
Tiburon, California
May 1, 1979

Love is the way I walk in gratitude.

FOREWORD

Love Is Letting Go of Fear is the sweetest, gentlest healing
melody to my heart. Its principles have had a profound
effect on me. It has influenced how I see and hold myself,
how I conduct my relationships with others, and how I
look at the world. It has helped me find a sense of inner
peace, joy, and happiness beyond what I had ever experienced before—or ever thought possible.

This amazing book for personal growth has been
helping millions of people around the world since it was
first published in 1979. After thirty years and even more
than before, it offers a timely tonic in these complex and
often troubling times. I love the straightforward practical-
ity of the lessons and the thought-provoking illustrations
that make the book cross-culturally appealing and so
reader-friendly for, literally, all ages. Jerry's writings have
a heartfelt honesty, simplicity, and integrity about them,
just like him, which really works for me when dealing with
complicated issues in everyday life.

The inclusion in this new edition of how people can
deal differently with financial insecurity and the fear that
comes with it is always timely. Especially useful are Jerry's
thoughts on how applying Attitudinal Healing principles

can help get us out of a state of victimhood, no matter what has happened to us. Living these principles has proven to me that I can choose to be in a state of inner peace and outer harmony even when there is chaos going on all around me. This revelation was life-changing for me as it will be to many readers, regardless of their politics, culture, or faith.

Whether it is my music, my band, my family life, my audience, or my business—when all's said and done, it is my relationships and how I handle them have become the top priorities in my life along with my spiritual growth. Seeing the value of releasing guilt and grievances about myself and others has opened up new vistas for me. I love quoting Bishop Desmond Tutu, who said, "There can be no future without forgiveness." I have been fortunate to know Jerry and his partner and spouse, Dr. Diane Cirincione, for a number of years, and it has been inspiring for me to witness how diligent they are in practicing these principles in their own lives.

It is my hope that this treasure of a book will empower people to heal all of their relationships, to motivate themselves and inspire others to make a difference, and to bring love and light into a world that is suffering in darkness. So if you wish to find a way of removing all the barriers that block you from experiencing love; if you wish to learn how to create a future that is different from the past; if you wish to learn to take responsibility for your own happiness and have a lasting sense of inner peace, then read on.

Peace.
Carlos Santana

INTRODUCTION

Love Is Letting Go of Fear has had an amazing journey since its first edition was printed in 1979. No one could be more surprised than I at the journey this book has taken. It has sold millions of copies, has been published in dozens of languages, and continues to be a classic after all these many years. This book is about inner healing and spiritual transformation. In many ways, I wrote this book for myself. Being dyslexic and a slow reader, I like books that are reader-friendly, have larger print than usual, and have cartoons to help make the writing easier to understand.

The core principles are about having a willingness to see the world differently; seeing value in letting go of our control issues, judgments, and grievances; and making forgiveness as important as breathing. The principles in this book apply to every aspect of our lives, including our relationships with other people and with objects such as money and material things.

In celebrating the third edition of this book some thirty-plus years after its first edition was published, it seemed like it would be helpful to take a look back. I wanted to contrast my impressions about what I was like during those first fifty years with my reflections about the second part of my life after I began to incorporate the lessons in this book.

The first part of my life I thought of myself as not being good enough and not being very smart when it came to academics as I usually was in the bottom of my class. I was an undiagnosed dyslexic, a very fearful kid who grew up to be a fearful adult. I was shy, judgmental of myself as well as others, always wondering when the next brick was going to come down from the sky and hit me on the head. My fear made me overly controlling and at the same time fearful of intimacy. On the one hand I always had a mission of wanting to help other people, and on the other hand I wanted to make a lot of money.

Although the world saw me as successful, I was not a very happy camper and my inner life was miserable. I married when I was twenty-nine years old, had two sons, and had a marriage that looked great from the outside but was very challenging from the inside. What was important to me was financial security, how much money I had in the bank, and the kind of house and neighborhood I lived in. What other people thought of me seemed terribly important. I was a fault finder to others, but also to myself. Emotionally, I was on a treadmill machine going at high speed, and I was not capable of slowing the machine or stopping it to get off. My ego seemed to have me in a stranglehold.

No matter how much money I made, it was never enough. We seemed to be always spending more than we were making. At one point I bought a green Austin Healey and had a green hat that went with it. I was sure it would bring me lasting happiness. And of course, that did not happen. I projected my unhappiness onto my wife, and a twenty-year marriage ended in a painful divorce. I soon turned to alcohol to hide my pain.

I denied I was an alcoholic even after I was stopped by the police for driving under the influence of alcohol. Most of my friends were either heavy drinkers or alcoholics who denied they had an alcohol problem. During this time I was an atheist, and in my judgmental way I thought that people who were religious or spiritual were this way because they were fearful. I remember being proud of my atheistic stand and how I viewed life.

I do remember brief times of happiness. But most of what I remember of those days was a life where I had little if any inner peace. A lingering feeling kept bobbing up that I didn't deserve to be happy.

I was fifty years old when I consciously started my spiritual journey. Before that I had no idea how hard I could be on myself or others. The word forgiveness had little meaning. However, I began slowly but surely to see the beneficial effects of being willing to forgive others—and, especially, myself.

By practicing the lessons in *A Course in Miracles* and *Love Is Letting Go of Fear*, I began to experience a sense of inner peace that I never had before, and I had never thought was possible. I began to sense, then believe in, what I call "inner knowing" and that there is a Higher Power that could, if I were willing, direct my life into a consciousness of love, giving and helping others. My focus on money and material things began to disappear. I was totally absorbed in helping as I started the first Center for

Attitudinal Healing. I began to experience how everyone I met, or even thought about, was my teacher. Finally, I discovered I could make inner peace as my only goal, and forgiveness as my only function. I learned to listen to an inner voice of love directing what I thought, said, and did.

As I have advanced in chronological years, I have become more mellow and realize that I don't know what is best for others but that each of us has an inner teacher that can show us the way. If I find myself in stress, I am more aware now that I have some more forgiving to do. As I have let go of some of the blocks I have put in the way of my experiencing love, I am more compassionate and focused on living in this present moment than doing what I used to do by getting caught in worrying about the fearful future and the fearful past.

❧✦❧

In general I am more of a happy camper. I am not trying to change other people or their attitudes. I do my best to be a vehicle of love with everyone and not withhold or exclude my love from anyone, including myself. I laugh a lot more as I keep the six-year-old kid inside me—active, alive, curious, and playful. I don't take myself so seriously. I am more careful about what I eat, and I exercise regularly and go to the gym several times a week.

Working with families with children who are facing death has shown me that there is another way of looking at living and dying and life and death. They have also taught me the value of living one day at a time and the great importance of discovering that it is always possible to have gratitude in one's life. They have taught me that it is possible to experience peace of mind even when chaos is going on all around me or in my body.

The people who I spend most of my time with are no longer alcoholics. They are like-minded and like-hearted people who are also on a spiritual pathway and who believe that nothing is impossible. They also, like myself, tend to believe that it is possible to retrain our minds to believe that there are only two emotions—love or fear—and to see our fear as a call of help for love.

The year 1981 was another turning point in my life when Diane Cirincione showed up. I believe the angels were working overtime that day when I discovered my soul mate. I don't think that was an accident or would have happened if I had not been able to let go of the shame and guilt I had been harboring in my own jail cell, resulting in my lack of self-love. Diane became an amazing partner and teacher for me of unconditional love, patience, gentleness, kindness, and forgiveness. Our joint goal became to demonstrate and teach only love. It has been a miraculous journey where our Higher Power, our Source, God, or whatever word you might wish to call it has become the most important thing in our relationship.

As far as how I look at my aging process is concerned, I now believe it is more important to count your smile wrinkles than your aging wrinkles. I think that age is but an abstract number, and that my mind knows no limitations. In the first part of my life I was fearful of aging and of death, but now I no longer have these fears.

I feel the age I am now is the best one yet and the best is yet to come.

And in those first fifty years I believed there was a pot of gold at the end of the rainbow, and it was my goal to find that pot of gold. Now I realize that we are the rainbow, the pot of gold is love, and that is what we actually are.

❦❦❦

Am I always in a blissful spiritual space? Of course not. I am a work in process and believe I will be a work in process as long as I remain in this body. Every day there are challenges around judgments of others and myself. I have periods of impatience and irritation and not feeling at peace with myself. What is different now is that these periods are much shorter in duration, when I choose to remember, as constantly as I can, that it is only my own thoughts and attitudes that can hurt me.

As I look at the world and what has happened to it since this book was first published, there has been amazing progress made in the field of medicine and in the treatment of diseases and traumas, and in the scientifically established relationship between the body and the mind. There has been awesome progress in so many different areas of technology. The first edition of this book I wrote in longhand on a yellow pad. The advancement of computers, the ability to communicate information instantaneously any place in the world on the Internet, and the advent of social networks . . . and on and on . . . all these have changed the world.

There are many people and philanthropic organizations, businesses, and individuals who are doing important work to help the disadvantaged in the world. But at the same time, again through my eyes, fear continues to play a major role in why we are not more loving, compassionate, kind, gentle, and understanding with each other and ourselves.

We continue to have major problems in getting along and living in harmony with our families, with our communities, with our country and other countries, and with our planet. There are millions of children and adults who are starving and others who are living below the poverty line, who do not have enough food to eat or proper health care.

Addiction problems are on the increase as are physical and sexual abuse. The rate of suicide is increasing in the armed services as it is in several countries. More jails are being built. Our educational system is in dire need of help, even as our military budget continues to go sky high. There are fears and concerns among many about the economic toll and political and spiritual impacts that wars throughout the world have been taking. There are fears about the possibility of nuclear war, fears about global warming, and whether or not these problems can really be solved. There are fears about drug wars, culture wars, religious wars, and wars over natural resources, and how they affect the world.

But perhaps the fears at the top of the list for many people are about financial instability and of terrorism. Because I am on a spiritual pathway does not mean there have not been those moments when I have had my own fears around money or the harm that could come to me through terrorist activity.

It is my impression that my attitudes and thoughts have a direct effect on how I and others deal with safety, money, and material possessions. There is certainly nothing wrong with money. What gets us into trouble is our attachment to money, which can lead to our making it have more value to us than our relationships. At the end of our lives when we reflect back on what has been most important to us, most people will agree that it has been loving relationships, not how much money we had in the bank.

In recent times, as in many other times in history, there has been a cyclic phenomenon where there is a tremendous focus on money and material things, on not having enough. People's worst fears seem to have come true, in that so many have lost their jobs, their homes, and even their retirement savings that they had planned for and worked so hard to achieve.

The financial crisis has had serious consequences around the world. People got angry, blaming everyone and everything they could think of. It has been all too easy to fall into the deep hole of victimhood. Many found it impossible to experience any sense of peace when the force of these economic failures entered their lives. When the traumatic events of life happen, some never recover and people continue to feel bitter, angry, and unhappy the rest of their lives. They continue to scratch their injuries so continuously that their wounds never heal.

Others seem able to experience their fearful and bitter emotions but not get stuck in them, to forgive the past, and choose to make their loving relationships more important than money and material things. These people refuse to live in the past; they choose not to worry. They see worry as a waste of time because, in actuality, worrying doesn't work! Against the majority of current world belief, they refuse to believe that the fearful past is going to predict a fearful future. They refuse to allow themselves to be pessimists and choose instead to live with an optimistic attitude. They seem to know they can choose to be peaceful internally no matter what is happening in the external world.

Fear can be known as the most virulent and damaging virus known to humankind. Most of the world's belief system of how we communicate with each other and ourselves is based on fear. Let's explore just a few of the beliefs of the world's ego thought system as it is related to money and material things.

Our ego's laws are based on the belief that our happiness depends on how much money we have in the bank and how many possessions we own. Its voice of fear bombards us with an attitude of greed, thinking of ourselves first, and getting as much as we can and holding on to it. The fear that is the nucleus of our egos gives us an insatiable desire and hunger to consume more, more and an unending consumption of more. Our ego's cardinal rule is that nothing is ever enough: "Seek but never find what you are looking for. Build your life with the fear of scarcity every step of the way."

For example, our egos can deceive us into believing if we just could have one million dollars in the bank, we would have peace of mind for the rest of our lives, and we would feel secure. Our fearful ego mind, the king of deception, would then come in with the thought that one million dollars is not enough to give me peace of mind and happiness; what I really need is two million dollars to feel consistently happy and peaceful. Our egos would not want us to believe that love, peace, and happiness are the enemy.

So what generally happens when we follow the belief in the world's fear-based laws around attitudes when there is financial insecurity and we have lost our jobs, our homes, and our retirement savings that were going to make for a safe and secure future?

Our egos motivate us to believe that we will feel more peaceful and happy if we find someone to blame and direct our anger at that person. So we develop an attitude that our egos call "healthy," which is to have a raging anger at bankers, mortgage loan officers, and politicians; we make up an "enemy list" in our minds. And when our "justified anger" does not seem to be enough, we add on to the list our anger at the world, God, and finally ourselves. The trouble is, we soon discover that it is just about impossible to experience peace of mind and justified anger at the same time.

When we get caught in the ego's thought system, our beliefs are created from the fear that the past is going to predict the future and the future is going to be just like the past. I have witnessed some people who, when financial insecurity comes their way, continue to feed on their anger and bitterness and lack of trust the rest of their lives. They seem to go around and around in circles, with peace, intimacy, and love escaping them. They do not still their minds and find new creative solutions for the problems they face. They superimpose the past onto the present and future and thus continue to re-create what they least want to experience.

There are others I have known who have faced their human feelings without getting stuck in them and have forgiven the world and themselves. They spend their lives in a giving and helping attitude. The attitude they carry with them is an optimistic one, believing that when one door closes, another door will open. They are on the lookout for ways they can help others even during bad times, and they are not afraid to reposition themselves. They remind themselves with gratitude that the love they have and give to others is the greatest treasure they could have, and it's a treasure that no one can ever take away from them.

Some years ago, Diane and I were guest lecturers on a conference titled, The Power Healing Power of Laughter and Play in Boston, Massachusetts. We were surprised to be met at the airport by two clowns. I started a conversation with the clown next to me and asked him his story about how he became a clown. His story was amazing.

He was a sixty-three-year-old businessman who had been quite successful. In 1987 he lost almost everything he had in the economic downturn. He stated that he became depressed and angry at himself for his poor judgments, and he was always feeling fearful of the future. One day he read in the newspaper that there was going to be a night course on clowning to be given at a local college near him.

He could not believe it when he found himself signing up for the course. He told me that this decision saved his life. He changed his lifestyle, including where he lived. He goes to hospitals and schools and helps children learn how to laugh. He enjoys giving his love to children and making them laugh, and the more he does this the happier he is. His last words to us were that he had never known he could be this happy.

People like him show us that we can suffer economic loss and see it as an opportunity for a spiritual transformation. We can make giving more important than getting; we can begin to see love as more important than material things. We can begin to feel that love actually is the answer to all our problems.

There are many of us who would rank our huge fear of terrorists along with fears about money and the lack of it at the top of our pyramid of fears. So far I don't think that anyone has come up with a successful plan that people agree on to rid the world of terrorists; they seem so elusive and hard to find.

Would you consider that the hate, anger, grievances, lack of forgiveness, and murder, either in words or actions, seem justified to the persons performing the acts of terrorism? Would you be willing to consider that such decisions are based on fear rather than love? And would you rewind our history and observe that since the beginning of humankind, there has been an amazing amount of fear and terror in one form or another that we have passed along in our teachings from one generation to another?

Terrorists come in many different forms, political persuasions, skin colors, sizes, and have different religious beliefs—they are rich people, poor people, governmental agencies, and heads of state. Their attacks are often sudden and unexpected where thousands upon thousands of innocent people have been killed, and the perpetrators often feel righteous and justified about what they have done.

In attempts to understand the world and myself, I have found cartoons to be extremely helpful and insightful. I, along with thousands of others, remember the famous Pogo cartoon that stated, "We have met the enemy and he is us." Dr. Elisabeth Kubler Ross, famous psychiatrist, now deceased, was known for her work on death and dying. She once said, "There is a little bit of Hitler in each of us."

When I first heard this statement, I resented it. I said to myself, "I hate Hitler, and there is no Hitler in me." I was then in denial of my ego, whose center is fear, conflict, hate, revenge, and murder.

Then I began to remember when my sons were in grammar school and they left their rooms a mess, how there were occasions when I lost my temper and would shout at them, trying to control them by making them fearful, not realizing I was causing terror in them by my loud outbursts of anger. Is not a terrorist someone who causes another person to feel terrified? And what about bullies in school who create terror in kids who are smaller than them? Isn't bullying another form of terrorism? Another form of fear?

Many of us have had the experience of being so angry that in our minds there is a wish that the other person would die or just disappear from the face of the earth, a wish and thought that can be considered as a disguised form of murder. If our thoughts are as powerful as our actions, could that be considered as the beginnings of a terrorist thought within ourselves?

Is it just possible that Pogo was correct and that the enemy is within our minds when we allow ourselves to believe that anger and hate will get us what we want? Is it not possible that to heal the outside world we first need to do inner healing of our own fears, attack thoughts, and hatred?

Questions and more questions continue to be asked. Can we get out of the mess that the world we see seems to be in? Is there an alternative to destroying each other and ourselves and the planet we live on? Will hate and violence always be a part of our lives? Is this a dream world, a world of illusions and insanity made up by our egos that blocks the awareness of the presence of love?

The concepts in this book can help heal our minds and our hearts. They can open the door to making all of our decisions based on love rather than fear. They can assist us in committing ourselves to go through each day with the vigorous determination that we will have no thoughts, attitudes, words, or actions that are hurtful to others or ourselves. The lessons in this book are based on the belief that only our own thoughts and attitudes create our reality, and that it is only our own thoughts and attitudes that can hurt us . . . or heal us!

I like reminding myself of my friend, Hugh Prather, who states, "There must be another way of going through life besides being pulled though kicking and screaming."

I do believe that there is another way of going through life, and it requires an open mind, a willingness to change our beliefs and to change our goal.

There is increasing recognition among people everywhere that we are destroying ourselves and the world in which we live. Many of us, myself included, have felt the futility of trying to rid ourselves of frustration, conflict, pain, and illness, while still holding on to old belief systems. We do not seem to be able to change the world, to change other people, or to change ourselves until we are willing to change our own minds.

Today there is a rapidly expanding search for a better way of going through life that is uncovering a new awareness and a change in consciousness. It is like a spiritual flood that is about to cleanse the earth. This transformation of consciousness is prompting us to look inward, and as we explore our inner spaces we recognize the harmony and at-one-ment that has always been there.

As we look inward, we also become aware of an inner intuitive voice that provides a reliable source for guidance. When the physical senses are hushed, and we listen to the inner voice and surrender to it, moments of true healing and growth occur. In this silence, where the conflict of personalities has ceased to interest us, we can experience the joy of peace in our lives.

Although we want to experience peace, most of us are still seeking something else that we never find. We are still trying to control and predict, and therefore we feel isolated, disconnected, separate, alone, fragmented, unloved, and unlovable. We never seem to get enough of what we think we want, and our satisfactions are highly transitory. Even with those people we are close to, we often have love/hate relationships. These are relationships in which we feel a need to get something from someone else; when the need is fulfilled, we love them, and when it is not fulfilled, we hate them. Many of us are finding that, even after obtaining all the things we wanted in terms of job, home, family, and money, there is still an emptiness inside. Mother Teresa of Calcutta, India, called this phenomenon "spiritual deprivation."

Throughout the world there is a growing recognition of the need to feel fulfillment within, rather than to rely on the external symbols of success. When we have a desire to get something from another person or the world and we are not successful, the result is stress expressed in the form of frustration, depression, perceptions of pain, illness, and death. Most of us seriously want to get rid of the pain, illness, and frustrations, but we still want to maintain the old self-concept. Perhaps that is why we are going in circles, because we rigidly hold on to our old belief systems.

The world that seems so insane is the result of a belief system that is not working. To perceive the world differently, we must be willing to change our belief system, heal our relationship with our past, and expand our sense of now by releasing the fear in our minds. This changed perception leads to the recognition that we are not separate, but that we have always been joined.

There are many valid ways that lead to transformation and inner peace. This small book has been written as a primer for those of us who are motivated to experience personal transformation toward a life of giving and love, and away from getting and fear. In brief, this is a book about self-fulfillment through giving. The words and drawings present practical applications of steps for transformation in everyday situations that all of us face. This book is intended to help us remove the blocks to the awareness of love's presence in our lives.

We can learn to retrain our minds to have the single goal of peace of mind and the single function of practicing forgiveness. Our fulfillment can come from listening to the voice of our inner teacher. And in so doing, we will learn to heal our relationships, experience peace of mind, and let go of fear.

My present happiness is all I see.

PART I

PREPARATION FOR PERSONAL TRANSFORMATION

All fear is past and only Love is here.

What Is Real?

Most of us are confused about what is real. Even though we sense there is something more, we attempt to settle for a reality based exclusively on feedback from our physical senses. To reinforce this "reality," we look to what our culture defines as normal, healthy, and therefore real.

Yet where does Love fit into this scheme of things? Wouldn't our lives be more meaningful if we looked to what has no beginning and no ending as our reality? Only Love fits this definition of the eternal. Everything else is transitory and therefore meaningless.

Fear always distorts our perception and confuses us as to what is going on. Love is the total absence of fear. Love asks no questions. Its natural state is one of extension and expansion, not comparison and measurement. Love, then, is really everything that is of value, and fear can offer us nothing because it *is* nothing.

Although Love is always what we want, we are often afraid of Love without consciously knowing it, and so we may act both blind and deaf to Love's presence. Yet, when we help ourselves and each other let go of fear, we begin to experience a personal transformation. We start to see beyond our old reality as defined by the physical senses, and we enter a state of clarity in which we discover that all minds are joined, that we share a common Self, and that inner peace and Love are in fact all that are real.

With Love as our only reality, health and wholeness can be viewed as inner peace, and healing can be seen as letting go of fear.

Love, then, is letting go of fear.

Replaying the Past

We all manufacture our own dust and static that serve only to interfere with seeing, hearing, and experiencing Love within ourselves and others. This self-imposed interference keeps us stuck in an old belief system that we use repeatedly, even though it doesn't get us what we want.

The mind can be thought of as containing reels and reels of motion picture film about our past experiences. These images are superimposed not only on each other but also on the lens through which we experience the present. Consequently, we are never really seeing or hearing it as it is; we are just seeing fragments of the present through the tons of distorted old memories that we layer over it.

If we are willing, we can with increasing effectiveness use active imagination to wipe away everything from those old reels except Love. This requires letting go of our past attachments to guilt and fear.

Prediction versus Peace

Sometimes we put more value in predicting and controlling than in having peace of mind. At times, it feels more
important for us to predict that we are going to be miserable the next moment, and then find pleasure in being
right, than to have true happiness in the present moment.
This can be looked upon as an insane way of trying to
protect ourselves. It produces a short circuit that confuses
pleasure with pain.

   We often believe that the fears of the past can successfully predict the fears of the future. The results of this
type of thinking are that we spend most of our time worrying about both the past and future, creating a vicious
circle of fear, which leaves little room for Love and joy in
the present.

Choice for Reality

We can choose our own reality. Because our will is free, if we wish we can choose to see and experience the truth. We can experience the truth of our reality as Love. To do this, we must, each instant, refuse to be limited by the fearful past and future and by the questionable "realities" we have adopted from our culture. We can choose to experience this instant as the only time there is, and live in a reality of *now*.

Because our minds have no boundaries, they are actually joined. In fact, our minds have only the limitations we place on them. For example, when we see value in making a fearful past "real," we limit our minds to using it as our reality. As a result, our minds can only look fearfully at all that is to come, and cannot pause for an instant to enjoy the present in peace. When we use words such as *can't* and *impossible*, we have imposed the limits of a fearful past on ourselves.

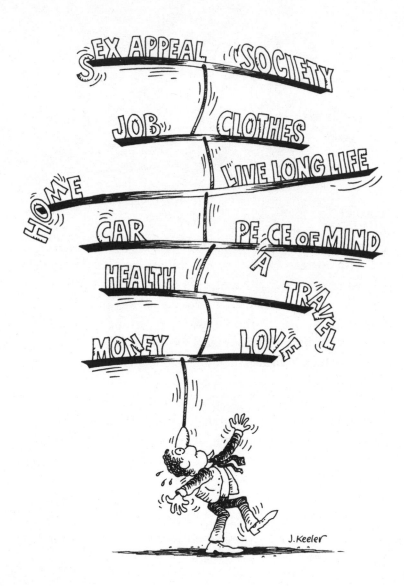

Singleness of Goal

Peace of mind as our single goal is the most potent motivating force we can have. To have inner peace we need to be consistent in having peace of mind as our single goal. Instead of having a single goal, we are all tempted to try to juggle multiple goals. Juggling can only serve to deflect our focus and increase our conflict. We can achieve consistency in keeping this single goal in mind by reminding ourselves of the singleness of purpose we would have if we suddenly found ourselves drowning in the ocean. We would, in that situation, put all of our attention into the single goal of staying afloat and breathing for survival.

Peace of Mind Through Forgiveness

With peace of mind as our single goal, forgiveness becomes our single function. Forgiveness is the vehicle used for correcting our misperceptions and for helping us let go of fear. Simply stated, to forgive is to let go.

Our first step in mind retraining is to establish peace of mind as our single goal. This means thinking of ourselves first in terms of self-fullness, not selfishness. The second step is forgiveness.

Many of us become frustrated when we make the mistake of trying to love others as the first step. In light of our past distorted values and experiences, some people simply seem unlovable; because of our faulty perception of their behavior, it is difficult to love them.

When we have peace of mind as a single goal, we can then take the second step, forgiveness, and choose to see others as extending Love, or being fearful and calling for help in the form of Love. With this new perception, it becomes easier to give both total Love and acceptance to the other person and therefore to experience inner peace at the same time.

Other people do not have to change for us to experience peace of mind.

Mind as Split

It may be useful to think of the mind as the film, the camera, and everything else involved in movie production. What we experience is really our state of mind projected outward upon a screen called "the world." This world and those in it become the mirror of our thoughts and fantasies. What the mind projects becomes our perception, which limits our vision as long as we hold to it.

The mind functions as if it were split; part of it acts as if it were directed by our egos, and part of it by Love. Most of the time, our mind pays attention to this pushy pseudo-director that we call the ego, which is simply another name for fear.

The ego directs "movies" about separation and conflict, although it makes them appear as if they were the realization of our romantic fantasies. It directs movies that project the illusion that we are all separate from each other. Our true director, Love, does not project illusions; it only extends the truth. Love directs movies that unite and join us to one another.

The mind is actually the director, producer, scriptwriter, film editor, cast, projectionist, audience, and critic. The mind, being limitless, has the capacity of changing the movie and everything about it at any time. The mind has the power of making all decisions.

The ego part of the mind acts like a curtain of fear and guilt that blocks out Love. We can learn to direct our minds to open the curtain and reveal the light of Love that has always been there and remains our true reality.

When we choose only Love as the director of our mind

we can experience the power and the miracle of Love.

Themes to Live By

In making practical application of the material covered in this book to everyday solutions, it will be helpful to keep the following underlying themes in mind:

1. Peace of mind is our single goal.

2. Forgiveness is our single function and the way to achieve our goal of peace of mind.

3. Through forgiveness, we can learn not to judge others and to see everyone, including ourselves, as guiltless.

4. We can let go of fear when we stop judging and stop projecting the past into the future, and live only in the now.

5. We can learn to accept direction from our inner intuitive voice, which is our guide to knowing.

6. After our inner voice gives us direction, it will also provide the means for accomplishing whatever is necessary.

7. In following one's inner guidance, it is frequently necessary to make a commitment to a specific goal even when the means for achieving it are not immediately apparent. This is a reversal of the customary logic of the world, and can be thought of as "putting the cart before the horse."

8. We do have a choice in determining what we perceive and the feelings we experience.

9. Through retraining of the mind we can learn to use positive active imagination. Positive active imagination enables us to develop positive, loving motion pictures in our minds.

This day I choose to spend
in perfect peace.

PART II

INGREDIENTS
OF PERSONAL
TRANSFORMATION

I see all things as I would have them be.

Belief Systems and Reality

We are what we believe. Our belief system is based on our past experience, which is constantly being relived in the present, with an anticipation of the future being just like the past. Our present perceptions are so colored by the past that we are unable to see the immediate happenings in our lives without distortion and limitations. With willingness, we can reexamine who we think we are in order to achieve a new and deeper sense of our real identity.

We Are All Limitless

To experience this sense of total freedom, it is important for us to detach ourselves from past–future preoccupations and choose to live in the *now*. To be free also means not to be confined to the reality that seems limited by our physical senses. To be free allows us to participate in the Love we share with everyone. We cannot be free until we discipline and retrain our minds.

While all of us want Love, many of us seem unable to experience it. Our guilty fears from the past block our ability to give and receive Love in the present. Fear and Love can never be experienced at the same time. It is always our choice as to which of these emotions we want.

By choosing Love more consistently than fear, we can change the nature and quality of our relationships.

Attack and Defense

When we perceive another person as attacking us, we usually feel defensive and find a way, directly or indirectly, to attack back. Attacking always stems from fear and guilt. No one attacks unless he first feels threatened and believes that through attack he can demonstrate his own strength, at the expense of another's vulnerability. Attack is really a defense and, as with all defenses that are designed to keep guilt and fear from our awareness, attack actually preserves the problem. Most of us cling to the belief that attacking can really get us something we want. We seem to forget that attacking and defending do not bring us inner peace.

In order to experience peace instead of conflict, it is necessary to shift our perception. Instead of seeing others as attacking us, we can see them as fearful. We are always expressing either Love or fear. Fear is really a call for help, and therefore a request for Love. It is apparent, then, that to experience peace we must recognize that we do have a choice in determining what we perceive.

Many of our attempts to correct others, even when we believe we are offering constructive criticism, are really attempts to attack them by demonstrating their wrongness and our rightness. It may be helpful to examine our motivations. Are we teaching Love or are we demonstrating attack?

If others do not change in accordance with our expectations, we are likely to regard them as guilty, and thus reinforce our own belief in guilt. Peace of mind comes from not wanting to change others, but by simply accepting them as they are. True acceptance is always without demands and expectations.

Forgiveness

Inner peace can be reached only when we practice forgiveness. Forgiveness is the letting go of the past, and is therefore the means for correcting our misperceptions.

Our misperceptions can only be undone *now*, and can be accomplished only through letting go whatever we think other people have done to us, or whatever we think we have done to them. Through this process of selective forgetting, we become free to embrace a present without the need to reenact our past.

Through true forgiveness we can stop the endless recycling of guilt and look upon ourselves and others with Love. Forgiveness releases all thoughts that seem to separate us from each other. Without the belief in separation, we can accept our own healing and extend healing Love to all those around us. Healing results from the thought of unity.

As inner peace is recognized as our single goal, forgiveness becomes our single function. When we accept both our goal and our function, we find that our inner, intuitive voice becomes our only guide to fulfillment. We are released as we release others from the prison of our distorted and illusory perceptions, and join with them in the unity of Love.

Getting and Giving

It is important to remember that we have everything we need now, and that the essence of our being is Love. If we think we need to get something from another, we will love that person when we get what we think we want, and we will hate that person when we do not. We frequently have love/hate relationships in which we find ourselves trading conditional love. The getting motivation leads to conflict and distress and is associated with linear time. Giving means extending one's Love with no conditions, no expectations, and no boundaries. Peace of mind occurs, therefore, when we put all our attention into giving and have no desire to get anything from, or to change, another person. The giving motivation leads to a sense of inner peace and joy that are unrelated to time.

Retraining the Mind

To aid in retraining your mind, remember to ask yourself the following questions in all circumstances, private or interpersonal.

1. Do I choose to experience *Peace of Mind* or do I choose to experience *Conflict?*

2. Do I choose to experience *Love* or *Fear?*

3. Do I choose to be a *Love Finder* or a *Fault Finder?*

4. Do I choose to be a *Love Giver* or a *Love Sender?*

5. Is this communication (verbal or nonverbal) *Loving* to the other person and is it *Loving* to me?

Many of our thoughts, statements, and actions are not loving. If we want peace of mind, it is essential that our communications with others bring about a sense of joining. To have inner peace and to experience Love, we must be consistent in what we think, say, and do.

Words to Eliminate

Another process for retraining the mind has to do with recognizing the impact of the words we use. The words in the list that follows are commonly used in the messages we give to ourselves and others. The use of these words continues to keep the guilty past and fearful future active in our minds. As a result, our feelings of conflict can only be reinforced. The more we recognize that using these words interferes with our inner peace, the easier it will be to practice eliminating them from our thoughts and expressions. You may find it helpful to carry an imaginary disposal bag in your mind; every time you use one of these words, visualize yourself putting the word into the disposal bag and then burying it.

It is important always to be gentle with yourself. If you find yourself continuing to use any of the words that follow, merely regard it as a mistake to be corrected and choose not to feel guilty about making the mistake.

The words to avoid using are:

- impossible

- can't

- try

- limitation

- if only

- but

- however

- difficult

- ought to

- should

- any words that place you or anyone else in a category

- any words that tend to measure or evaluate you or other people

- any words that tend to judge or condemn you or someone else

Conclusion

This book provides guidelines for letting go of fear and bringing about inner peace. Its practical applications can help shift our perceptions so that we no longer feel separate, fearful, or in conflict, but rather experience joining, Love, and peace. Inner peace is experienced as we learn to forgive the world and everyone in it, and thereby see everyone, including ourselves, as blameless.

Each instant of our lives can be regarded as a present opportunity for a new awakening or rebirth, free from the irrelevant intrusion of memories from the past and anticipations of the future. In the freedom of this present moment, we can extend our natural loving nature.

When we find ourselves irritated, depressed, angry, or ill, we can be sure we have chosen the wrong goal and are responding to fear. When we are not experiencing joy, we have forgotten to make peace of mind our single goal and have become concerned about getting rather than giving.

By consistently choosing Love rather than fear, we can experience a personal transformation that enables us to be more naturally loving to ourselves and others. In this way we can begin to recognize and experience the Love and joy that unite us.

Review

1. One of the main purposes of time is to enable us to choose what we want to experience. *Do we want to experience peace or do we want to experience conflict?*

2. All minds are joined and are one.

3. What we perceive through our physical senses presents us with a limited and distorted view of reality.

4. We really cannot change the external world or other people. We *can* change how we perceive the world, how we perceive others, and how we perceive ourselves.

5. There are only two emotions: one is Love and the other is fear. Love is our true reality. Fear is something our mind has made up, and is therefore unreal.

6. What we experience is our state of mind projected outward. If our state of mind is one of well-being, Love, and peace, that is what we will project and therefore experience. If our state of mind is one filled with doubt, fear, and concern about illness, we will project this state outward, and it will therefore be our experiential reality.

Forgiveness ends all suffering and loss.

PART III

LESSONS FOR PERSONAL TRANSFORMATION

How to Proceed with the Lessons

The specific principles and guidelines found in this book gain personal meaning through the practice of the daily lessons. You may find some of them difficult to accept or have trouble seeing their relevance to the problems you face in your own life. These uncertainties do not really matter. However, your willingness to practice the lessons without exceptions is important. It is the experience resulting from the practice that will help you approach your goal of greater personal happiness. Remember that willingness does not imply mastery—only a readiness to change one's perceptions.

Suggestions for deriving maximum benefit from the lessons:

1. Beginning with Lesson 1, do the lessons sequentially, one each day.

2. Every day on awakening, relax and use your active imagination. In your mind's eye, put yourself somewhere you would feel comfortable, relaxed, and at peace.

3. Spend a few minutes while you are in this relaxed state repeating the lesson title and related thoughts

several times, allowing them to become part of your being.

4. Each day ask yourself the question, "Do I want to experience *PEACE OF MIND* or do I want to experience *CONFLICT?*"

5. Put the lesson title on a card and keep it with you, review it periodically throughout the day and evening, and apply the lesson to everyone and everything without exception.

6. Before retiring, relax and take a few minutes to review the day's lesson. Ask yourself if you would be willing to have these ideas incorporated in your dreams.

7. When you have considered all of the lessons, your learning will be facilitated if you begin again with the first lesson and repeat the entire series.

8. This form of practice may be maintained until you find that you are thinking about the lessons and applying them consistently without needing to refer to them.

LESSON 1

ALL THAT I GIVE IS GIVEN TO MYSELF

All That I Give Is Given to Myself

To give is to receive—this is the law of Love. Under this law, when we give our Love away to others we gain, and whatever we give we simultaneously receive. The law of Love is based on abundance; we are completely filled with Love all the time, and our supply is always full and running over. When we give our Love unconditionally to others with no expectations of return, the Love within us extends, expands, and joins. So by giving our Love away we increase the Love within us and everyone gains.

The law of
what we give aw
something away,

The world's
holds that we a
feel empty as we
Love and peace
to think of as d

The problen
nal world will c
the world's law,
frequently think

in need. We then try to fulfill our imagined needs through other people.

When we expect others to satisfy our desires, and they disappoint us, as they inevitably must, we experience distress. This distress can take the form of frustration, disappointment, anger, depression, or illness. As a result, we are likely to feel trapped, limited, rejected, or attacked.

When we are feeling unloved and depressed and empty inside, finding someone to give us Love is not really the solution. What is helpful is to Love someone else totally and with no expectations. That Love, then, is simultaneously given to ourselves. The other person doesn't have to change or give us something.

The world's distorted concept is that you have to get other people's Love before you can feel Love within. The law of Love is different from the world's law. The law of Love is that you are Love, and that as you give Love to others you teach yourself what you are.

Today allow yourself to learn and experience the law of Love.

I was mistaken in believing that I could give anyone anything other than what I want for myself. Since we want to experience peace, Love, and forgiveness, these are the only gifts I would offer others. It is not charity on my part to offer forgiveness and Love to others in place of attack. Rather, offering Love is the only way I can accept Love for myself.

Example A

The following is a letter from Rita, a friend who came into my life in the fall of 1978. Rita phoned me to ask for help for her teenage daughter Tina, who had leukemia. Tina died in January of 1979.

Rita has given me permission to share this letter, which, to me, states with beauty and clarity the essence of today's lesson:

All that I give is given to myself.

February 27

Dear Jerry,

I hope you don't mind being the recipient of these letters, which are my way of expressing my thoughts as they are starting to emerge from some deep, formerly untouched source.

If nothing else, you, as a psychiatrist, know this expression can be therapeutic.

Since I last wrote you, other little threads seem to be weaving into this tapestry of life.

On February 22, I went to hear Dr. Elizabeth Kubler-Ross speak. Needless to say, it was a real experience. One could hardly come away untouched or unmoved. She touched on some sore spots, and some portions of her talk were difficult to endure. But her words, her philosophy, and her work have made a lasting impression on me, and I feel that what she and you are doing is "what it's all about."

To continue the chronological events which are taking place, this is what happened the next day. I decided to go to work for that one day. During a break, I walked over to a small shopping mall, which I usually frequent. But as I walked over, I noticed a bookstore that hadn't been there previously. I couldn't help wondering from whence it had materialized. I just had to go and look in. I asked how long the shop had been there and I was told, a month. I looked around and noticed some books that had not yet been put on the shelf. One was a book I had heard about and thought I'd like to read one day. I decided to get it. It was Ruth Montgomery's *A World Beyond*. I can't even begin to express the way that book "hit" me. That's a story in itself. But I started to take still another look at my life and ponder where all this was taking me. But, as you said, if the question raised a conflict in me, it wouldn't do me any good. So I didn't dwell on the whys and wherefores. Instead, I reread your letter and thought about the line where you said that one of the best ways of dealing with what I was going through (mourning) would be to find someone to help. I didn't have to go out and search or even wrack my brain. I knew all along whom I was supposed to help.

As briefly as I can, I will tell you the story.

About a year ago, my daughter Tina was beginning to show signs of illness. At the same time, another young woman, twenty years old, who lived two doors away and whom I had known for fifteen years, also came down with a still-undiagnosed illness. The mother and I spoke about our concern and fears about their conditions. Sometime later, when Tina's illness was diagnosed, this lady could not bring herself to talk to me. She never spoke to me the entire time Tina was sick. When Tina was sick, she came to the Rosary, but she never said a word. A silent look passed between us. She came to the funeral and then was one of the kind neighbors who brought food to the house afterward. In all this time, she never said anything. I knew I was the "reality" of what could happen to her daughter. And so afterward I, too, stayed away so I wouldn't remind her. I always asked other neighbors how she was doing, and I always got my information secondhand. Then I thought of you and your letters and words. And I thought, "Why not?" I did care! And so I went to see her. As soon as she saw me, she came right over to me and we embraced. It was natural! We knew how each other was feeling! It was just beautiful! I felt so good when I left. I wondered why I took so long to walk those few feet to her house. I guess until that point, I just wasn't ready.

But again I say, though you are far away, geographically, spiritually you are close. I will not question anything that happens, but accept it and see where it takes me.

Peace to you, Jerry, now and always.

Sincerely,
Rita

Example B

Some years ago I had the good fortune of spending some time in Los Angeles with Mother Teresa, known for her work with the poor and dying in Calcutta, India, and throughout the world. I wanted to meet with her because I knew she demonstrated an almost perfect consistency of living a life of inner peace, and I wanted to learn from her how she did this.

We talked about our mutual work with people who were facing life and death situations. I experienced an inner stillness while in her presence. The power of the Love, the gentility, the peace of mind that emanated from her is difficult to describe. This was something I wanted to experience and demonstrate in myself.

It was the July Fourth weekend, and I learned she was flying to Mexico City that afternoon. I asked if I could join her because I wanted to continue being in her presence.

She smiled gently and said, "Dr. Jampolsky, I would have no objection about your joining me on the trip to Mexico. But you said you wanted to learn about inner peace. I think you would learn more about inner peace if you would find out how much it costs to fly to Mexico City and back, and give that money to the poor."

I found out the cost of the round-trip flight from Los Angeles to Mexico City and gave that amount to the Brothers of Mercy in Los Angeles.

The powerful lesson I learned from Mother Teresa was that I do not have to seek for guidance outside of myself to find out what to do. I learned that the time for giving is always now—not later—and that by giving with no expectations or limits, one has immediate inner peace. I learned in that one instant that all I give is given to myself.

Today I will give to others only the gifts I want to accept for myself.

LESSON 2

FORGIVENESS IS THE KEY TO HAPPINESS

Forgiveness Is the Key to Happiness

Inner peace can be reached only when we practice forgiveness. Forgiveness is the vehicle for changing our perceptions and letting go of our fears, condemning judgments, and grievances.

We need to remind ourselves constantly that Love is the only reality there is. Anything we perceive that does not mirror Love is a misperception. Forgiveness, then, becomes the means for correcting our misperceptions; it allows us to see only the Love in others and ourselves, and nothing else.

Through selective forgetting, through taking off the tinted glasses that superimpose the fearful past upon the present, we can begin to know that the truth of Love is forever present and that by perceiving only Love we can experience happiness. Forgiveness then becomes a process of letting go and overlooking whatever we thought other people may have done to us, or whatever we may think we have done to others.

When we cherish grievances, we allow our mind to be fed by fear and we become imprisoned by these distortions. When we see our only function as forgiveness, and are willing to practice it consistently by directing our minds to be forgiving, we will find ourselves released and set free. Forgiveness corrects the misperception that we are separate from each other and allows us to experience a sense of unity and at-one-ment with each other.

Forgiveness, as defined here, is different from the way most of us have been trained to understand it. Forgiveness does not mean assuming a position of superiority and putting up with or tolerating behavior in another person that we do not like. Forgiveness means correcting our misperception that the other person harmed us.

The unforgiving mind, contrasted with the forgiving mind, is confused, afraid, and full of fear. It is certain of the interpretation it places on its perceptions of others. It is certain of the justification of its anger and the correctness of its condemning judgment. The unforgiving mind rigidly sees the past and future as the same and is resistant to change. It does not want the future to be different from the past. The unforgiving mind sees itself as innocent and others as guilty. It thrives on conflict and being right, and it sees inner peace as its enemy. It perceives everything as separate.

Whenever I see someone else as guilty, I am reinforcing my own sense of guilt and unworthiness. I cannot forgive myself unless I am willing to forgive others. It does not matter what I think anyone has done to me in the past or what I think I may have done. Only through forgiveness can my release from guilt and fear be complete.

Example

The following is a personal vignette that demonstrates some principles about grievances and forgiveness.

One morning my secretary brought in a huge pile of bills. She reminded me that my income was down because of the increasing amount of time I was spending on a non-fee basis. She said there was a man who owed me $500 for services rendered to his daughter the previous year, and reminded me how well and quickly the daughter had responded to working with me. Then she said that she was tired of sending the bill and suggested I send it to a collection agency.

I told her I had never sent a bill to a collection agency, and didn't plan to do that now, but I would give some thought to the matter. As I looked at the unpaid bills I owed, I began to feel what I thought was justified anger, and I felt I had a legitimate grievance. After all, I had done my part, and he and his daughter had benefited from working with me. I knew her father could well afford to pay the fee, and I began to think he was a louse for not paying. I made up my mind to phone him that afternoon.

While meditating on my daily lesson from *A Course in Miracles*, which was "Forgiveness is the key to happiness," a picture of this man who owed me money came across my mind. I heard an inner voice state that I was to let go of the past and my attachment to the money. I was to practice forgiveness and heal my relationship with him.

So I phoned him. I told him about my meditation and my decision to send no more bills. I told him of my past anger and of my determination not to retain it. I said I was calling to heal our relationship, and that the money was no longer an issue. There was a long pause before he said, "Well, if I don't pay your bill, certainly God is not going to."

I said I thought it important to let go of the money issue and the anger I had felt toward him regarding the bill. I told him I was releasing myself from the thought that he had hurt me in any way.

There was another silence, and his voice became warm and loving. He thanked me for phoning and then to my surprise he said he would mail the check next week (which he did).

The next hour I saw a mother of an eleven-year-old girl who had cancer of the spine and was a member of one of our groups at the Center. The mother had been receiving public assistance, but because of many complexities was not able to obtain money through this or other channels. Her car had been repaired and was waiting for her at the garage, but she could not pay the $70 repair bill. Because of the car problem, she had missed essential appointments for her daughter's chemotherapy treatments. My inner voice said, "Give her the $70 since you have just found money that you thought you didn't have." When I did this, I experienced inner peace. I continue to be impressed by how quickly I experience inner peace when I let go of my attachment to the past belief that someone is guilty and someone is innocent.

Today I choose to let go of all my past misperceptions about myself and others. Instead, I will join with everyone and say: I see you and myself only in the light of true forgiveness.

LESSON 3

I AM NEVER UPSET FOR THE REASON I THINK

I Am Never Upset for the Reason I Think

Most of us have a belief system based on experiences from the past and on perceptions from the physical senses. Have you considered that what we believe is what we see? Or, as the late Flip Wilson put it, "What you see is what you get."

Because our physical senses appear to relay information from the outside world to our brain, we may believe that our state of mind is controlled entirely by the feedback we receive. This belief contributes to a sense of ourselves as separate entities who are largely isolated and feel alone in an uncaring and fragmented world. This can leave us with the impression that the world we see causes us to feel upset, depressed, anxious, and fearful. Such a belief system presumes that the outside world is the cause and we are the effect.

Let us consider the possibility that this type of thinking is upside down and backwards.

What would happen if we believed that what we see is determined by the thoughts in our mind? Perhaps we could entertain an idea that at the moment seems unnatural and foreign to us; namely, that our thoughts are the cause and what we see is the effect. It would then make no sense to blame the world or those in it for the miseries and pain we experience, because it would be possible then to consider perception as "a mirror and not a fact."

Consider once again that the mind may be like a motion picture camera, projecting our internal state onto the world. When our mind is filled with upsetting thoughts, we see the world and those in it as upsetting to us. On the other hand, when our mind is peaceful, the world and the people in it appear to us as peaceful. You can choose to awaken in the morning and see a friendly world through glasses that filter out everything except Love.

It may be helpful to question our need to attempt to control the external world. We can, instead, control our inner world by consistently choosing what thoughts we want to have in our mind. Peace of mind begins with our own thoughts and extends outward. It is from our peace of mind (cause) that a peaceful perception of the world arises (effect).

We all have the power to direct our minds to replace the feelings of being upset, depressed, and fearful with the feeling of inner peace.

I am tempted to believe that I am upset because of what other people do or because of circumstances and events that seem beyond my control. I may experience being upset as some form of anger, jealousy, resentment, or depression. Actually, all of these feelings represent some form of fear that I am experiencing. When I recognize that I always have the choice between being fearful or experiencing Love by extending Love to others, I need no longer be upset for any reason.

Example

For many years I had been bothered by chronic disabling back pain. Through those years I was not able to play tennis, garden, or do many of the things that I liked to do. I was hospitalized several times, and at one point the neurosurgeon wanted to perform surgery on what was called an organic back disease—a degenerative disc. I chose not to have the surgery.

I thought I was upset because of the pain and the distress caused by it. Then one day there seemed to be a small voice inside that said, even though I had an organic back syndrome, I was causing my own pain. It became clear to me that my back condition became worse when I was under emotional stress, particularly when I was fearful and holding a grievance against someone. I was not upset for the reason I thought.

As I learned to let go of my grievances through the practice of forgiveness, my pain disappeared. I now have no limitations on my activities.

I thought I had been upset because of back pain. I found, however, I was upset because of unhealed personal relationships. I had let myself believe that the body controls the mind, rather than realizing that the mind controls the body. I feel certain that most people who have back problems have the potential to learn to let go of their grievances, their guilt and fears, and through forgiveness of others and themselves experience their own healing.

Throughout the day, whenever you are tempted to be fearful, remind yourself that you can experience Love instead.

LESSON 4

I AM DETERMINED TO SEE THINGS DIFFERENTLY

I Am Determined to See Things Differently

The world we see that seems so insane may be the result of a belief system that isn't working. The belief system holds that the fearful past will extend into a fearful future, making the past and the future one. It is our memory of fear and pain that makes us feel so vulnerable. It is this feeling of vulnerability that makes us want to control and predict the future at all costs.

I would like to present a personal example. I was reared in a family where a fearful attitude always seemed to prevail. I bought into a philosophy that said, "The past was awful, the moment is horrendous, and the next moment is going to be worse." And, of course, we were all correct in our predictions since we shared the same assumptions.

Our old belief system assumes that anger occurs because we have been attacked. It also assumes that counter-attack is justified in return, and that we are responsible for "protecting" ourselves, but are not responsible for the need to do so.

If we are willing, it is possible to change our belief system. However, to do so we must take a new look at every one of our cherished assumptions and values from the past. This means letting go of any investment in holding on to fear, anger, guilt, or pain. It means letting the

past slip away and with it all the fears from the past that we keep extending into the present and future.

"I am determined to see things differently" means that we are truly willing to get rid of the past and future in order to experience now as it really is.

Most of my life I have acted as if I were a robot, responding to what other people said or did. Now I recognize that my responses are determined only by the decisions I make. I claim my freedom by exercising the power of my decision to see people and events with Love instead of fear.

Example A

When I was in medical school, a surprising percentage of the class came down with whatever disease was being discussed. It made no difference what the disease was; it could have been hepatitis, schizophrenia, or syphilis.

My thing was tuberculosis. When I was an intern in Boston I had to spend one month on the TB service, and I was scared to death that I would catch it and die. My fantasy plan was to take one deep breath as I went on the ward and not breathe for a month. I was a total wreck at the end of my first day.

That night about 11:30 I received an emergency call. I ran to the ward where a fifty-year-old woman, who not only had tuberculosis but was also an alcoholic with cirrhosis of the liver, had just vomited blood. She had no pulse. I massaged her heart and removed the blood from her throat with a suction machine. The oxygen machine would not work at first, and I administered mouth-to-mouth resuscitation. Her pulse came back, and she began to breathe.

After I went back to my intern quarters I saw myself in the mirror, and I was a bloody mess. All of a sudden it occurred to me that I had not been fearful at any time during the episode.

That night I learned that when I was totally absorbed in what I might get, I was immobilized with fear and a help to no one, but when I was totally absorbed in giving, I felt no fear. By letting go of the past, by putting my full attention into giving in the now, I forgot about fear and could see things differently.

Perhaps it is needless to say I immediately lost my fear of tuberculosis. That patient turned out to be a very potent teacher for me.

Our state of mind is our responsibility. Whether we experience peace or conflict is determined by the choices we make, how we see other people, and whether we see them as worthy of Love or as justifying our fear.

We do not have to act like robots and give others the power to determine whether we will experience Love or fear, happiness or sadness.

Example B

This book emphasizes that a shift in perception can reverse our way of thinking; it helps when you put the cart in front of the horse.

I find that when personal guidance has established the goal (the cart), all I need to do is keep that goal firmly in my mind and the means (the horse) will take care of itself. Most of us expend so much energy in trying to find the means that we lose sight of the goal.

Here is an example. The children I work with who have catastrophic illnesses recently wrote a book. It looked as if it would take eighteen or more months to get it published at an established publishing house. Although we did not have any money, my guidance was not to wait but to publish the book ourselves, and to have faith that somehow the money would be provided. (In the past I would never have done anything like this without having

the money first. This time, however, I was determined to see things differently.)

I did make a personal commitment to the printer that I would borrow the money from the bank if we were not able to raise the necessary funds. On Friday at noon, the 5,000 copies of the book, *There Is a Rainbow Behind Every Dark Cloud*, were delivered. We had raised less than 10 percent of the money required.

I felt as if I were at the end of a high diving board and someone was about to push me off. However, one hour later we received a phone call from the executive director of the Bothin Foundation, stating that they had approved our grant application and we would immediately receive a check paying for the books in full.

Through this experience, I learned that nothing is impossible when we follow our inner guidance, even when its direction may threaten us by reversing our usual logic.

Whenever you feel tempted today to see through the eyes of fear, repeat to yourself with determination:

I am not a robot; I am free.
I am determined to see things differently.

LESSON 5

I CAN ESCAPE
FROM THE WORLD
I SEE BY
GIVING UP
ATTACK
THOUGHTS

I Can Escape from the World I See by Giving Up Attack Thoughts

Many of us feel at times that we are hopelessly trapped in the world we see. Try as we may, we just can't seem to change the world and escape from its seeming confines.

If we remember that it is our thoughts that make up the world, then we can change them. We change the world we see by changing our thoughts about it. By changing our thoughts, we are actually changing the cause. Then the world we see, the effect, will change automatically.

A changed thought system can reverse cause and effect as we have known it. For most of us, this is a very difficult concept to accept, because we resist relinquishing the predictability of our past belief system and so resist assuming responsibility for our thoughts, feelings, and reactions. Since we always look within before looking out, we can perceive attack outside us only when we have first accepted attack as real within.

We forget this premise when we perceive another person as attacking us. We try to hide from our conscious awareness that the attack we perceive is coming from elsewhere actually originated in our mind. When we recognize this, we can become aware that our own attack thoughts are actually hurting us. We may then choose to replace attack thoughts with Love thoughts in order to stop hurting ourselves. Our higher self-interest brings with it the understanding that the Love we give others strengthens the Love we have for ourselves.

Once again, it may be worthwhile to remind ourselves that attack thoughts do not bring us peace of mind and justifying our anger doesn't really protect us.

I recognize today that my attack thoughts about others are really directed against myself. When I believe that attacking others brings me something I want, let me remember that I always attack myself first. I do not wish to hurt myself again today.

Example

The Center for Attitudinal Healing has recently received considerable national publicity through television and other media because of our work with children with catastrophic diseases. We have, because of the thousands of letters received, started a national and international pen pal and telephone network in which children around the world are finding peace by helping each other. This work was producing enormous telephone bills, and we were in need of money.

Because I was preoccupied with this problem, I was quieting my mind through meditation, and the thought occurred to me that I was to call the president of the phone company and elicit his financial help. I found this guidance difficult to accept for two reasons. The first was that I felt I had already paid my dues in asking people for money and just did not want to do that anymore. The second reason was that one of my pet hates was the telephone company. My phone was frequently out of order, and I often found myself irritated and angry at the telephone company.

However, my inner voice was persistent. I felt that I could not call them while I was still angry. So what I did was to spend the next two weeks practicing forgiveness and letting go of my attack thoughts. To my surprise I was then able to feel a sense of oneness, a joining, and Love between me and the people at the telephone company.

I then tried to phone the company president and, of course, couldn't get through to him. My fantasy was that there were about fifty people protecting him from callers who were angry and wanted to complain. I always got the same message. "The president is busy and can't talk to you now."

After calling him four times, I decided to try only once more. To my surprise, he answered the phone himself. I told him why I wanted to see him and, rather than referring me to their public relations department, he made an appointment with me.

He could not have been more cordial. Almost immediately, a committee from the phone company began to evaluate the center, and six weeks later we were awarded a $3000 grant.

Now, as far as I am concerned, *that was a miracle!* And in my heart I do not believe this miracle could even have happened until I was willing to let go of my attack thoughts and allow the Love, that was already there, to be revealed.

Throughout the day when you are tempted to hurt yourself through attack thoughts, say with determination:

I want to experience peace of mind right now.
I happily let go of all attack thoughts
and choose peace instead.

LESSON 6

I AM NOT
THE VICTIM OF
THE WORLD
I SEE

I Am Not the Victim of the World I See

Have you noticed how often you feel that you are a victim of the world in which you live? Because most of us perceive many aspects of our surroundings as insane, we are tempted to feel helplessly caught in a trap. When we allow ourselves to think we are living in an unfriendly environment where we must fear being hurt or victimized, we can only suffer.

To be consistent in achieving inner peace, we must perceive a world where everyone is innocent.

What happens when we choose to see others as free from guilt? How can we begin to look at them differently? To begin with, we might have to look on everything in the past as irrelevant except the Love we have experienced. We could choose to see the world through the window of Love rather than the window of fear. That would mean we would then selectively choose to see the beauty and the Love in the world, people's strengths rather than their weaknesses.

What I see without is a reflection of what I have seen within my own mind. I always project onto the world the thoughts, feelings, and attitudes that preoccupy me. I can

see the world differently by changing my mind about what I want to see.

Example A

In the past, I thought it was healthy and culturally supported to feel paranoid when walking into a dealership to buy a car. Car salesmen were not to be trusted. To be suspicious of them was as normal as it was wise, and I could have given you selected experiences to prove my case. What I did not realize was that all this approach was doing for me was to eliminate my choices. I found myself with only one attitude, that of fear and suspicion. Peace of mind was impossible.

I was not even aware that the salesman was probably operating from his own set of selected past experiences that "taught" him to be distrustful of customers. He had "learned" that they were disrespectful and had only some

form of degradation to offer. By seeing himself as being perceived by his customers as a second-class citizen, all he was accomplishing was to see himself that way.

The car salesman and I had one thing in common—a perception of each other that was totally distorted. And the means by which we had blurred out vision was the same. We had selected only certain aspects from our pasts to form a judgment by which we measured each other in the present.

I am now consulting at a large car agency, and I find that my attitudes are changing. Together, we are exploring letting go of our past grievances, and we are putting our efforts into practicing forgiveness.

What would happen if customers and car salesmen clearly saw the past as irrelevant and could thereby release it, and so become Love finders rather than fault finders, Love givers rather than Love seekers? Perhaps, then, we would all be free to approach each other with the extension of peace as our only motivation. The misperception "I am the victim of the world I see" could then be changed to "I am *not* the victim of the world I see."

Example B

Through others hearing about our work at the Center, I was asked to see Joe, a fifteen-year-old boy whose head had been run over twice by a tractor. He was rendered blind, mute, and sensationless, with a bilateral spastic paralysis. He was in a coma for months, and the doctors felt even a miracle would not help him.

However, his family never gave up hope for Joe's improvement and tried to live one day at a time, making the utmost of their *now*. As Joe began to regain consciousness, he worked hard and was determined to recover completely. Then, what seemed like a series of miracles began to happen. Joe recovered his speech and began to walk. Throughout this period he spent much time helping others.

When I saw him, Joe's spirits seemed to be up almost all the time. I asked him how he maintained this mood, and he replied, "Oh, I just look at the positive things in everyone—and pay no attention to the negative things, and refuse to believe in the word 'impossible'."

Joe doesn't often feel sorry for himself. He could feel that the universe had dealt him a horrible blow. However, he chooses peace instead of conflict by deciding to see the world and those in it through the window of Love. *There is a choice.*

To me, Joe is pure Love. He just exudes it. He and his family are powerful teachers of Love for me and many others. He perfectly exemplifies the statement, "I am not the victim of the world I see." Sometimes when I am feeling down, I think of Joe. I am then reminded that I, too, can choose not to see myself as a victim of the world I see.

Throughout the day, whenever you are tempted to see yourself as victimized, repeat: Only my loving thoughts are real. It is only these I would have in this situation (specify) or with that person (specify).

LESSON 7

TODAY
I WILL JUDGE
NOTHING
THAT OCCURS

Today I Will Judge Nothing That Occurs

Have you ever given yourself the opportunity of going through just one day concentrating on totally accepting everyone and making no judgments? Most of us think we would find that a very difficult task, since it is a rare occurrence to spend a few moments, let alone a whole day, with someone without making a judgment. When we think about it, many of us will be appalled at how often we condemn others and ourselves. We may even feel that it is almost impossible to stop being judgmental. However, all that is really necessary is our willingness to practice being nonjudgmental, without expecting instant perfection. The relinquishing of old habits that we do not want comes with repeated and sustained practice.

Most of us manifest a condition that could be called tunnel vision. We do not see people as a whole. We see just a fragment of a person, and our mind often interprets what we see as a fault. Most of us were brought up in a home and school environment where emphasis was placed on constructive criticism, which actually is usually a disguise for faultfinding.

On those occasions when we observe ourselves repeating this same mistake with our spouses, our children, our friends, or even someone seen only casually, it may be

helpful for us to quiet our minds, observe our thoughts, and become aware that being a faultfinder is totally dependent on our past experiences.

Evaluating and being evaluated by others, a habit from the past, result at worst in fear and at best in conditional love. To experience unconditional Love, we must get rid of the evaluator part of ourselves. In place of the evaluator, we need to hear our strong inner voice saying to ourselves and others, "I totally Love and accept you as you are."

As we reinforce our decision to be only Love finders, it becomes easier for us to concentrate on the strengths of others and overlook their weaknesses. It is important that we apply this lesson to everyone, including ourselves. That means that we can also see ourselves in a Loving way.

Not judging others is another way of letting go of fear and experiencing Love. When we learn not to judge others—and totally *accept* them, and not want to *change* them—we can simultaneously learn to accept ourselves.

Everything we think, say, or do reacts on us like a boomerang. When we send our judgments in the form of criticism, fury, or other attack thoughts, they come back to us. When we refrain from making judgments and send out only Love, it comes back to us.

Today, be willing not to make a condemning judgment against anyone you meet, or even think about. See everyone you meet or think about as either extending Love or as being fearful and sending out a call for help, which is a request for Love.

Example A

I recently had a powerful learning experience in regard to my attack thoughts. It had been a particularly busy day. I had arranged to have a boy with terminal brain cancer and his mother fly from Connecticut to California late in the afternoon. That evening I brought them to the Center. There was a meeting that night with other children who had catastrophic illness. After it was over I took them back to my home and returned to the Center to assist in another meeting of adults who had various forms of cancer.

That meeting was to be over at 9:30 P.M., and I was to go to a friend's house to meet some guests from India. When I started to leave the Center, there was a young man of about eighteen years of age waiting to see me. He had a beard, was untidy in appearance, and smelled like he had not had a bath in weeks.

He said he wanted to talk to me. I was tired and anxious to leave and didn't really want to see anyone who had a problem. He said he had just arrived after hitchhiking from Virginia, that he had seen me on a national television show and felt guided to meet me.

My inner thoughts became quite judgmental. "He must be disturbed to come across the country to meet me because he saw me on television." His request seemed like a demand and an attack. I told him I had another appointment that evening and that I could see him the next day if he thought he could wait. He said he could wait.

The next day he was not able to be specific about what he wanted except to say there was something in my eyes that made him want to see me. Since neither of us seemed to know why he was there, I suggested that we meditate together and that perhaps we might get an answer.

As we meditated, I was surprised to hear a clear inner voice state, "This man came across the country as a gift to you to tell you he saw perfect Love in your eyes—something that you have difficulty seeing in yourself. Your gift to him is to demonstrate total acceptance to him, something he has never in his life experienced."

I shared with him what I had heard, and we embraced each other. I was amazed to realize that the awful odor I had smelled only a moment before had totally disappeared. Tears came down both of our faces, and a mutual peace and Love was experienced that is difficult to describe.

A healing had taken place for both of us. Attack thoughts had been replaced by Love thoughts. We truly had been teachers and psychotherapists for each other.

We departed in extreme joy. I had a feeling I would never see him again but that I would never forget the lesson of forgiveness that he had taught me.

Example B

I think most of us can identify with the man who goes to a fashionable restaurant for dinner and finds the service simply awful and the server brusque, rude, and unfriendly. We can also identify with what would seem like justified anger, a reasonable grievance, hostile fantasies—and his decision to leave the server no tip.

To have inner peace as our single goal, we need to correct the erroneous belief that justified anger or grievances

bring us peace. Anger and attack simply do not bring peace of mind.

Now let us start this small drama over again. This time I whisper into the patron's ear, just as he sits down, that the server's husband died two days ago and that she has five children at home who are solely dependent on her for their support.

Now, he can see the waitress as fearful, and recognize that she is giving a call for Love. He can now respond by seeing her strength and devotion, and he finds he can overlook (forgive) her behavior. His response now is a loving, accepting attitude that he demonstrates by leaving an extra-large tip.

The external form of what is seen by the eyes and ears is the same in both dramas. However, in the first script, the events are seen through the window of fear, and in the second, through the windows of Love.

Today, allow yourself to have the single goal of inner peace by putting all your attention on the following thoughts: Today, I will view without judgment everything that occurs. All events provide me with another opportunity to experience Love in place of fear.

LESSON 8

THIS INSTANT IS THE ONLY TIME THERE IS

This Instant Is the Only Time There Is

I have often thought that we have much to learn from infants. They have not yet adapted to the concept of linear time with a past, present, and future. They relate only to the immediate present, to right *now*. My hunch is that they do not see the world as fragmented. They feel that they are joined to everything in the world as part of a whole. To me, they represent true innocence, Love, wisdom, and forgiveness.

As we get older, we tend to accept the adult values that emphasize projecting past learning into the present and anticipated future. It is difficult for most of us to have even the slightest question about the validity of our past–present–future concepts. We believe that the past will continue to repeat itself in the present and future without the possibility of change. Consequently, we believe we are living in a fear-filled world where, sooner or later, there will be suffering, frustrations, conflict, depression, and illness.

When we hold on to, invest in, and become attached to our guilty experiences and grievances form the past, we are tempted to predict a similar future. The future and the past then become one. We feel vulnerable when we believe that the fearful past is real and forget that our only reality is Love, and that Love exists this instant. Feeling vulnerable, we expect that the past will repeat itself. We see what we expect, and what we expect we both invite and seek. Past guilt and fears are thereby continually recycled.

One way of letting go of our "archeological garbage" is to recognize that holding on to it does not bring us what we want. When we see no value in recycling it, we remove the blocks to our being free to forgive and Love completely now. Only in this way can we be truly happy.

"This instant is the only time there is" can become an eternity. The future becomes an extension of a peaceful present that never ceases.

My preoccupation with the past and its projection into the future defeats any aims of present peace. The past is over and the future is yet to be. Peace cannot be found in the past or future, but only in this instant.

I am determined to live today without either past or future fantasies. I will remind myself: This instant is the only time there is.

Example

The following letter is from a nurse named Karol who has become a dear friend. We had previously talked together about how healing (the inner peace that comes from letting go of fear) can take place in an instant.

February 23

Dear Jerry,

Recently I've been in numerous situations where I've talked on and on about unconditional love and the importance of honoring the very essence of one's own being by letting go of fear. I guess we talk most about the very things we are learning.

In a dream, I was sitting face-to-face with a human being—ugly, fearful, deformed, and miserable. For a brief instant I wanted to run away. But as I relaxed into myself, I saw the very real connection between us and I loved this connection. As I saw the illusional aspect of the ego interpretation fade away, a bright light emitted the radiance, divinity, and innocence nobody had seen before. I embraced this person with a genuine love I'd never experienced. This person received my love, and there was a rejoicing and a communion with a spiritual merging of souls. This person was myself and I was this person; we celebrated our oneness. I knew the real feeling of love, honor, and forgiveness. I shall never forget the absolute and complete healing that took place in an instant. I truly understand what you were saying now.

> In Truth and Love,
> Karol

I wanted to share this beautiful letter with you because gifts are to be shared. I continue to find Karol's letter helpful to me at those times when I become attached to the past and am having trouble forgiving myself and others.

This instant is the only time there is.

LESSON 9

THE PAST IS OVER–
IT CAN
TOUCH ME NOT

The Past Is Over—It Can Touch Me Not

When we think we have been hurt by someone in the past, we build up defenses to protect ourselves from being hurt in the future. So the fearful past causes a fearful future, and the past and future become one. We cannot Love when we feel fear. We cannot Love when we feel guilt. When we release the fearful past and forgive everyone, we will experience total Love and oneness with all.

We seem to consider it "natural" to use our experiences of the past as reference points from which to judge the present. This results in our seeing the present with distorted dark-colored glasses.

Familiarity may not always breed contempt, but it is likely to dull our perceptions of those with whom we have close relationships. If we are to see our spouse, boss, or coworkers as they truly are, we must see them now, by recognizing their past and our own have no validity in the present.

To let each second be a new birth experience is to look without condemnation on the present. It results in totally releasing others and ourselves from all the errors of the past. It allows us to breathe freely and experience the miracle of Love by sharing this mutual release. It allows for an instant healing where Love is ever present, here and now.

It is our investment in wanting to control and predict that keeps us attached to the painful and guilty experience of the past. Guilt and fear, which are allied and which our minds make up, stimulate us to believe in this continuity of time.

If we feel that someone rejected us, criticized us, or was unfair to us in the past, we will see that person as attacking us. This reinforces our fear, and we attempt to attack back. Releasing the past means not blaming anyone, including ourselves. It means holding no grievances and totally accepting everyone, making no exceptions. It means a willingness to see only the light in others, and not their lampshade.

Fear and Love, guilt and Love, cannot coexist. Only if I keep reliving the past in the future am I a slave to time. By forgiving and letting go of the past, I free myself of the painful burdens I have carried into the present. Now I can claim the opportunities for freedom in the present without my past distortions.

Example

In 1975, I conducted a seminar on *A Course in Miracles* a few months after I had become a student of these writings. At the intermission, a couple in their sixties came up to me and said they were going to visit their thirty-five-year-old son, a chronic schizophrenic, in the state hospital the next day. They asked my advice about how to apply the principles of the *Course* to their visit.

I didn't really know what to say, so I asked my intuitive self for guidance. What came out of my mouth surprised me. The words didn't seem like mine, although they will be familiar to you because they have since become part of me and therefore part of this book. I responded by saying:

"Spend as much time as you can before tomorrow ridding yourself of all the past, painful guilty, fearful thoughts and experiences you have had with your son. Release yourselves from any guilt you have about your son's condition. Use your active imagination and put all your fears, guilt, and pain in a garbage can and attach it to a yellow balloon filled with helium. Print on the balloon, *I forgive my misperceptions.* Then watch the balloon and garbage can disappear into the sky. Pay attention to how much lighter and freer you feel.

"When you go to the hospital and the doctor talks to you about your son's behavior, do not be attached to what he says. Look past what your eyes and ears report. Choose to see your son only through the window of Love. Choose to see your son only as light—the light of Love. See the light

of Love in your son and the light of your Love as one light. Feel the peaceful bliss and know that the function of Love is to unite all things unto itself."

A week later I received a beautiful gift, a letter from the parents saying that they had experienced the most peaceful visit with their son they had ever had.

Today I choose to claim my release from past pains and suffering by living only in the immediate present.

LESSON 10

I COULD SEE PEACE INSTEAD OF THIS

I Could See Peace Instead of This

Most of us go through life with the belief system that our happiness or unhappiness is largely determined by the events in our environment and reactions of other people to us. Frequently we feel that our happiness is dependent on good or bad luck for which we bear little responsibility.

We forget to instruct our minds to change our perceptions of the world and everything in it. We forget that peace of mind is an internal matter and that it comes from a peaceful mind that a peaceful perception of the world is experienced.

The temptation to react with anger, depression, or excitement exists because of interpretations we make of the external stimuli in our environment. Such interpretations are necessarily based on incomplete perception.

When we dwell on past events or anticipate future happenings, we are living in the realm of fantasy. Whatever is real in our lives can only be experienced now. We block the possibility of fresh and novel experiences in our lives when we attempt to relive in the present our memories of episodes from the past, whether painful or pleasurable. We are, therefore, in a continual state of conflict about the actual happenings of the present and are unable to directly experience the opportunities for happiness that are all about us.

Most of the time I see a fragmented world where nothing seems to make much sense. The bits and pieces of my daily experience reflect the chaos I see within. Today, I welcome a new perception of myself and the world.

Example A

When my mother was eighty-eight years old, I was a fifty-four-year-old man who frequently found himself wanting to please her, and to change the many situations that made her unhappy. When I found my efforts were unsuccessful, I felt uneasy, and I was tempted to perceive my mother as demanding and rejecting when she was simply asking for help.

I find that I need to remember that I am responsible for the emotions I experience, and that my mother didn't cause my lack of peace—I did.

The lesson, "I could see peace instead of this," reminds me that the choice is between peace and conflict. When consistently practicing this lesson I then can choose to see my mother differently. I can choose to accept my mother without wanting to change her. This perception leads to seeing the Love that exists between us and the recognition that she continues to be a most significant teacher of mine.

Example B

When we are ill, the temptation is to complain, pity ourselves, focus attention on our bodies, and feel disabled by our discomfort and pain. In this state, our feelings of anger, irritability, and depression only reinforce a generalized sense of helplessness and hopelessness.

We are finding in our work with the children at the Center that through our willingness to help others we can learn to be happy rather than depressed. These children are teaching us that when we are ill or disabled, we can choose to direct our minds away from our bodies and their ailments and focus all our attention on being truly helpful to others.

The moment we put our attention on helping someone, we cease to perceive ourselves as ill or in pain, and find meaning in the statement, *To give is to receive.*

Repeat to yourself whenever you feel that your peace is threatened by anything or anyone: I choose to see the unity of peace instead of the fragmentation of fear.

I could see peace instead of this.

LESSON 11

I CAN ELECT
TO CHANGE
ALL THOUGHTS
THAT HURT

I Can Elect to Change All Thoughts That Hurt

That free will and choice are inherent attributes of the mind is something most of us tend to forget. We have all had the experience of feeling trapped in a situation where there seemed to be no escape.

Here is a suggestion that may prove helpful under such circumstances. You can use active imagination to find a way out. Picture a wall and let it represent your problem. On this wall, paint a door and hang a red exit sign above it. Imagine yourself opening the door, walking through it, and shutting it firmly behind you. Your problem is no longer with you, since you have left it behind. Experience your newfound freedom by imagining yourself in a place where you have no worries and there is nothing to do other than what you would enjoy. When you are ready to leave your happy retreat, bring with you this newfound sense of release from past problem-solving attempts. In the freshness of your new perception, solutions previously unavailable to you will now occur.

If we perceive things not as problems but rather as opportunities for learning, we can experience a sense of joy and well-being when the lessons are learned. We are never presented with lessons until we are ready to learn them.

In my mind are thoughts that can hurt me or help me. I am constantly choosing the contents of my mind, since no one else can make this choice for me. I can choose to let go of everything but my Loving thoughts.

Example

The following personal vignette may help to illustrate today's lesson. The episode took place in 1951 at Stanford Lane Hospital, which was then located in San Francisco.

The situation was one in which I felt trapped and immobilized by fear. I experienced emotional pain and thought I was being threatened with potential physical pain. The past was certainly coloring my perception of the present, and I was surely not experiencing inner peace or joy.

I was called at 2 A.M. one Sunday morning to see a patient on the locked psychiatric ward who had suddenly gone berserk. The patient, whom I had not seen before, had been admitted the previous afternoon with a diagnosis of acute schizophrenia. About ten minutes before I saw him, he had removed the wooden molding around the door. I looked through the small window in the door, and saw a man six feet four inches tall weighing 280 pounds. He was running around the room nude, carrying this large piece of wood with nails sticking out, and talking gibberish. I really didn't know what to do. There were two male nurses, both of whom seemed scarcely five feet tall, who said, "We will be right behind you, Doc." I didn't find that reassuring.

As I continued to look through the window, I began to recognize how scared the patient was, and then it began to trickle into my consciousness how scared I was. All of a sudden it occurred to me that he and I had a common bond that might allow for unity, namely, we were both scared.

Not knowing what else to do, I yelled through the thick door, "My name is Dr. Jampolsky and I want to come in and help you, but I'm scared. I'm scared that I might get hurt, and I'm scared you might get hurt, and I can't help wondering if you aren't scared, too." With this, he stopped his gibberish, turned around and said, "You're goddamn right, I'm scared."

I continued yelling to him, telling him how scared I was, and he was yelling back how scared he was. In a sense we became therapists to each other. As we talked, our fear disappeared and our voices calmed down. He then allowed me to walk in alone, talk with him, give him some oral medication, and leave.

That was a very powerful and important learning experience for me. At first I saw the patient as a potential enemy who was going to hurt me. (My past told me that anyone who seemed disturbed and had a club in his hand was dangerous.) I chose not to use the manipulative device of authority, which would have only served the purpose of creating more fear and separation. When I found a common bond in our fearful attitudes and sincerely asked for his help, he joined me. We were then in a position of helping each other. When I saw this patient as my teacher rather than my enemy, he helped me recognize that perhaps we are all equally insane and that it is only the form of our insanity that is different.

I am determined today that all my thoughts be free from fear, guilt, or condemnation, whether of myself or others, by repeating: I can elect to change all thoughts that hurt.

LESSON 12

I AM
RESPONSIBLE
FOR WHAT I SEE

I Am Responsible for What I See

I choose the feelings I experience, and I decide

upon the goal I would achieve.

And everything that seems to happen to me,

I ask for, and receive as I have asked.

**Teach only Love for that
is what you are.**

EPILOGUE

Let us consistently choose the single goal of peace rather than multiple goals that lead to conflict. Let us continue to practice forgiveness and to see each other and ourselves as blameless. Let us look lovingly upon the present, for it holds only knowledge that is forever true. Let us continue to be involved in a process of personal transformation in which we are only concerned about giving, and not about getting.

Let us recognize that we are united as one Self and illuminate the world with the light of Love that shines through us. Let us awaken to the knowledge that the essence of our being is Love, and, as such, we are the light of the world.

For information about Dr. Jampolsky or Attitudinal Healing International lectures, workshops, centers, or groups, please go to www.AHInternational.org or contact us at jerry@jerryjampolsky.com or info@ahinternational.org.

Gerald Jampolsky, MD
Attitudinal Healing International
3001 Bridgeway, Suite K-368
Sausalito, CA 94965
415-435-1622, ext. 0